LETTERS TO LORNA

BY

BILL BIRCH REYNARDSON

Published in Great Britain
by
WILTON 65
Hernes Keep, Winkfield, Windsor, Berkshire SL4 4SY
2008

Copyright © William Birch Reynardson

All rights reserved.
No part of this publication may be
reproduced, stored in a retrieval system, or transmitted,
in any form or by any means, electronic, mechanical,
photocopying, recording or otherwise,
without the prior permission
in writing of the
Copyright Owner.

ISBN 978-1-905060-10-8

Contents

Introduction		1
Prologue		3
Footnotes to Prologue		19

Part I March 1943 – April 1944 ... 27
Learning to be a Soldier

Britannia Barracks, Norwich	March 1943
Blackdown, Camberley	April 1943
R.M.C, Sandhurst	July 1943
24th Lancers, Bridlington	Jan 1944
Embarkation for North Africa	April 1944

Footnotes to Part I ... 65-67

Part II April 1944 – August 1944 ... 68
Regimental Soldiering

Arrival in Algiers	April 1944
Embarkation for Italy	May 1944
Regimental battle training	May-Aug 1944

Footnotes to Part II ... 89

Part III August 1944 – May 1945 ... 90
Active Service

Travelling North	Aug-Sept 1944
First contacts with enemy	Sept 1944
Second contacts with enemy	Oct-Nov 1944
Wounded	5th Nov 1944
Return to Regiment	Dec 1944
Winter operations	Jan-March 1945
Third contacts with enemy	April-May 1945

Footnotes to Part III ... 136

Part IV May 1945 – August 1946 ... 137
Victory and the Aftermath

Royal Salute on R. Po	5th May 1945
Having fun in Italy	May-Nov 1945
Course in UK (Old Sarum) and Christmas at Adwell	Nov 1945-Jan 1946
Return to Regiment	Feb 1946

	Victory Parade, Trieste	May 1946
	More fun in Italy	May-Aug 1946
	Leave Regiment	7th Aug 1946
FOOTNOTES TO PART IV		216-219

PART V SEPTEMBER 1946 – APRIL 1948   223
    A CIVILIAN ONCE MORE

Return to Christ Church, Oxford	Oct 1946
Hunting, Beagling, Hunt Balls	Oct 1946-Mar 1947
Shooting, Summer and Autumn	Aug-Oct 1947
Hunting during Winter	1947-1948
Trying to work for degree	Jan-April 1948
The end of the Affair	26th & 30th April 1948

    FOOTNOTES TO PART V   293-297

EPILOGUE   298

APPENDIX 1   Song, by H.B.R.   309

APPENDIX 2   Verse written by H.V. Sones for W.B.R.   310

APPENDIX 3   Extract from article describing the battle at Montecieco on 20th September 1944   312

APPENDIX 4   W.B.R's Address at Michael Joicey's Memorial Service   314

APPENDIX 5   P.M.B.R's Obituary   319

APPENDIX 6   Humphrey Prideaux   321

APPENDIX 7   Extract from *Illustrated*. The evacuees at Adwell   322

APPENDIX 8   Kit Egerton's award of the MC   328

APPENDIX 9   Scotsgrove and the Ashtons   329

APPENDIX 10   The 400   332

ACKNOWLEDGEMENTS   334

ILLUSTRATIONS

	Page
Lorna as a F.A.N.Y. in 1943	2
Portrait by Munnings of Nancy Tree with Michael riding Moonstone	20
Dickie, William, Rosamund and Cynthia on Neddy. Adwell 1928	21
Dickie B.R. 1932	21
Adwell from the West. 1949	22
Farm Pond at Adwell	22
H.B.R. with Bungie	23
H.B.R. in his office	23
Ann Bewicke. 1942	24
Loading wheat stooks at Adwell. 1942	24
Clothes coupons	25
Loders Club. 1942	26
The Silver Staircase at Manderston	29
Manderston, the garden front	30
Douglas Bailie	62
W.B.R. in Algiers. 1944	73
Portraits of Diana and Henry Birch Reynardson	91
Map showing Battle of San Savino	96
Sgt Jack Edmunds MM. San Savino 1944	97
W.B.R's tank at San Savino. 1944	99
John Joicey's tank crew. Battle of Coriano Ridge. September 1944	100
Lt Colonel Jack Price DSO. 1945	117
David Wentworth Stanley. February 1945	118
Lt Colonel R.S.G. Perry DSO. 1944	122
Map of Italian campaign	124
88mm German gun overrun by B Squadron. April 1945	128
'B Squadron firing indirect.' 1945	129
Captured German 155mm gun. April 1945	129
Gen-Adm von Friedenburg signing surrender terms 1945	132

Photograph of Officers at Palmanova, Italy. 1945	135
Leaving for U.K. on 'Python Release' August 1945	135
RSM Harwidge and Lancer with Tim Gilmour	153
W.B.R. on Quicksilver. 1945	155
W.B.R. with Jack Price and Quicksilver	155
Petrol coupons	215
Nik Humphreys. 1940	220
Envelope with post mark of Royal Tour. April 1947	221
Ships telegram sent by Nik B.R. December 1946	222
W.B.R. with Christ Church Beagles. 1947	226
Walter Clinkard after Peterborough Hound Show. July 1947	254
Eleanor, Mrs Bailie and Lorna at Manderston	299
Eleanor's Ball at Manderston. 1949	300
Extract from Manderston Visitors Book	301
Red Hat Ball, Grosvenor House. 1950	302
W.B.R. and Nik's Wedding. November 29th 1950	303
W.B.R. Inner Temple. 1952	304
Charles Ponsonby, Gladys Ponsonby and Leslie Jones. 1958	304
Lt. Colonel David Laurie MC. 1960	305
Nik B.R. 1975	305
Nik, W.B.R. Clare and Juliet at Adwell. 1960s	306
Thomas and Nik with Glenny at Adwell. 1960s	307
The family at Adwell. 1995	308
Michael Joicey	314
Humphrey Prideaux	321
The Evacuees at Adwell. 1939-1945	322-327
Kit Egerton	328
Ash tray from the 400	332
Lavinia Lascelles and Delia Holland-Hibbert as WRNS	333
W.B.R. 2008	335

Introduction

This book is for you, my grandchildren. It would not have been produced had it not been for Adrian Palmer who, most thoughtfully, gave me the collection of over two hundred letters which I had written to his mother, Lorna, between the years 1943 and 1948. He had found them in a locked box, all neatly tied in bundles of twenty, and each letter numbered on the envelope. Adrian and I met, by chance, at a concert given in the Hall of Lincoln's Inn in aid of Lord Renton's charity (he was in his 99th year) and Adrian told me of his discovery. We made a plan for me to go up to Manderston to collect them. I am most grateful to him. (The letters which Lorna wrote to me were burnt, on two occasions, when my tanks were destroyed in the War by fire.)

Some of you have said that you would like to read them, so I have selected about half of them, the other half being of little interest. But when I read them I thought that I should, for the sake of continuity, add explanatory notes as background to some of the letters. And then I wondered whether it would be an improvement to write about my early life between coming to Adwell in the mid 1930s up to 1942, and then a final short section covering the period between leaving Oxford in 1947 and getting married at the end of 1950. I concluded that I should do this and you will see that I have written a Prologue and an Epilogue.

This is certainly not a biography, nor even a part biography. I have had a very happy life but not a particularly distinguished one. It would have been presumptuous of me to have written about it. It was only the discovery of the letters by Adrian which prompted me to reproduce some of them in a form for, I hope, the enjoyment of my family and friends.

Perhaps I should add that, before she died, Lorna told her sons that, although she had destroyed her letters to and from Gordon, she wished these letters from me to be preserved in the expectation that they should be made available, particularly to the younger generation.

Adwell, Autumn 2008

LORNA AS A F.A.N.Y.
IN 1943

Prologue

We (my sisters Cynthia Prideaux and Rosamund Egerton and my brother Dickie) arrived at Adwell in 1936. Of course we knew the place very well because the whole family had been 'waiting in the wings' for three years (after our return from South Africa) during which time my grandparents made up their minds, after much dilly-dallying, to move to Woodstock Road in Oxford.

My father had had an unhappy upbringing at Adwell, finding his parents out of sympathy with his way of life. From Oxford, where he had lived in some style (a member of Loders and Bullingdon Clubs, whipped in to the Christ Church Beagles, rode in Point to Points, drove horses in tandem[1a] and not as a pair, etc, while still getting a First[2a]), he left to join the Army. In that way he got away from home.

He was badly wounded in 1916 but married my mother, Diana Ponsonby, in 1917 - still in a wheel chair. In the end he had to leave the Army (which he had much enjoyed) and, in about 1927, became Private Secretary to the Governor General of South Africa, Lord Athlone, and, later, Lord Clarendon. This job, of course, entailed a number of voyages to and from South Africa when my father went on leave or on business. One of these voyages in, I think, 1928 was particularly memorable as we travelled with the Prince of Wales (later Edward VIII), my father acting as a temporary equerry. The Prince didn't like my father because the latter was constantly trying to make the Prince behave and not ogle the prettier girls on board, etc, (the 'etc' covering quite a wide range of activity!). But he liked us children – and I became a particular pal (aged 5 or 6) of his. As the future King of England, I reckoned that he must have intimate knowledge of such matters as the locomotion of the ship, the position of the stars, the making of glass and other essential topics.

As a result the Prince arranged for me to visit the ship's engine room, to sit on the bridge at night to observe the stars through a telescope and to obtain saltpetre and sand in order to make glass in the ship's hospital where there was a Bunsen burner. He arranged for a dressing up party for all the children on board.

But the incident which I remember particularly clearly occurred when the ship was about to dock at Cape Town. There we all were on deck as the ship slowly manoeuvred into the harbour, the Governor General in full dress with Princess Alice[3a] clearly visible standing on an elaborately decorated dais. But where was the Prince? Nowhere to be seen. So my father hurried down to his cabin, accompanied by me (unknown to him). There was the prince wearing a cream coloured silk suit and a straw Botha hat. My father suggested that it was time for him to change. "No, it's too hot for uniform." My father explained that his uncle, the Governor General, was waiting to welcome him in full dress (as was my father). There was quite an argument but, in the end, the Prince most unwillingly changed into uniform. He was, as a result, in a fearful sulk when he met the Athlones!

The six years which we spent in South Africa were, I believe, the happiest period of my father's life. He was a close adviser to both Lord Athlone and Lord Clarendon (who succeeded him) and, at the end of his appointment, received the C.M.G. in recognition of his service to them. He seemed to thrive away from England and, so far as I can remember, his health was always good there. We lived in a charming staff house in the gardens of Westbrook, the residence of the Governors-General. We brought with us my mother's maid, Mrs Walker, and our nanny, Miss Turner, to be joined by Amy, the cook, and Thomas, the 'house boy.' He took me to school at Bishops on my pony Joey, which he led. My mother and father were great friends with both the Athlones and the Clarendons, though Lady Clarendon was rather more distant than Princess Alice who we all loved. They often lunched or dined with us. When Princess Helena Victoria was staying with the Athlones they all came to dinner and I was allowed to stay up to meet them. I was fascinated by Princess H.V.'s jewellery - she was wearing some particularly beautiful pink pearls of huge size. "Are they real?" I asked. Dead silence. Then she whispered to my mother "I had them copied before coming to South Africa. Is it so obvious?"

My father returned to England in 1933 to find half the Adwell estate sold without his prior knowledge and certainly not his consent.

Our first house on our arrival back in England from South Africa was a dreadful little semi-detached house in Lathbury Road, North Oxford. It was from here that I was introduced, aged nine, as a day boy at the Dragon School in Bardwell Road. Even in those days, there were over 300 boys (no girls, of course, except daughters of masters). I had been at Bishops in Rondebosch when we had lived in South Africa and I found the Dragon School much tougher, with frequent beatings for every sort of offence. Jock Lynam (the son of the founder and owner of the school, Hum Lynam) would call one into his study and, after haranguing you about your offence, would say "Well, do you want me to beat you with a cane or with this chair leg?" It was an extremely painful proceeding and what made it worse was that Lynam obviously revelled in the event.

And another thing of which I gradually became aware was the somewhat affectionate way in which many of the masters embraced their charges! This came to a head when one of them kissed me very warmly when I was returning from swimming. I didn't like this! I went to Hum Lynam and explained what had happened. He told me to come to his house and I was shown into the drawing room, where I'd never been before. There then followed a long (and straightforward) explanation of homosexuality: "This means that some men like boys and not girls. Many of the masters here like boys; that is why they are such good teachers. But I quite agree that Mr – should not have kissed you and, if he does that again, you must tell me." The offence was not repeated but the master in question left to run a hotel nearby!

Later on in my career as a Dragon School boy, John Mortimer and I attended a sex talk by Hum Lynam, again in his drawing room. The whole subject was so concealed by references to "birds and bees" that neither of us understood one word of his explanation. Nevertheless, neither of us was prepared to reveal this, so when John said "Could you explain exactly what all that was about" I was completely flummoxed and had to admit that I had no idea! Seventy years later, I went to John's play *Voyage Round my Father* when this scene was re-enacted by two teenage boys (representing John and me). It was a hilarious occasion with John sitting behind me in the theatre! The audience did not understand the laughter coming from rows 3 and 4 of the stalls!

And here I think I should pause to write something more about my mother and father (your great grandmother and great grandfather).

First then, my mother: I adored her and we had a very close relationship – though if I behaved in a way which she considered unacceptable she would certainly let me know! Sometimes we had rather awful rows, as only people who love each other can. She had been brought up at Woodleys (near Woodstock) in a very Victorian household, presided over by her charming, but somewhat pointless, father. Her mother died when she was six and it is said that, on the day of her death, her father sent for her and said "Your mother is dead; you will sit at the head of the table at dinner this evening." She became very ill with tuberculosis as a teenager and, to help in her recovery, her father sent for the Heythrop hounds so that she could see them from her bedroom window. She and her father (but not her brothers) hunted regularly with the Heythrop and, even in her old age, we could never cross the river at Islip without her saying "That's where I gave Dad a lead on my grey mare, jumping the river just upstream from here."

Her religious beliefs were central to her life and, before she married, she wrote two little books of prayers of great depth of feeling. She had made a little chapel from a dressing room next door to her bedroom. We were bidden there most mornings to say our prayers with her. But she never forced her very strong religious beliefs on us; she merely expected us to accept them – no discussion, let alone any argument, was considered necessary. Religious instruction was given by Bible reading. On birthdays we would meet in the Chapel when my mother would read the Christmas Gospel of St John 1.1 ('In the beginning was the word . . . . .').

She sacrificed herself in caring for my father and it was he who took priority over us children. Because he was physically unable to hunt, she never hunted again, although she took a great interest in my riding and hunting.

She was a very loveable person and made us all laugh a great deal. Once, when watching the Trooping the Colour, she turned to her neighbour and commented on the wonderful drilling of the troops. "You know," said her neighbour "that all the guardsmen have to be a certain size." And she then turned to sister Cynthia, who was sitting next to her, and said "How interesting, did you know that all the soldiers had to be circumcised?" One other bon mot, describing her great friend Dorothy Maud and her decision to be a nun, she said "Of course she will have to be a prostitute [postulent] first." And I can't resist just one more malapropism. My mother was a J.P. (Justice of the Peace). On hearing, in advance of the court sitting, that there was to be a case of alleged incest, she told Humphrey that she couldn't understand the reason for a case of incense – "something to do with the church I suppose."

In later years, immediately after the War, my father began to suffer serious depressions. She comforted and nursed him through these difficult times with great courage and devotion. And then it gradually became apparent that her vagueness, which we had all experienced over the years, had taken on an exaggerated form. Some kind of dementia was diagnosed and, after a year or two, we had to resort to a full time companion. In the end she became unmanageable; the only person who could control, and indeed bath her, was Leslie Jones (about whom I write later). After a rather desperate family conference it was decided that she had to have proper nursing care and we found a wonderful group of Catholic nuns, the St Joseph's Community, who looked after her till her death in 1962. I still miss her every day after all these years.

I feel that I hardly knew my father. He was a distant figure in my life. I think I bored him. He disapproved of my Eton friends whom he suspected of keeping me away from my books (probably correct!). Certainly the reading of my school reports each holiday produced an atmosphere of 'could do better', with little encouragement. He wrote three or four books (including *The Mesopotamia Campaign* which became a recommended book for Staff College candidates, *High Street Africa* describing the drive from Cape to Cairo which he accomplished with my mother, Cynthia and Rosamund in 1933, and *Black Coffee*, a detective novel which he wrote at Oxford as a bet that he would be able to get it published). He also wrote many articles for *Blackwoods* and other similar magazines and some (rather depressing) poetry. [There is an example of one in Appendix 1.]

But we never had a row, sometimes 'rockets'. I well remember two occasions. Once, after an exceedingly wet day's hunting, Audrey Holland-Hibbert (Mrs, of course, to me all my life) told me to ring up and get our chauffeur Jim Hedges to come in a car to fetch me, my pony being left for the night with the Holland-Hibberts. This (quite rightly, I suppose) was considered monstrous behaviour and I received a mammoth ticking off. The punishment was no hunting for a month. An appeal to my mother got this period reduced to a week.

The other rocket concerned my financial mismanagement. I had lately gone on an allowance, paid into my bank monthly. I had, mistakenly, thought that I had a sufficient balance to buy a suit from Austin Reid – very smart, dark blue with a pin stripe. I was immensely proud of it. I was having my bath after hunting when there was a tap on the door. It was Leslie Jones saying that I was wanted by the Colonel in his study. "Oh, thank you," I said. "I'll finish my bath and get dressed." Mr Jones replied "No Master William, I think that this is a dressing gown occasion." So down to the study I went. My father looked at me in a most unfriendly way. "Why have you overdrawn on your account by two pounds, twelve shillings?" I had no explanation. "A gentleman never overdraws on his bank account and I am ashamed of you." As a matter of fact the suit was a dismal failure. George Holland[4a], always impeccably dressed, asked after church where I had obtained it. I told him that I had bought it at Austin Reid. "Ah, I thought as much. Please remember that your clothes must be made for you by a tailor, as mine are."

I do not want to leave the subject of my father without making it clear that, although our relationship may not have been very close, he was, nevertheless, a charming, intelligent and thoughtful man. He had a crowd of devoted friends. He was constantly encouraging his children and grandchildren with wise advice as they grew up. His kindness as a host was well known throughout Oxfordshire and elsewhere. He was a thoughtful employer, his staff remaining with him often throughout their lives. But, above all, he trusted me as the next custodian of Adwell and made it possible, financially, for me and my family to live here.

My father inherited a large outdoor and indoor staff at Adwell in 1936. The garden was well, but somewhat unimaginatively, kept by Wixon and four others. There was a large greenhouse (occupying the space which is now the tennis court), vinery, peach houses and extensive kitchen gardens both sides of the drive (there were a lot of people to feed!). The Home Farm was run by the bailiff, George Holland, who had under him two men in the stables (six draught horses – no tractors), two herdsmen (we milked forty or fifty cows) and two or three general farm labourers.

The shoot was keepered by Wilby, quite strict with me but I was a great admirer of him because, not only did he produce a lot of good wild pheasants and partridges (no birds were put down then), but also he grafted lovely roses onto the briars in the hedges on the estate.

The domestic staff was headed up by Sones. He wrote a poem for me [in Appendix 2], but was soon to be replaced by Leslie Jones. There was also a footman called Thomas Abbott and a chauffeur, Jim Hedges. There were three in the kitchen, four housemaids, a lady's maid and dressmaker for my mother and sisters. We children always addressed heads of department with the prefix Mr or Mrs (cooks were always Mrs) and woe betide any of us who behaved in a way considered disrespectful to any of them.

Of course life was then somewhat formal and much more organised than it is today. The main reason for this was the occupants of the servants' hall. There they all were and, in a way, they ruled or certainly set the pattern of our lives. We had to get up and dress by 8 o'clock (latest) because the maids, who had called us with hot water for our basins, had to return to make our beds and empty our wash basins before doing the housework. Lunch was at 1 o'clock because Mr Jones announced that "Luncheon is ready" at 12.55. And dinner, well that was quite something. First there was a gong at 6.30 pm to announce that we should dress for dinner and we had to be down by 7.30 for sherry beforehand (no spirits were allowed in either the Drawing Room or the Library – only in the Billiard Room). Dinner began at 7.45 sharp.

When I went to Eton I was promoted from supper in the School Room (later Clare's bedroom) to dinner in the Dining Room. Of course the men (of which I was then one!) wore dinner jackets (certainly not velvet coats). My clothes were laid out by Wallace Merritt, the Footman, on the first night of my promotion and I went downstairs looking, I thought, extremely smart. But when I entered the Drawing Room my father walked up to me and felt my shirt which was not starched (as, of course, his was). "Are we playing tennis this evening?" he asked.

We had people to stay most weekends. Often they arrived with a lady's maid and a chauffeur, but most of our guests were contemporaries of my sisters and were not encumbered in this way. Tipping, on leaving after the weekend, was not only expensive but also sometimes a problem as to whom one should give a tip. To solve this my mother had notices put on the dressing table of every spare room which read: "Our guests are the guests of the whole household and visitors are requested to refrain from offering tips." At the end of every year the visitors' book was examined and a per capita levy applied and distributed to all concerned.

Perhaps this is where I should mention the extraordinary procedure which occurred every day in the servants' hall at lunch time. Mr Jones presided, sitting on a curved bench with a sort of canopy, at the head of the table; Mrs Shuttle (the cook) sat opposite him at the other end of the table. When the pudding was brought in Mr Jones, Mrs Shuttle and Mrs Turner (the Head Housemaid) were served and then, carrying their plates before them, they filed out of the servants' hall (now the kitchen) and sat down in the Housekeeper's Room (now the small sitting room) opposite. Here they finished their lunch, ringing a bell to have their plates cleared by the kitchen or scullery maid. Talk about class distinction! I believe that this charade went on in many houses in those far off days.

I can only just remember morning prayers held by my grandmother before breakfast in the Library. But, here again, it was quite a performance with the Butler (then Mr Sones) heading the procession of the members of staff (kitchen and house) who curtsied when my grandmother entered, prayer book in hand! My mother did away with all this and, instead, had private family prayers in the little chapel upstairs. She disliked anything approaching ostentation. She addressed her father, The Hon Edwin Ponsonby (the son of Lord de Mauley), as plain Mr (most unusul and discourteous in those days). When in South Africa my father met her with a Crown on his car (as was his entitlement) she had it immediately removed!

We all had a lovely time with our dogs and ponies. We even had a swimming pool which was a rarity in those pre-War days (no heating or filtering!) Our riding lessons were extremely rudimentary and my first pony's main job in life was to take the washing to the laundry in South Weston. (Mrs Rixon was our laundry maid. When I offered to instal a water supply to take the place of the well, she at first refused. Later she changed her mind but insisted that the tap should be placed next to the well and certainly not in her house.) I was first taught by George Holland, then later with the South Oxfordshire Pony Club which was run by Gwen Evetts, an ardent spiritualist.

The Pony Club was, for us children, the social centre of our lives and it was all great fun, devoid of 'parental ambition' which is, sadly, so evident today. The summer Pony Club camps were the main feature of the whole year. They were held on various South Oxfordshire estates including Adwell. Run on cavalry lines, there was always 'the Adjutant' (a volunteer Cavalry officer including, one year, my brother-in law, Humphrey Prideaux. Colin Balfour was batman to Humphrey). The participating children were divided into troops and the ponies were tied in troop lines. Each troop had an instructor and instruction in equitation was taken seriously.

We slept in 'bell' tents hired from the local army barracks at Cowley and, of course, there was strict segregation between girls and boys. Nevertheless there was an occasion when one young lady (whose name cannot be revealed) said to me "If you kiss me on the lips, I'll show you my crack." So instruction was not limited to matters of equitation!

My first 'proper' pony was a chestnut Welsh gelding called Punch. I can just remember setting off from Adwell with my mother to view him (she always chose our ponies and, later, our horses). No sooner had she seen Punch (unridden) but she said that was the pony for me. Having ridden him round a rather basic sort of manège I jumped him over some small obstacles and he was purchased for £40 (in notes!). I rode him for three or four seasons. And then, out hunting, Colonel Muirhead (who lived at Haseley Court with his old mother; a friend of my father's), rode up to me and said "William, that pony is too small for you. I think I know of a very nice 14.3 pony which would suit you well. She belongs to a lady called Mrs Tree and I will make a plan for us to go over and see her."

So, a week or so later, the two of us drove over to Ditchley to see Moonstone (that was her name). I'd never seen Ditchley before or Nancy Tree (later Lancaster) or, indeed, such an awe-inspiring set up. First of all the Tree hunters (both Nancy and Ronnie Tree hunted, not only in Leicestershire but also in Virginia where they had another stable full of horses). There were about fifteen of them at Ditchley. Then the skewbald ponies for the various carriages driven by the Tree sons. Finally, the ponies and horses ridden by the two boys, including Moonstone. She was, I thought, the most beautiful thing I'd ever seen; extremely good-looking and obviously well behaved. Munnings painted a picture of Nancy with Michael Tree riding Moonstone. Although it is not, perhaps, a great picture in itself, it is very good of Moonstone. (See reproduction of picture on page 20. I am grateful to the present owners who have allowed me to include it in this book.)

One of the many grooms (meticulously turned out in breeches and boots) helped me on and we trotted down to a grass paddock where I tried her. "Jump over that little post and rails" shouted Nancy. This I did without mishap. After a few minutes I was called in and asked whether I liked the pony. Of course I was quite speechless but managed to say that I did. "But, Mrs Tree, how much do you want for her?" "Well, my dear, I think that the two of you will get on very well together and I'd like to give her to you. Go off now and have a proper ride and jump some fences." Of course I was completely overjoyed. But such was my excitement that, having jumped a small fence, I set sail at something more substantial, not realising that there was a wide ditch on the landing side. I ended up on my head, unconscious! I was put to bed and the doctor sent for. The verdict was concussion – and to be kept quiet. Nancy decided that this was not the best way to recovery. She spent much time in my bedroom, telling me stories in her inimitable way – both of us laughing uproariously. I had to tell her to stop because she made my head ache!

So began a life long friendship. She moved to Haseley after the War, turning it from a featureless bachelor apartment into one of the most beautiful houses and gardens I know. It was she who inspired me to change the garden at Adwell – and to paint the hall from what she called 'battleship grey' to the present burnt orange (John Fowler mixed the colour and oversaw the painting by Symms, the Oxford builders). It was she who really got me gardening.

But I have deviated and must return to Adwell. My father never seemed to enjoy the place. Remember that he had only three years to settle in before War was declared in September 1939. Then the house was taken over by the Evacuees and the five or six girls who volunteered to look after them (see later). My father's war work was of a hugely hush-hush nature. He rejoined the army – much to his joy – and worked at the War Office, living at Denham at night to escape the London bombing. None of us had any clear idea of the precise nature of his work. He was certainly very glad to be out of the hurly burly of life at Adwell.

In those days Army officers were not allowed to marry before they were 25. Therefore, when Humphrey (aged 23) asked my father's permission to marry Cynthia (20), it was not forthcoming. "Come back again in two years' time and we'll talk about it." But then it became clear that war was imminent and my father relented. "There's going to be a war and you'll probably be killed before Christmas, so you'd better get married now." And so they were – and Humphrey is still very much alive at 92!

The reading of the banns of marriage by Canon Henderson in Adwell Church caused my brother Dickie and me immense pleasure. "I publish the banns of marriage between Humphrey Treverbian Prideaux, bachelor, and Cynthia Birch Reynardson, spinster and infant of this parish." It was too good to be true. Here was this rather bossy (but always kind) elder sister described as an infant (she was under 21). Her authority over us had received a most serious dent.

The evacuee children (aged between 3 and 6 years) arrived at Adwell just after the last guests had left the reception following Cynthia's wedding to Humphrey on 30th August 1939. I remember well that the whole family were relaxing in the library (now the dining room), all rather exhausted, when two double-decker London buses appeared in the drive. "What the devil are those bloody buses doing in our drive, damn fool's lost the way I suppose ....." shouted my father. My mother went very quiet. Of course, she had quite forgotten that a year earlier (at the time of the Munich Crisis) she had volunteered that we would have up to 50 Evacuees in the event of war. But she had omitted to consult my father; he took the news badly.

There was, however, little time for recrimination as furniture had to be cleared from four rooms to provide space for 50 children and six 'keepers'. And the cots for the children had been forgotten. Our neighbours, the Woods, were sent for and furniture removal commenced, including that of the billiard table and other heavy pieces of furniture. My father retired from the scene in a major sulk and my mother took control of proceedings with relaxed authority. Fortunately the South Oxfordshire Pony Club Camp had recently taken place at Adwell and we were able to use the palliases (filled with straw) as temporary bedding for the children.

Gradually life returned, not to normal – how could it? – but to something approaching it. The 'keepers' (nurses from the Middlesex

Hospital) were considered totally unacceptable by my mother and were replaced by Doris Sayer (who took charge, under my mother) and girl friends of my two sisters – Disney Mann, Honor Mahoney, Annette Burt-Smith, Delia Holland-Hibbert, Viola Head, Anne FitzRoy and others. They made their headquarters in the west room, the drawing room was the reserve of the members of the family, and the other rooms on the ground floor (the billiard room, study and dining room) were occupied by the children. (My father's study was turned into the 'potty room', containing two rows of wooden benches with chamber pots fitted below!) Mrs Shuttle presided over the kitchen and Edna Gibbs ran the domestic side of the house.

You will find in Appendix 7 some photographs (extracted from a magazine called *The Illustrated*), of life at Adwell with the evacuee children. I believe that the happiness which my mother was able to give them was, perhaps, the greatest achievement of her life. There were constant expeditions into the Chiltern Hills with huge picnic teas. (On one of the early trips a little girl came up to my mother and said "Please could I have a picnic contraption like Tommy has as I do want to pee.") Later on there were lessons and visits to Oxford. At the end of the War a house was purchased for them in Oxford where the children, who had no parents, grew up.

How well I remember Canon Henderson, our Rector, announcing in the Church "I must tell you that we are now at war with Germany. May God bless you all." My mother was sitting between Dickie and me. She clasped our hands and said "So be it." She had lost a beloved brother, Ashley, 23 years earlier. After church we walked together in the shrubberies (her favoured place for serious conversations) and she broke down in tears. This was the only time in my life that I ever saw her cry.

In these early days of the War I was sixteen and Dickie thirteen. We were both at Eton. There had been an alarming suggestion that we, together with Mary Ponsonby, should be sent to South Africa for the war years. This was strongly opposed by us and the plan dropped.

Hunting continued on a reduced scale but my choice of horses was widened because Sir Robert Fanshawe[5a] (Dick Fanshawe's uncle) mounted me on top class horses sent, for the duration of the War, to his stables at Lubbersdown by his nephews. Ruth Fanshawe (Dulverton) hunted hounds (in place of her husband) and Rachel Clerke-Brown and I whipped in to her. We had two glorious seasons before I joined the Army and I am ever grateful to Ruth for the fun she gave us. The sight of her and Dick riding across our lovely South Oxfordshire country – then all grass with little wire – is a sight which I'll never forget. And, thanks to Sir Robert's generosity, I was able to keep up with them riding Ginger Rogers, Wagon Lit, Koran and other splendid horses which he lent me.

During the summer of 1940 Sir Robert formed a mounted troop of what was then called the L.D.V. (Local Defence Volunteers, to be replaced by the Home Guard). Our Sergeant Major was Jack Castle, a well known yeoman farmer who lived in Thame. Sir Robert instructed us in cavalry drill, dating back to the Boer War, and my job was to dismount and hold the troop horses when their riders stalked 'the enemy' on foot. We drew our Lee Enfield rifles from the Regimental Museum in Cowley. Such was the state of national defence at that time!

But I am running ahead of myself because I have not mentioned going to Eton in 1936 and meeting there two people who were to play such an important part in my life, my Tutor, Charles Gladstone and my life-long friend, Kit Egerton.

First then, my Tutor: He was a fairly 'silent' man – anyway at the start of my time at Eton. But gradually we made friends and conversation became easier. The breakthrough came, I think, when he set himself the task of improving my speaking. I have a very high roof to my mouth and my tutor determined to correct my poor enunciation. So, every evening when he came to say goodnight, he sat down and made me read to him for five minutes.

Although he never hunted himself, he was one of the few House Masters who allowed Lower Boys to go beagling. This, so far as I was concerned, qualified him as a 'good man'. Indeed, at the end of my time at Eton (which was far from distinguished) he gave me a key to the house so that I could come in after 'lock up' when I had been made late after hunting.

He was certainly a strict disciplinarian and, with his permission (given to the Captain of the House), we were all beaten regularly for any misdemeanours. He was held in great respect by all of us and, during his goodnight visits (which occurred every night), we discussed a wide variety of subjects (excluding sex, which was never mentioned!).

Kit Egerton and I arrived at Eton on the same day. His father, Admiral Jack Egerton, and my father were both trustees of some charity so knew each other slightly. Neither Kit nor I had sat our Common Entrance exam but that did not seem to matter in those days! We messed together from day one (that is, we cooked tea together at the end of the passage and ate it in my room) and, after a short time, asked Other Windsor (now Lord Plymouth) to join us. Not only did we like him but Kit pointed out (he was keen on his food) that Other was being supplied with grouse, pheasants and partridges from his father's various estates and felt that an additional advantage!

Kit and I more or less lived together and became inseparable friends. Neither of us were much good at games - though we enjoyed the Field game – so we became closely involved with the beagles from the start of our careers at Eton. We had a wonderful time with Mike de Chair and Hugh Arbuthnot as masters. The kennel huntsman in our day was Will Perkins, a remarkable man. Not only did he feed and exercise the hounds (sometimes with our help) but he taught us, very tactfully but firmly, the art of venery. Out hunting (always perfectly dressed in his white breeches and Eton brown velvet coat) he would arrive, from nowhere, when hounds had checked and whisper a possible (and usually correct) solution. He was a wonderful contributor to all the fun we had in those gloriously happy days where we were welcomed by farmers all over Berkshire, Buckinghamshire and Oxfordshire.

Kit met my sister Ros during one of the early Fourth of June picnics and fell in love with her! Of course I ragged him endlessly about this. In the holidays, he was either at Adwell or I was hunting at his home, Sheriff Hutton in Yorkshire. He was a wonderful friend. Ros, as you will see from the letters, married Jimmy Marriott in 1943. He was a most charming and courageous man (he won the George Medal). He was killed in Normandy in 1944, Christopher having just been born. But Kit had never ceased to love Ros and, although she was three years older than him, they were married in 1949. They went to live first in Northumberland and then in Yorkshire, near Nunnington, where he 'farmed', hunted, shot and became a famous commanding officer of the Yorkshire Hussars. Sadly, he was very nearly defeated by drink. After a huge struggle he was able to give it up but he never truly recovered his former joie de vivre.

I also want to tell you about two other people who influenced my early life. They were George Holland and Leslie Jones, both of whom I've already mentioned briefly. First George Holland: He had come to Adwell (from Wheatfield where he was born) as a 14 year old boy in the early 1900s. He worked for my grandfather in the stables, looking after the carriage horses. When my grandfather purchased his first car in about 1912, George (or Mr Holland as we addressed him), was promoted to be his senior chauffeur.

The second chauffeur, Jim Hedges, and George Holland, both dressed in dark blue suits with silver livery buttons and wearing breeches and black leather leggings, would travel in the front of the car, George driving, while my grandparents would sit in the back. There was a 'speaking tube' connecting the chauffeurs with the passengers. This consisted of an air tube with mouth and ear pieces. I asked George why it was necessary for Jim Hedges to travel with him. "In case I have a puncture" he replied. Changing a wheel was clearly below his sphere of activity.

As the years passed, George became my grandfather's constant companion and, by the time we came to Adwell, he was running the two farms – my grandfather taking little interest – reporting to our agent, Mr Monck, a disagreeable and unscrupulous man, who did not long survive my father taking over at Adwell.

I owe a huge debt of gratitude to George (he was said to have been the illegitimate son of a local aristocrat) who taught me as a boy all the different aspects of country life. I was introduced by him to the different skills required in agricultural management (I learnt to milk, to drive horses, to mend machinery, etc), to ride a horse, to plant trees, to rear partridges and pheasants and even to dress (he was always impeccably turned out)! One could not have had a kinder or more knowledgeable tutor. He was one of the best mannered men I ever met.

Then our butler, Leslie Jones. He came to us a year or two before the War. He was also a 'man in my life'. He taught me the finer points of his job and, later on, was my father's 'shadow', going to Scotland with him every year. I have already mentioned the way he lovingly looked after my mother, who allowed no one to come near her except Jones. Not only did he bath and dress her, but also performed the necessary personal duties required of a disabled person. He spared us much of the distress of her illness. He stayed to see us into Adwell in 1959, notwithstanding the onset of Parkinson's disease. I was extremely fortunate to know him.

So I've now come to the end of this Prologue having covered, very briefly, those very important formative years of my life between my early childhood and my youth.

Some of you will, I'm sure, remember the opening sentence of Tolstoy's *Anna Karenina:* "All happy families resemble one another, each unhappy family is unhappy in its own way." Looking back I don't think that we were an entirely happy family; I believe that we did live rather 'in our own way'. This was, I suspect, because of the shadow cast over all of us by my father. As I've already mentioned, he did not have a happy childhood and, later, his relationship with his parents (particularly his father) was very far from close. I don't think he ever really loved Adwell. And then there was this depression which permeated our lives. This, I am sure, was the result of his wounding in Mesopotamia (now Iraq). The (Turkish) bullet which pierced his backbone left a fearful hole, the size of a clenched fist, half way down his back. He would certainly have died on the battlefield but for the courage and tenacity of his soldier servant and a colleague who carried him on a stretcher for miles across the desert to the safety of the allied lines. Although, thanks to the nursing by my mother, he was able to dispense with his wheel chair, he never made a complete recovery either physically or mentally. My mother was constantly on the alert for yet another bout of serious mental illness which frustrated his life. I want to explain the effect which this episode had on his future life and acknowledge the patience and fortitude with which he bore it. With her Christian charity my mother accepted these frustrations which she tried to modify, but with only limited success.

Footnotes to Prologue

Frontisepiece. The picture of Lorna was taken from the icing sugar portrait on her wedding cake on her marriage to Gordon Palmer, May 5th 1950.

1a. It was considered a bit swanky to drive horses in tandem and not in pairs. I believe that the Dean of Christ Church remonstrated with my father, demonstrating 'cocking a snook' (hands in front of each other) compared to hands in prayer (hands together).

2a. When asked to write a letter of recommendation for his post in South Africa, Robin Dundas wrote 'He was one of the cleverest men I ever taught.'

3a. HRH Princess Alice. Her husband, Earl of Athlone, was Queen Mary's brother.

4a. George Holland, our bailiff. See later.

5a. Sir Robert Fanshawe was a wonderful friend to me – though I never met him till he was over sixty. His father had been the Rector of Adwell. He had three sons, all generals and all knighted. Once, when riding down the gated road from Clare crossroads to Haseley with his brothers and me, I took rather a long time to open one of the gates. As I struggled, head down, with the gate catch, they all jumped the gate. "A bit slow, aren't you!" Sir Robert cried as he flew over it! They were all over seventy.

Nancy Tree (as she then was) with Michael (her son) riding the pony Moonstone which she gave me.
By Munnings, 1930s

DICKIE, WILLIAM, ROSAMUND AND CYNTHIA
ON NEDDY, ADWELL
1928

DICKIE B.R.
"I PUT THE SMALLER
ONES BACK."
1932

ADWELL FROM THE WEST 1949
(BEFORE DEMOLITION OF GARDEN ROOM)

FARM POND AT ADWELL

My Father

H.B.R.
WITH HIS BELOVED TERRIER BUNGIE

H.B.R. IN HIS OFFICE

Ann Bewicke, 1942

Loading wheat stooks at Adwell in 1942
with landgirl Molly and Head Carter Jones

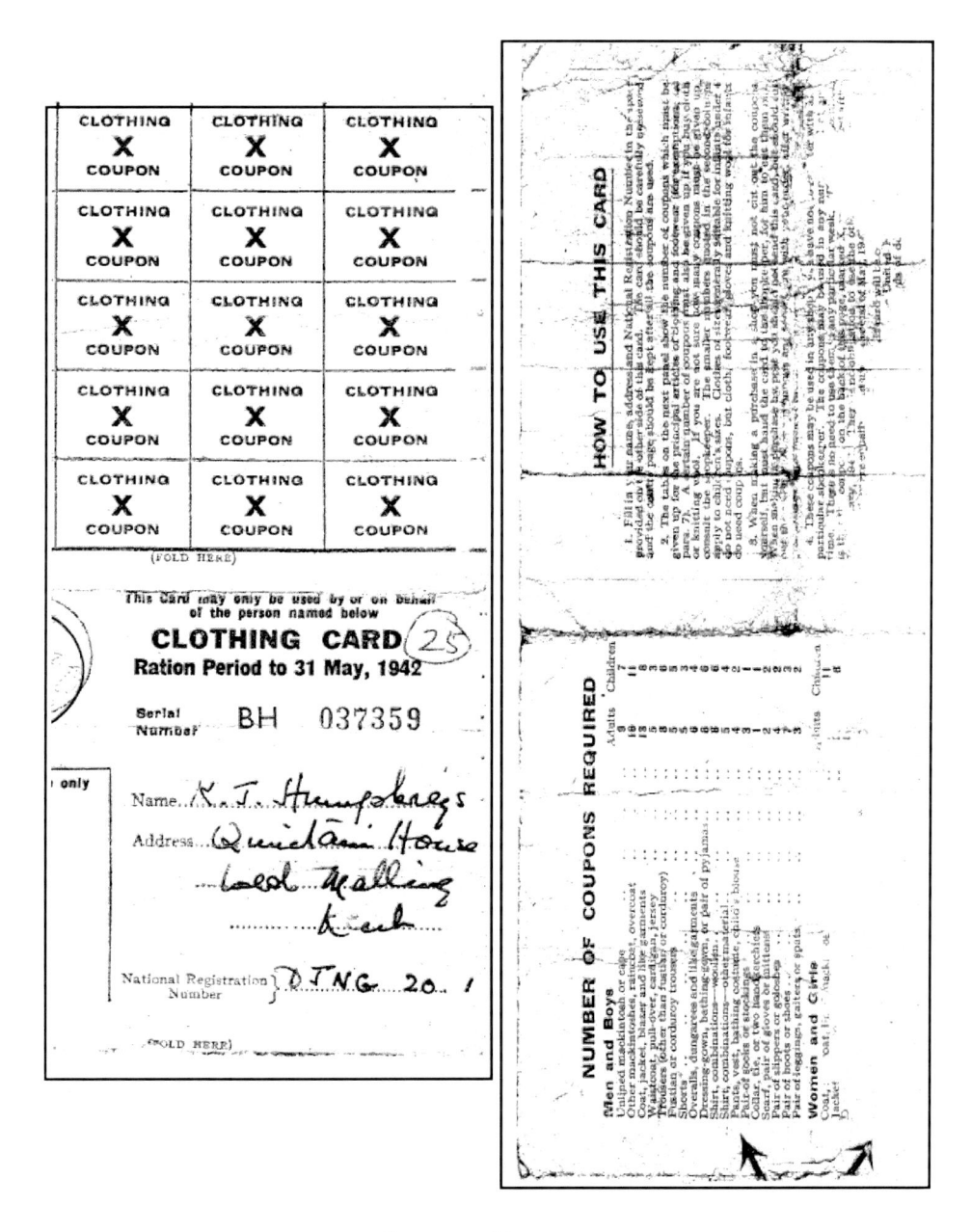

CLOTHES COUPONS

LODERS CLUB 1942

J. R. SYNGE　　D. D. BOLTON　　HON. C. E. STOURTON　　MARQUESS OF LOTHIAN　　W.B.R.
EARL OF DALKEITH

Part I
March 1943 – April 1944
Learning to be a Soldier

After leaving Eton, I went up to Christ Church, Oxford, in April 1942, for two terms to read General Science. I went down at the end of the Michelmas term in December that year.

It was at the end of this rather brief sojourn at Oxford that I first met Lorna. She was doing a typing course in Oxford at the 'Ox and Cow' (short for the Oxford and County Typing School) but I can't remember (how very unromantic of me) the precise circumstances of our meeting. I believe that, as her father had been in the same regiment as mine, Hugh Bailie had written to my father asking him to be nice to his daughter. Anyway I do have some recollection of her coming out to Adwell for lunch and, after that, giving her lunch at the Mitre Hotel (then a rather expensive and select Restaurant).

Soon after this I joined the Army. At that time everyone was required to serve as a private soldier for a short period before going to Blackdown and Sandhurst for training before being commissioned.

I was sent to the Royal Norfolk Regiment in Norwich where I spent about 8 weeks or so. It was quite a change living in a Barrack Room full of fairly uncouth soldiers, but I enjoyed the experience very much – even though I was knocked out in the boxing ring by a huge soldier who had been the middleweight boxing champion of the Metropolitan Police! This happened the second night of my sojourn with the Royal Norfolk Regiment.

I knew quite a few families in Norfolk including my cousin Priscilla Bacon (nee Ponsonby) at Raveningham. Her husband, Mindy, introduced me to the Divisional Commander, General Ozanne. He was hunting a pack of beagles with which I hunted a few times before he was posted overseas and I then hunted them on two or three occasions in his place, before being sent to Blackdown.

This first letter was written after my first visit to Manderston[1]. (An earlier letter, which is not included in the collection describes the wonders of the house - together with a reference to the mass of orchids in the hall - it was the third year of the War!) I remember that I found the house very large and somewhat daunting but, nevertheless, I enjoyed being there very much. Mrs

Bailie was quite frightening. When I came down the silver stairs before dinner, I commented with considerable surprise, on the silver bath which I'd used. "Well," she said, "it's rather ignorant of you to be unaware that silver is an excellent conductor of heat and that therefore when you get into the bath it is warm on your back - not cold like an enamel bath."

From Britannia Barracks, Norwich:
23rd March 1943

I did love seeing your mother – and I feel that I know her already! Give her my love, please.

After I left you, I wandered along and caught the underground for Hendon, feeling sick – I was so vilely depressed. But then I remembered how lucky I had been and how I loved you – and all was well.

But I made little progress towards Norwich until at last I got one of those long R.A.F. lorries to stop. When I said that I wanted to get to Norwich, the driver had the audacity to laugh!

I did very well till I got to Thetford (about 25 miles from Norwich) – then things weren't so good and I walked for two hours and a half without a thing stopping. It was such a lovely evening, though, that nothing seemed to matter. The cock pheasants and partridges were calling to each other under that lovely moon which seemed almost brighter than it had been in Leicester Square!

At last I got to a station and there was a train due in at Norwich at 11.38. However, we are in England and the train didn't fancy arriving until 12.45! This was rather a pity – but I was far too tired to mind and I don't think anything is going to happen anyway!

But I seem to have been writing all about my travels! I wonder what it was like last night for you. I thought of you going up to Scotland as I was walking along last night – with the pheasants and the partridges and the moon. I hope it wasn't a beastly journey. You couldn't be as tired as I am now!

I must go to the office now.

Well, there is, as usual, nobody here. It really is ridiculous.

I hope that my letter was waiting for you at Manderston – otherwise it means that it must have been lost which is most peeving.

HALL AT MANDERSTON
THE SILVER STAIRCASE

It's a lovely day again. I don't know quite what I shall do this evening. If I hadn't walked such miles yesterday I might have gone for a walk! But my feet are too sore!

I haven't heard anything about going to Blackdown yet – I do hope that it doesn't mean that I won't go on Thursday.

Evening: I have been talking to a poacher most of the evening. He is the typical Northamptonshire countryman – knowing all about nature. He loves so much what he sees – and has a rather lovely description for everything – and because of his real, deep down, heart-beating love for life, he has a deep rugged religious zeal. But that he does not know. Perhaps he has lived so much with realities that he cannot understand …

The men have asked me "but do you believe I would be a better man if I believed in God?" Of course I do because I can't see how man can live without spiritual help – we are not nearly strong-minded enough to live up to the ideal that has been set for us. But it is awfully hard to explain …

The whole subject came up the other day when a Church Army man came into the barrack room and began distributing leaflets to us. No one is so brave as these men who enter into a room filled with so many uncouth uneducated men and try to teach them about God. But they are not very inspiring looking individuals! And it is the worst thing for the men as they rather laughed at him and then religion on the whole. It is such a problem. The main attack should, I am certain, be made through education. And that will come.

MANDERSTON
GARDEN FRONT

Blackdown, near Camberley, was the pre O.C.T.U. (Officer Cadet Training Unit) before going on to Sandhurst.

The Beveridge Report was published in 1942, having been commissioned by the Government. In 1945 the Labour Party defeated the Conservatives and Clement Attlee (the new Prime Minister) announced that he would introduce the Welfare State as outlined in the Report, namely to defeat the five "Great Evils" of Want, Disease, Ignorance, Squalor and Idleness. This was the start of the National Health Service in 1948.

From Britannia Barracks and arriving at Blackdown: 26th March 1943

I came along to the office today (Wednesday) feeling furious with the thought of at least a fortnight more of doing nothing. Then I was sent for by the Commanding Officer and I am going to Blackdown TOMORROW. I am so pleased to be able to get on with the job. But I really will be sorry to leave them all here, because I have made such a lot of friends and really the whole two months have been tremendous fun. I will always be thankful for this experience – I have learnt such a terrific lot about men – and I know that it will help me to be a better leader. And that, Lorna, is what I want to do in life. I must learn as much as possible about people, though, before I can begin to think myself qualified to lead.

I got a most lovely letter from Mother yesterday – she is a marvellous mother too. I have finished reading the Beveridge Report. I have come to the conclusion that the main value of the Report is that it has made people think. That sounds rather cruel and condemning – but I do think that a good deal of it is sound. The big snag, I think, is that a man and wife unemployed can get 56/- a week with other benefits according to children etc. Now Beveridge says that, although it appears a good deal, man is not naturally idle and he will try and be employed again. But surely the answer to this is that he will pick up odd jobs (to satisfy his will to work) and go on drawing his unemployment benefit? However, perhaps all this is rather dull!

I just might be able to see Ann[2] tomorrow if I go through

London – but I don't yet know what time I am going, or which way.

Friday: I am so sorry that I have not got on with this letter but an awful lot has happened since Wednesday.

I left the Barracks in a great hurry on Wednesday evening – but not before I got your letter which was lovely. It was really sad saying goodbye to them all – I had to go round the Barrack Room shaking hands with them and a real lump came in my throat. Bill Wilson (the poacher) made me promise to come and see him when I was next in Northants – and said that he would like to take me out with him. It was all very sad and touching .

I got to London at about 10.30 and rang Ann up – but she must have been asleep, and I couldn't get hold of her in the morning – so I never saw her which was awfully disappointing.

I got hold of Father though, and just as I was going out to lunch with him, who should turn up but Dickie! He had just come up from Eton and was in awfully good form. We had a lovely lunch with Father at his Club and he told us that Cynthia and the two boys were coming up in the afternoon. So we had a grand family party before I left!

I got here in time (just!) I rushed around (though rather slowly as I had a very heavy kit bag and case to carry about!) till I was told that I had to report to the orderly room. Needless to say, I walked straight into the Colonel's office by mistake! However he recognised me and was awfully nice. "So you've arrived at last" he said. "I'm very glad – but we have heard some most amazing stories about you." These, I imagine, had come to him via Dick![3] Colonel Monck examined me at Oxford in that awful Certificate B! And was there when my late Commanding Officer began teasing me about my hunting . . . . .

I have, in fact, started with a doubtful reputation! I must take it really seriously here – I can't go through life laughing at everyone and everything! And I do mean to do well! I have already discovered that the discipline here is really strict. We work till seven o'clock every evening which seems a bit much.

But to the events of yesterday: I wandered about the Barracks till a corporal found me and brought me to Dick (Dick Fanshawe) my

Squadron Leader. It really was rather embarrassing seeing him in the capacity of my O.C. – and having to salute him rather demoralised me!

But this morning was much worse – we all had an interview with the C.O. and Dick was there. It was just awful! As soon as I came into the room, they both roared with laughter and said that they knew all about me – and therefore suggested a conversation about hunting! They both flung questions at me – what direction is the wind blowing, what sort of scent would there be, etc. I came out most exhausted!

From Blackdown:
6th April 1943

I am sitting in the sun in Cynthia's garden at Camberley. It is all very lovely – and to be near those two who are so happy together makes me happy too. I didn't go home this weekend as the family have gone to Wales to fish.

I have been seeing a good deal of the men at Sandhurst who I knew at Oxford – including Sandy Faris, John Sutton and John Ambler. It is so lovely talking to them again.

Your two letters were lovely – and Manderston does look most beautiful. Thank you so much for sending it to me.

I have written to Eleanor[4] – all very technical, but I hope that she will gather what I mean and that it will be a help to her! How nice of her to write.

Poor Sergei Rachmaninoff – how we both loved his music – he did have a hard life, but he was triumphant.

Yes I think you are quite right in your thinking that a crisis must be met and passed by a genius. Some time in the life of most men and women, good and bad very nearly coincide. It is at this point – this critical point – where one has to choose the right way in life. And it is the good in the person that leads him down the right path.

I am sorry about the rather depressing thought of a job in Edinburgh for you. But you will gain something out of it – if you try to – and experience is never learnt in vain. I know, though, how beastly this idea must seem.

I suppose that Ann will be at Manderston now – how lovely for you. Give her my love, won't you? I do so hope that she is getting straight about everything. It made me unhappy to see her so unhappy that night in London.

Cynthia and Humphrey have gone out for a walk with Nicholas[5] now – so I have come in and am now listening to the *Pastoral* – Beethoven's 6th. It fits in very well with today. I am afraid that I can't think very hard today. I don't know what is wrong with me! Perhaps the lovely day has gone to my head. So, I will stop for the moment and later – after tea – I may, perhaps, have something to say!

Tea has revived me a bit – it was great fun – and I had another one with Hum and Cynthia when I returned! But I can see that this letter won't get off tonight – as I've now got to leave Camberley and walk back to Blackdown. Most energetic!

Monday: Today was too lovely. We went out map reading. All this means is that you drive for miles and miles in the sun looking at the most beautiful views the whole time. We went over the Hog's Back to Hindhead. You have never seen such beauty – and the sun was hot. We lunched (very well!) at a hotel in Hindhead and got back here for tea. But since then I have been working rather hard and have only just finished my notes – and it's almost time for lights to go out!

From Adwell (sick leave after operation on finger):
6th May 1943

I got another lovely letter from you today – you are simply marvellous writing to me so often, but you know how I love your letters and they are not, I think, in vain.

I am finished with the hospital[6] – and do not even have to go in daily for dressings – it is a blessing as it was such a bore going in so often. But Oxford is up now and I really had awful fun there with them all. On Monday I spent a lovely evening – who with, do you think? Cuffie[7] – no less! But she isn't nearly as bad as you make out – really!

She gave me an excellent dinner and then we talked to Mary MacNeal and Foxy – they were most interesting about the Beveridge

Report. Then we played the gramophone. The Poulenc *Concerto and Trio*, some Stravinsky and Bach – most lovely. Do you know the Poulenc – it is really rather lovely – most unusual. It is recorded by Decca. Actually I tried to get it with you that day we went to HMV's.

Last night I dined with Jimmy Galbraith[8] and Tim[9] and other members of the Gridiron Club. I am so hopelessly 'sloppy' about Oxford – but I do so love being there – and trying once again to live the life of an undergraduate. I wish it had all gone on a bit longer – but perhaps it was a good thing that it didn't. I will go up there again after the War I suppose – but it won't be the same, Lorna. I'm not sure that I really want to go back at all. So many of my friends have now been killed – so many that I loved. People who I used to talk to until three o'clock in the morning without knowing how the time would go so quickly. But I mustn't be depressed.

I have had rather a bad day – I came back here and found Mother gone to see Rosamund who doesn't seem very well – I imagine that it is more nerves than anything, poor old girl. I felt rather lonely – then Colin Balfour[10] came to say goodbye. He is going to sea for the first time and will be away for two years. It is so awful – I will miss him. He lives very near here and I saw a tremendous lot of him and we always went out together.

How very sad John Chaworth Musters being killed. I did not know him well but I remembered what a friend he was of Doug's and of course I know his brother very well.

It is a lovely evening – I am writing from where I can see out into the park. Koran (my grey horse) looks so perfect with the evening sun shining on him. I love him very much. When I go down to the gate he comes up, taking those long Araby strides of his, looking so pleased with life. What a lovely life too. Lazing away all the summer – and then in the winter he is made fit again and comes hunting. I'm sure he is very happy.

I'm playing some piano music now – an odd selection of Debussy, Chopin and Brahms. I so seldom play these single records now – some of them are lovely. They were mostly bought by Mother and Father when they were married. Now the Chopin *Nocturne in E Flat* is playing. Most lovely. It is getting dark. Koran is eating under the elm avenue which stretches from the lawn right away out of sight. But how I love Adwell. When will you see it? Come soon.

Blackdown:
20th June 1943

Thank you so much for your letter. I should have answered it before but didn't have time! Now the weekend is here though – and my War Office Board has been cancelled! I go next weekend instead – which means that I will have next to no leave, unless Dick has thought out some wonderful plan!

I forget now what your plans are – when do you go up to Scotland? I shall have Saturday free next week and then Tuesday and Wednesday (the 28th and 29th). I wonder if you will still be in the land of the living.

I don't like the idea of you not writing to me so much one bit. It is a very unfair arrangement. You are writing about ten letters to my one – but I am the one who gains – so, knowing as you do how I love your letters, you will not lessen them, will you?

I dined with Kit and a large party of men from Sandhurst on Thursday. It was such fun – Dickie Pearce was dining too. He has just got the Belt of Honour and deserved it too, by all accounts. He is most awfully nice.

Hectic plans are going on for Rosamund's wedding – they are all very involved at the moment but I have an idea that they will be alright at the end of it all! We have a system of our own, we BRs!

I was on guard on Friday night. Really rather fun as it was such a lovely night. Anyway I had 4 hours spare to think while I marched up and down alone. I suppose I thought most about you – but also about this queer world that we are living in. So seldom do we have time to think. But Lorna, we are all striving at the moment to kill and destroy. That is our job. Pretty ghastly, isn't it? How amazingly easy we humans can adapt ourselves – now we do not hear how many men were killed on a raid – but rather how many aeroplanes were shot down. For we are fighting against machines. And God is with us all.

I then thought about Ann – but it is too hard a problem. I do pray for her very hard.

I did post that letter to Lady Trenchard – did I tell you about the A.T.S. dance? No, I haven't written since I went. I got a telephone call from Dick Fanshawe saying that I had got to get hold of ten other men from the Squadron to go to a dance at the A.T.S. O.C.T.U. at Windsor. I duly found ten who thought it would be funny enough to make it worthwhile and we started off.

Seldom have I laughed so much! First of all we had a badge pinned on our breasts bearing a name – mine had Derby on it – and it was our duty to find our partners amongst the A.T.S.! Mine, I was told, was Joan. Needless to say, we all went in, and there was Joan – fat, grey haired and hideous!! Of course all the others were overjoyed to see me dancing with her!

So the evening went on until we felt that we would die of exhaustion unless we had something to eat (food appeared to be non-existent in the whole O.C.T.U.) so we stole out and hailed a marvellous old man – complete with bowler hat and whip – who was driving a horse and cab. He duly stopped and took us to the Old House at Windsor! Of course they were closed but we did get something to eat in the end at a Y.M.C.A.

Then we returned to the fray – and saw the cabaret. This consisted first of 3 A.T.S. singing 'in harmony' very sloppy songs, very out of tune – then two girls, both hideous, with rather too few clothes on tap dancing for ten minutes. Their style was their own – they were, shall we say, at least original! I'm afraid we behaved rather badly!

I had to run in a race on Wednesday – very bad time I did too – but it wasn't very fair after London and the A.T.S.! It was three miles over awful country. I can't tell you how ghastly I felt after it!

Sunday: I'm at Adwell! I decided that Blackdown was no place for me at the weekend and that really there wasn't any reason why I shouldn't go. I have been having a lovely day listening to lots of music and talking much too much! Lots of people seem to be here – Viola Head and Anne Symonds who both worked at Adwell, Sylvia Nott who is a great friend of Rosamund's and mine – lovely seeing her again. We had a great talk and she is getting married to somebody in the fairly near future. Brilliantly clever, she got a first at

Cambridge in Economics last year and spends most of the time trying to make me a Socialist! But she is pretty level-headed about it, unlike most of her colleagues!

I came through Oxford and saw Jimmy and Euan Graham. Jimmy has got an exhibition at the house – isn't it good because he really does deserve it as he worked jolly hard. He gets his degree next term.

Do you recognize the smart paper? The Chatham Club – I stole it from Tim! It was rather a bogus political club where the members spent most of the time smoking cigars (!) and drinking port – but it was all great fun!

Oh dear, I will be rather pleased to get to Sandhurst – B'down is awfully monotonous! I forgot to say that Gay Cropper came out this afternoon. She really is rather amazing – but I went to see Koran and stayed for an hour with him! He's so nice to talk to and he smells so good.

I must stop now or I shan't catch the post – anyway this won't get to you till Tuesday which is awful.

I forgot to tell you a great bit of news! I got an amazing letter from Robin Lyle's solicitors saying that he had left £10 to the President of Loders at the time when he was killed – that's me! Wasn't it good of him though – it was so sad his being killed. But I've got to buy something for the Club I suppose, which is a bore – I should have so much rather been selfish and bought £10 of records! What shall I buy – simply can't think! We'll go to Aspreys and choose something.

From Adwell (still at Blackdown) – Interview:
2nd *July 1943*

It was so lovely seeing you at Eton on Saturday – it would have been awful to have you go away up to Manderston before seeing you again. It made all the difference. But it was pretty vile saying goodbye, wasn't it? I remember so well saying goodbye to Kit when he left Eton. We had both been dreading it so dreadfully and I will never forget the feeling of actually seeing him go. He was such a friend of mine that I felt that Eton could never be the same without him, nor was it – but I loved it just as much somehow. I suppose I missed him very little after a time – perhaps because I find it easy to adapt myself quickly – it is very lucky.

I got rather the same feeling on Saturday night – Scotland seems an awful long way. But Ann is such a marvellous 'connecting link' – and I shall see her tomorrow. She seemed so sad – but you say she isn't so bad. I am sure that there is no need to worry about her being 'flighty' – it is rather natural. She is so starved of sympathy – so starved of love that she is now almost greedy. But who wouldn't be? Her father never taking any notice of her, and instead married to this woman. I will talk to her tomorrow night though.

I do so hope that you both got back all right last night – it was such a bad 'hitch', you going back so late. I arrived at Camberley at about eleven and didn't get to bed till rather late as I talked to Hum and Cynthia.

I went back to the Barracks in the morning, and after rather hectic dressing got onto Parade in time to go to the Selection Board. And here I am. We have been spending most of the time filling in the oddest forms and rushing about over obstacle courses – but now we are free.

It is really a lovely place. The house is, I think, designed by Lutyens as also is the garden. Very typical of his architecture. Well-proportioned red brick and a verandah overlooking a garden in three terraces, lawns and Surrey trees – rose gardens and fish ponds. Very pretty – but perhaps a little bit too "arty" and proportional. But the view from the terrace where I am writing is most beautiful. First of all I can see a typically English park surrounded on three sides by woods. There are some cows lying down in it – looking so contented with the evening sun catching their bodies in its warm golden light. And then underneath the elm trees – all in a cluster there are some good looking horses standing head to head whisking the flies off each other. Then behind the wood at the bottom of the park I can see right away to the horizon. The country is covered with trees – but they look quite lovely this evening. Most of them are conifers of one sort or another – and somehow they appear to be in a mist – the blues and greys and greens all mingling together. It is a nice place, in fact, to attend a Board which more or less decides my future! I only hope I pass!

The Interviewing Officer is in the VIII Hussars and seemed nice – anyway we had a long talk about hunting. But it is so awful feeling one is being watched the whole time.

My Troop Officer is really deadly and lacks any form of sense of humour badly. I had to give a lecture this morning. It was so suddenly flung on me that I couldn't think of anything to talk to my rather dull Troop about. I began to ramble about foxes – the Troop seemed interested – but not so the officer! Very silly little man.

I wonder if you got a sleeper last night. I thought of you and hoped you had.

However Ann turned up looking so pretty (wearing that pink and white dress with lace collar) and in time to get to *The Moon is Down* just as the curtain went up. The play was very well acted and I think she enjoyed it – though it was rather sad and 'shattering'.

But we soon forgot our sadness and danced while Carol Gibbons[11] played the piano too beautifully – perhaps it was a bit risky but I asked him to play *Night and Day* and got a large lump in my throat as a result! Ann was in very good form really – we had a long talk and I think it did us both a lot of good. We both decided that you were really rather nice. So we danced and talked till we thought that it was time to stop – it was a lovely evening. But I did miss you so terribly . . . . .

I wonder if you will be able to come down here before you join up. It is really rather an unbearable thought if you can't. But I suppose that a bit of discipline would do us no harm. We have been jolly lucky this last month – how lovely it has been. Not that we've ever been alone. It is all so difficult. However . . . . .

I was left asleep until nearly eleven o'clock on Wednesday morning! But after a lovely breakfast I recovered and went out and 'looked at the shops'. After lunch I went to see Tom Fairfax[12] who has been in bed since March. I have never seen anybody look so awful – his mother says that he won't be allowed back to his regiment till October at the very earliest – isn't it awful for him? Poor chap, he seemed really pretty depressed . . . . .

I then went down to Oxford and got there about six thirty. I went to the House and saw Jimmy and after a quick dinner went up to the Eltons and danced there. It was great fun and I talked for a long time to Ld. E. He is most awfully interesting. Jimmy was there too.

Mother told me – or rather asked me – if I would go to the Headington High School dance as Mary Ponsonby's partner. I thought that it was awfully kind of me to accept! But thank goodness it was all a mistake and she meant the Eltons! I don't think that I would be very good with girls of all ages varying from ten to seventeen! In fact I'd have been quite terrified! But it was great fun.

I had breakfast with Jeannine, Marigold, Anne Balfour and Juliet[13] this morning! And a very good one too. I did at least stay at our house! Then I had another breakfast with Tim and Jimmy and Archie Dunn! We talked for ages – in fact till my bus went – missed it of course, but got home quicker by hitching!

Such a lovely surprise – telegram from Molly[14] asking me up to London on Friday – but I don't think I'll go! You make me sound catty though. It is jolly kind of her to ask me! And so I'm back – for a week. It's just too lovely.

Our course at Sandhurst was to last six, rather hectic, months. (Now the course lasts for a year.) Blackdown, quite frankly, had been slightly boring but when one got to Sandhurst we were Cadet Officers and military life had started! The main activities were drill on the Square, 'assault courses', map reading and 'schemes ' away from Sandhurst, often in Wales, when live ammunition was used - so one had to be careful!

Our Squadron Leader and chief instructor was a charming fellow in the Scots Guards called Reggie Gordon Lennox. Under him were a number of Guards Sergeant Majors and Sergeants headed up by Regimental Sergeant Major Britain, Coldstream Guards, a man of huge frame with an amazingly loud voice on the Square. It is said that when a small aeroplane (a Leander) had the temerity to fly over the Square when the R.S.M. was present, he looked up at the aeroplace and shouted "Get out of my air space." The aeroplane immediately complied.

When drilling, the Sergeants, who always called us 'Mr' and ended any remark with 'Sir', cursed and swore at us in most politically incorrect language. Once, when I had failed to about turn correctly, the drill sergeant yelled 'Mr Birch Reynardson you're marching like a pregnant crab, Sir.'

The assault courses were designed to make us fit and courageous. We had to run in 'full order' (large pack, small pack, rifle and ammunition) for considerable distances over (and under) obstacles, ending up with the order 'fix bayonets'. We men had not only to pierce the sacks filled with hay (representing Germans) but to twist the bayonet so that the enemy was not wounded but killed!

Map reading was a wonderful relief as we drove round the country in comparative comfort. But, in order to make life difficult for the invading Germans, all signposts had been removed so that one had to be alert not to lose the way! I always enjoyed Wales and the 'schemes'. We lived in 'battle conditions' sometimes without the provision of food or drink.

The six months passed very quickly and I think we all enjoyed it. The passing out parade was a very grand affair. I can't remember which general took the salute after which Major Arthur James (the Adjutant) rode his little grey horse up the steps of the main building (as was the custom) and we were then dismissed. We had made it!

Arriving at R.M.C. Sandhurst, Ros's wedding: 13th July 1943

I haven't heard from you for years – you aren't trying that awful fortnightly letter system are you?! But then I haven't written to you either – and there is so much to tell you about.

I got back to Blackdown on Wednesday and, after rather hectic packings and signing forms, got finished in time to dine with Dickie F[15], Lavinia Holland-Hibbert and Mike Leslie Melville[16]. It was great fun but I was rather sad at leaving Blackdown. Dickie has been so frightfully kind to me – and anyway it has been rather fun!

I went to Sandhurst on Friday. We marched in with full band and colours etc! I am sharing a room with Bill Geddes, Brian Cummins and John Althorp.[17] They are all quite charming – and, though six months is an awful long time to be in such close contact, I think it will be great fun being with them.

Anyway a horn has been duly established in its place of honour on the dressing table! Slowly the room will attain a more civilised semblance when a few Lionel Edwards and Munnings pictures and brushes and masks are added to the walls! Oh yes – we all hunt!

Sandhurst is certainly going to be fun – there are so many people here that I know. I saw Kit[18] on the Friday night – just finishing work at 11.30 pm. Apparently when one has been at Sandhurst for about three months the working hours become quite impossible.

Then on Saturday, after spending a morning listening to various lectures, Humphrey and his sister, Nicholas and I started off to Adwell. We changed taxis half way and got to the wedding with two minutes to spare! It was so lovely. Rosamund really did look rather beautiful in her dress and the Queen's Choir sang most awfully well. But, oh dear, how selfish one is! I can't tell you how sad I felt all the way through the service – I couldn't make myself remember that she was going to be happy and that it was all right. But I am going to miss her terribly.

There seemed to be hundreds of people there. The whole Ponsonby family – lots of the Oxford and Bucks – Hugh Euston[19] – but it would bore you if I went on telling you who I saw. Let it be that it was a perfect wedding except for the weather which was vile! She got some really lovely presents – particularly jewellery and silver – and an awful lot of them.

I do like Jimmy[20] – I am certain that he will look after her.

I had to get back to Sandhurst by 12 – a most maddening arrangement – but I managed it all right – just!

I am writing this at Cynthia's listening to the *Bach Prom*. I wonder if you did. So lovely. Particularly the *A Minor Concerto for 4 Pianos*.

Ann will be up with you by the time that this gets to you – what fun you will have together. I wonder if she has found a place to live yet. Give her by best love.

If you do have the chance read *Christian Behaviour* by the same man who wrote *The Screwtape Letters* and *The Problem of Pain* – but I can't remember his name for a moment. He was – or rather is – a don at Magdalen. The book is very interesting and most amusing. I think you will like it.

Must stop now – Nicholas has been put into my charge and is proving definitely tiresome.

Kit Egerton's party on leaving R.M.C.:
1ˢᵗ August 1943

This will only be a short letter I'm afraid – but it is just to tell you that I am thinking so much about you now. It will all be a bit difficult at first, I know – as it was for me – but you will be all right. You will find things in your new life that you will hate and despise – you will see and hear things that you would not have believed, but remember that God is with you, and be brave (as I know you will).

I am writing to you feeling rather tired as Kit had his party last night. It was awful Ann not being able to come – you will no doubt be amused to hear that Molly took her place. But it was a really lovely party – Kit, Carli Tufnell, Molly, Elizabeth Lambart and Jane Ruggles Brice and me. They are all very nice – I shall miss Kit so much. He missed the Belt of Honour by one – wasn't it bad luck? He will make a first class officer I think.

I never told you that John Althorp and I crept out of Sandhurst last Tuesday night and went to a Prom! Actually we could only just hear the 1ˢᵗ part of the programme as we had to catch the 9.24 down to Camberley but it was worth it.

I wonder how much leave you will have. It would be so lovely going to some concerts together. Such a pity that you couldn't get off today – but I rather doubted it all the time. I'm afraid the first few days 'in the Services' are rather ghastly – inoculations, etc, which make one feel beastly.

ROYAL MILITARY COLLEGE
CAMBERLEY, SURREY.

Exercise in Wales:
17th August 1943

I got back from Wales to find two lovely letters waiting for me. So marvellous hearing from you again – we were allowed no letters while we were in Wales, and I missed them so terribly.

I am so glad that all is well now – and I only hope that you have had a good leave. As soon as I got back last night I rang up the Lansdowne and Hook – but to no avail. Ann was out and so I am writing this without having any idea where to send it! But I will ring up Ann again this evening and try to get hold of your new address. Otherwise I will just have to wait until you write to me again.

I am still rather tired after Wales – it was a tremendous experience. We left Sandhurst early on Sunday morning and got up to London at about 8.30. We had about an hour to wait and so I rang Ann up from the Euston Hotel but, as usual, she was out – I have very bad luck with my telephoning to her!

Then we went on down to Llandudno and arrived in the pouring rain at about six. The country was rather lovely through which we went – passing right through the cream of the Pytchley country. We could see Althorp from the train – rather awful for John who was in the same carriage as me. He is such a nice fellow – so kind and unselfish, and a very good soldier. We stayed the first night at a hotel in Capel Cure – most beautifully situated in the bowl of the Welsh hills near a loch.

On Tuesday we marched for miles all over the hills in the most lovely weather. It was very hard work – but we were always rewarded by a most heavenly view when we had reached the top – often right to the sea. One day we could see right down into the valley of the Conway and over the castle to the Isle of Man. And in this most godly country we fired thousands upon thousands of rounds – we charged with fixed bayonets – it is rather a ghastly thought isn't it? But somehow we were all so hardened to it – so excited that it didn't seem so vile. It is something to know that one does forget when fighting hard. Just like when hunting we do not think of the fox or the rather terrifying obstacles which somehow are met and overcome!

It was a week of terribly hard work – we never had more than three hours sleep a night – and one night we slept in two inches of water! But enough of Wales – let it be that it was great fun, though why I don't quite know!

We have changed over from the Old Buildings to the New Buildings now. It was an awful job packing everything up and getting it over – but now it's done we are really better off.

Later: I've been asleep! I suppose that I must be tired – I do love coming here so much. It is such a happy family. I will miss them terribly when they go at the end of next month. Hum has got a very good job – but very hush-hush – in fact I hardly know what it is. Cynthia is going to live down in Sussex near Eridge which is fairly near his work.

I must go back to the R.M.C. now or I won't get organised for the new course tomorrow.

Sandy Faris plays the piano:
28th August 1943

I got your letter this evening when I got in after a very hectic day's driving. Oh Darling – such a lovely one, thank you so much. Yes, it probably was a good thing that you tore your first two up!

I have been having such a lovely evening listening to Sandy Faris playing the piano. It was so like the old Oxford days when he used to play right into the night and go to sleep over the piano. He is such a marvellous person – so wonderfully blessed with so many talents. There he sat in the Mess playing whatever people asked him. He started off with some Chopin – then veered into some of his own compositions – ending with *Night and Day* – I was hoping that no one would ask but John Althorp loves it too, but not quite in the same way.

I dined with Cynthia and Hum last night and rang up Ann. I'm going up to see her on Sunday afternoon. She sounded rather tired, but in very good form and terribly happy about Verly. That is a good thing, isn't it? I will be so lovely seeing her again.

Can you read any of this? I'm writing in bed and it's all very difficult. We sleep in bunks – Brian Cummins on top and I below!

Everything looks pretty good about seeing you soon. I'm sure I could get up to London on Saturday 4th – but not till the afternoon. Could we have an early dinner – or do you have to get back earlier? Perhaps you could catch a train back in time to get the bus back at 10.30. But I don't know the trains to Oxford. Mine goes at 9.24. Anyway, think of something! It's not worth coming to Oxford as I would have to start back as soon as I arrived!

I'm dining with Dick Fanshawe tomorrow night, and Lavinia H-H too. It will be fun – they always make me laugh so much.

We had an awful tidying up this morning as the Commandant inspected our rooms. Absolutely hectic – Brian and I are quite hopeless together and just roar with laughter instead of taking it seriously. However all went off all right – and I'm told he liked my Ackerman prints and, of course, the hunting horn!

Did I tell you that I found the other part of my Oxford diary that I lost in the hills above Adwell? I was so pleased – they are so funny to read now, though they make me rather sad. Amazing mentions of you! Even the first time when I saw you with D singing in the Bach choir! I'll show it to you one day.

I've tied all your letters up in a bundle now – there are a marvellous amount. What a good correspondent you are! I'm trying to read then again – but never seem to have time.

Criticism of Church Parades:
29th August 1943

I got your Thursday letter this morning – a lovely one – thank you so much. The Gillette razor blade is much appreciated!

I am writing this at Cynthia's listening to rather a lovely concert – at the moment the Scottish Orchestra is playing the Elgar *Enigma*

Variations – do you know them – I have heard them before.

I am on guard again tonight – isn't it the limit. But I shall be off in time to go to Holy Communion tomorrow morning.

We are being inspected by the Commandant at church parade tomorrow which is rather a bore as one has to be so maddeningly smart!

I wonder if you have read the letters in *The Times* lately about compulsory church parades. In all the units that I have ever been in they have been a definite failure.

There are two faults in the system. First and foremost, the men are forced to church – it should be much easier for them to be able to have leave off it – and secondly the church parade itself is far too long and formal. Men do not exactly prepare themselves for church by polishing endless buttons and pressing trousers.

Of course, I think the standard of padres in the army today is low. Some seem to care little for their men. And what an opportunity to teach them – so many all gathered together in a community. It seems so awful, such a chance being missed by them.

It's lovely being alone, isn't it? Do you remember how I used to love it in Norwich? I often think of the days when I used to dine alone at The Bell - and write to you from there. And I too thought I should hate it. There is always something to think about though.

Now, about your education! What a good idea about the history. The books that I think you want to read for a start are:

(a) Trevelyan's *History of England*, then
(b) *The Years of Endurance*, Arthur Bryant, and if you like that:
(c) *English Saga*.

I have got them all if you would like me to send them, though perhaps it would be simpler for you to get them from The Times Library. But Trevelyan is the most important – a really first class history.

I am longing to see Ann tomorrow – though it won't be for long as I'll have to catch the 9.24 down to Camberley. But it will be lovely seeing her and hearing all the news.

Nanny has just been in with Julian – he has had his curls cut off – but he looks so nice. He's the sweetest little chap.

Cynthia and Humphrey are out at the moment – and I don't know quite when I'm going to get my dinner. It's now 8.15 – and there's no sign of them! I'm on guard at 9.30! Oh! I am going to miss them so much when they go – and it's in a month's time now. Rather an awful thought.

Surely we can think out a plan for Monday other than your bicycling all the way to Adwell. It would take hours – it's much too far. Poor old Darling, you'll be quite exhausted when you arrive. Couldn't you catch a bus into Oxford and then another one to Adwell? Or catch a train out to Thame where I could fetch you?

Party at the Lansdowne Club and dancing at 400 and Astor: 7th September 1943

Oh Darling, it was so lovely talking to you yesterday – but I was so cross that Mother rang off. What did she say to you! I am so terribly sorry for you about the quarantine. I wonder if everything will work out all right though, and I shall see you on Monday after all. Now that we have been looking forward to it, it will be a beastly disappointment if the whole plan falls through, won't it?

I got a letter from you this morning – so lovely. What good news about Diana arriving. That will be a great boon. I don't know where Tom F is at the moment, but I will write to him at his home in Essex and try and get hold of him.

I had a lovely weekend. I felt that it would possibly be a good thing if I could get up to see Ann – so I went to Reggie Gordon Lennox and said that I had to go up, and he never asked any questions but just gave me a pass. He is a really nice fellow. This all happened on Saturday, so there was no time to let Ann know that I was coming. I rang her up when I arrived though and arranged to come to the Lansdowne at 7.

In the meantime I saw hundreds of people – Ronnie Wallace and Jean, Michael St Aldwyn and Peggy, Arthur Clerke Brown, John Mogg, Andy Martin – oh hundreds! But it was particularly lovely seeing Ronnie who I hadn't seen for years.

I then went to the Lansdowne and found Ann. She was really in very good form. The whole situation seems a wee bit complicated. The affair with Robin, however, seems to be under control now. I simply can't get over his father almost forcing Ann to marry him – too awful. She says that she doesn't know what to think about Noel but she is going down to stay with him soon which is a good thing I think.

Then there is the question about her living in the Lansdowne. Her father has now said that he will not pay for her living out at all. If Verly does come to London I think that she will probably go to him. Otherwise she will be stationed outside London. She talks rather vaguely of going abroad – but I think that it would be silly. Anyway she has got to get Major Bewicke's leave – and he obviously won't give it. It all seems frightfully vague at the moment – but all will be well in the end no doubt!

I talked with her until about a quarter to nine and then I went and had dinner with Ronnie. I thought that I was just going to talk to him and Jean and then go to bed. But when I arrived at Mannellia's a host of girls met me. It was maddening but I managed to talk to R quite a lot – it was lovely. However they wanted to go on and dance – I would have put the party out if I hadn't come – but, oh, I didn't want to.

We went straight to the 400. It was awful, but there were so many people there who I knew that I just sat and talked. Then we went to the Astor. That was better – at least we weren't in the dear 400 (our club!). There I saw John Sutton! I was so pleased to see him again. He is up in Yorkshire – and seems to be enjoying himself a good deal. He was with one of the Sankey girls – she looked so nice, though frightfully young – then there was Charles Laurie and Ann Cumming Bell – and lots of other Etonians. I again talked much more than danced! In fact I felt rather rude, I'm afraid. One of the girls in our party was called Matty Colt – she is at Englefield Green with Molly and Elizabeth. She's rather nice – I met her beagling with Ronnie last season.

I didn't get to bed in the end till awfully late – in fact it seemed very little time before I had to get up again for church. I called Ann at about eight and we went to St Peter's, Hanover Square. It was so lovely being with her – and we both felt much better afterwards.

I went back to 'the club' (!) and had breakfast and then I went to Park Royal (on the Western Avenue) and hitch-hiked to Adwell fairly successfully, getting there in time for lunch. It was so lovely being there. Actually Ros was with Jimmy – but Dickie was in very good form – though he rather failed in his School Certificate as he only got 5 credits – and he should have got more really. However, it's all right.

We shot all the afternoon. I was shooting very badly – but it didn't matter! We only got 3 ½ brace – but it was great fun and a lovely afternoon. Your ringing up just made it perfect. It is, as usual, rather an anti-climax being back here. But I am very lucky – and really it is the greatest fun.

Hunting at Waterstock with Dick Fanshawe: October 1943

I am writing to you in the drawing room and we are listening to Tschaikovsky's *No 6* – the *Pathetique* – it makes me want you so. And I know that you are sitting all alone in the cold.

I wonder if your shoes are dry yet? Have you got an awful cold? So far I am all right!

They had all gone to bed when I arrived last night (or rather this morning – did I really see you today?) It was a good thing. I simply couldn't have made it if they had all been waiting for me – ready to pounce on me.

I must write to Juliet – I got up at 6.30 and went and had breakfast at the Ross[21] – they were most amused and equally amazed to see me at such an early hour! Then I hitched out to Thame and drove back to Adwell. I just had time to have a cup of coffee and I then rode to Waterstock. And what is more, I was there absolutely on time – much to my surprise. Dick was hunting hounds – and lots of nice people out. But we didn't have much of a day. It was so lovely to be out though. I rode back with dear old Sir Robert. What a lot I owe to him.

Later: I have been having a long talk to Father. He is just a wee bit depressed about the politics of England at the moment. What an amazingly illogical method of legislation is democracy, that Father's vote counts exactly the same as the kitchen maid's. He feels so much that politics is becoming a professional race – we poor Conservatives organise ourselves so badly! Just look at the Labour Party – they finance all their members far above the £600[22].

Betsy Ponsonby[23] is here on leave from the W.R.N.S. – I am so fond of her. She is so full of sadness though. A mother and father and brother dying in a year is too much.

Mother is being so marvellous about Granny – what strength she must get through prayer. The funeral is on Monday, but I shan't go to it as I feel that I must get down to Sandhurst again as it will be the first day of the course.

Michael Holland-Hibbert, now Viscount Knutsford, I first met at a children's party at Beckley. His face was very scratched. I asked him the reason for this. "Well, my two sisters always hunt me round the garden, I'm the fox you see. And this morning they ran me to ground in a blackberry bush and they wouldn't dig me out." He was always very dressy and we much admired his Tyrolean hat.

Dining with Rachel Lambert; Death of Mrs Rigden:
Undated

I hope so much that you are feeling happier now – and that things are a bit less tense. I know so well how you felt – but you were not wrong to leave the dance, and I think that the others were merely rather impressed, but felt that they had to behave otherwise. Don't let it worry you.

I haven't written for days now. I have been pretty busy. This afternoon I did a very bad exam paper which is maddening. But I am going to Rachel's[24] for dinner and that will be lovely. No doubt we will play the Brahms *No 2*. I had fun there on Sunday – but she was in bed, as she had a tummy ache.

Father has bought me the most lovely sleeping bag. It is a Jaeger one! All wrapped in a waterproof case with a rubber sponge mattress under it. It will be frightfully useful on this course – and later on.

I got a very understanding and nice letter from Juliet. I am most awfully fond of her - most of all my cousins I think. You must get to know her better.

I walked over Bagshot Common on Saturday afternoon. It was so perfectly beautiful – all the trees a most glorious red – and the sun and the deep blue sky. I walked slowly and thought a good deal …

Then I hitched from Bagshot and saw Dickie at Eton. Did I tell you that Mrs Rigden[25] had died? Isn't it awful? She really was rather an institution – and it was very odd to go to The Cockpit and not have her 'all over you' the whole time. Dickie was in very good form – and had been playing football. I saw Michael Holland-Hibbert at a film in the school hall which was fun.

I played rugger yesterday afternoon – the first game that I have had since I left the Dragon School! It was rather fun – though I had forgotten a good deal about it and kept on playing the Field game!

I got a letter from Tom Fairfax yesterday. He wants to meet Diana.

On wireless exercise:
4th November 1943

I said that I wouldn't be able to write to you – but I had to, even if it does mean writing to you and listening to various dots and dashes at the same time. Oh Darling, wasn't it a lovely, really perfect weekend? It is pretty grim back here without a chance of seeing you for a fortnight. But we must harden ourselves to that.

You were marvellous in taking the news about me going so well – though I can't quite decide whether I should have told you now – particularly as all plans might be changed. But perhaps it is better to be prepared.

I have also bought a very smart primus stove with me so that I will not have to attempt to light a fire this evening with wet sticks! Most efficient. We won't get back from this scheme till 1 o'clock on Wednesday so I shan't be able to lunch with your mother which is a great pity. It would have been such fun – and it was terribly kind of her to say that she would come with me.

Tuesday Night: This won't get to you till Thursday – it is awful, but we never went near a post office all today, and only got back tonight. It was an exhausting and rather awful day – sitting attempting to receive morse. I am so awful at it and can never concentrate properly.

I saw David Laurie[26] tonight – he was very rude about me staying with you so long at the 400![27] I am dining with him tomorrow night. I sent a telegram to your mother before dinner – I do so hope that she gets it in good time tomorrow. I meant to send it yesterday – but couldn't.

I wonder if you have read about this new strike that has broken out in London. Of course it is natural to condemn them all without much thought – but if we pause for a moment, I'm not sure that we are quite fair. They have a pretty awful job – and it is a very thankless job. But there is also, I think, a much more far reaching reason. It is because the workers are fearful of the wages being too low after the War (when they will obviously be lowered) and they are trying to guard against this.

I am lunching with Dukie Hussey[28] and George Myrrdin Evans on Sunday. Will you be in Oxford on Sunday evening – or near a telephone? If so, I will dine with Rachel – but don't please go bicycling for miles! Let me know if you will be near a telephone anyway.

Written on my 20th Birthday:
8th December 1943

Here I am at the Y.M.C.A. – or almost, perhaps the Red Shield Clubs are not open to you F.A.N.Y! However, they supply quite excellent 'sanwidges' and hot tea!

My goodness, this is a slightly grim place – but it has all been quite fun and interesting.

Your lovely letters have made all the difference, and stopped me feeling quite uncivilised. They have been brought out from 'the Coll' – as my companions like to call it – practically every day.

Darling – have you given me a tie pin? How lovely – a most excellent and necessary addition to the otherwise well-dressed soldier. Actually it hasn't turned up here but no doubt it is awaiting me at R.M.C..

I have had lots of lovely letters, including one from Johnnie Dalkeith[29] who seems to be having a most exciting time sinking submarines! What a great age twenty is – I feel most superior. But how young we are still!

I must write a very long letter to Mother – I see so little of her nowadays that I never have time to talk to her properly.

I'm sorry that I never rang you up from here on Tuesday night – but I was on guard. It was quite icy. But as you guessed, I wore many jerseys.

I will never get clean again – I am absolutely filthy! We are out with the tanks all day and, ghastly thing, on iron rations! We had a big exercise today and no less than twenty two officers, including the Brigadier, came to watch us! However they say it was done rather well. We go back to Sandhurst on Friday night – it will be rather a relief.

I am terribly tired – must stop.

I return Angus's[30] masterpiece – it is awfully oily. I am sorry about this.

Margaret Elphinstone, the Queen Mother's niece, was living at Windsor Castle. I had known her well at Oxford. At the dance, the Queen (as she then was) asked me whether I could dance a waltz as she wanted the Princesses to learn to do so. After 'trying me out' with approval, the two Princesses were sent for to learn from me! First was Princess Elizabeth who was rather solemn compared to her sister. When dancing with the latter, she asked me whether I knew the 'old fellow' walking into the ballroom. I said that I didn't. "Well, he's painting my father and mother and he's taking a very long time about it. You see he likes the food here." The artist was Gerald Kelly.

Dance at Windsor Castle:
14th December 1943

I have had a most exciting time since I last wrote to you from the YM at Thursley. I was just getting up on Thursday morning when a message came through that John Althorp and I were to report back to the Adjutant at Camberley. We were in a great quandary as to know what on earth he wanted – but it turned out that we had been asked to the dance at Windsor Castle on Friday night.

It really was the greatest fun – and the Queen and the Princesses were most charming and natural. Lots of lovely people were there – including Molly and Elizabeth. We danced all night and arrived back here at five – only to rise once more at 6.30!

Can you read any of this? I've lost my lovely pen – can't get over it.

Your lovely birthday present arrived – or rather was waiting for me when I arrived back here from Thursley, and was first worn in front of the Queen!

Now look – move heaven and earth to get a pass over the night of Saturday 8th January – it will be alright won't it? What shall we do? Brian Cummins, Willie Geddes and John Althorp will also be in the party. I suggest that we dine at The Savoy and then pay the 400 a visit afterwards. But if you could get off in time we could all go to a play first. I do so wish that I was going to pass out and go on leave at the same time, instead of having to go on this exercise directly after the Passing Out Parade – but it can't be helped.

In the following letter I mention Dame Clara Butt: she had a wonderful contralto voice. I first me her when I was four! This was going out to South Africa when my father was appointed Secretary to Lord Athlone, the Governor General. I heard the singing in the ship's dining room where there was a piano. She always practised after breakfast so I managed to escape from my nanny (Miss Turner) and hid under the piano. And then she arrived with her husband Kennelly Romford (who accompanied her). It was after half an hour that I was discovered! She made me sit beside her husband and turn the pages when he nodded! The start of my love of music!

Christmas at Adwell
28th December 1943

It was so lovely talking to you yesterday – it made all the difference to my Christmas. Your letter sounded rather depressing –

you poor thing. I don't wonder either. I have had such a lovely time here – and you must have had a perfectly vile Christmas, the first time away from Manderston.

I got down to London for breakfast – it was lovely hearing Ann on the telephone and I met her at Fortnum's at eleven where we drank hot chocolate and ate buns till about twelve! Then we did some shopping together – such fun. I had lunch with Father, went to my tailor's etc and then came back and saw Ann having her hair done! There is nothing I have to learn about that side of a girl's dressing!

I drove down to Adwell with Father, Humphrey and the American. We got here too late for the Estate Party which was a great pity – and Dickie had to be Father Christmas – he was quite mad all Christmas Day.

Father gave me a most lovely watch, and Mother replenished my stock of leather waistcoats – but this one is lined with sheep's fleece!

We danced in the evening. It was such fun as we were a really good party. I like the American immensely – the right type of course, a cavalryman – he hunted in New York State and played polo. But he is awfully nice really!

And tomorrow I hunt – rather a good thought. Oh Darling, is it a bad thing to love it as much as I do! To think that I will be hearing those hounds again, and gripping a horse again between my legs – riding, riding, riding. How I miss it.

I just can't believe that you will not be with us on the 8th – it will be a really bad disappointment won't it? I wonder when you will know definitely what the plan is. You will let me know directly, won't you?

I have asked Kit to come down if he can. He wrote to me for Xmas – he had a motor smash coming back from a dance last Monday and was in hospital at Cambridge but managed to get back to Sheriff Hutton all right for Xmas. He has got a new horse – given to him by Mrs Simmonds, Master of the North Shropshire. Isn't he lucky? And to think you have never met him. Oh you must – he will be able to tell you so much about all that you don't know!

We are playing some lovely vocal records – *Little Things* by Ernest Lough, Clara Butt, etc. It is rather a nice change. No doubt we will play some slightly more serious music later! Do you think that *Rachmaninoff No 2* would do? Oh Darling, I wish you were here with me – I miss you so – and when am I going to see you again? Oh you mustn't go on the 8th.

The children acted a nativity play in the church this afternoon. It really was the most beautiful and the most moving thing that I have ever seen. One of them read the lessons and they all sang carols in between the different scenes. Ros taught them the play and deserves a lot of praise. I don't think that she is feeling too well now – poor thing. One doubts whether it is worth having babies until little fellows like Julian and Nicholas are to be seen. They really are too nice. Cynthia is the most marvellous mother – and so obviously brimming over with happiness.

John Ambler rang me up this evening – he had been out with Ann and June Capel etc on Christmas Day, and seemed to enjoy it.

Having passed out of Sandhurst and been commissioned into the 9th Lancers, I was sent to the 27th Lancers, the holding regiment of the 9th Lancers.

Joining 24th Lancers at Bridlington, Yorkshire: 20th January 1944

Well, I've got here! All these new experiences in life are worth having, but this one is certainly odd and, I think, rather unpleasant.

I arrived at 5.20 in a drizzling rain and was driven to the Squadron Office where I gave in my papers, and then I went on to the mess. Perhaps I was expecting too much – but the 24th Lancers evidently care little, or anyway succeed in obtaining little comfort. The dining room and ante room are really very dismal. No pictures and awfully ugly furniture, found only in boarding houses of seaside resorts (which is exactly what they are!)

All today was very dull, and I felt that I had no job to do. I saw odd bodies such as the Adjutant – and the rest of the time I spent filling magazines. Actually last night I was really rather depressed, but I've stopped that now – because it is quite pointless. I read the Twenty Seventh Psalm[31] instead, and that made me feel much better – but, oh Darling, you are such a help in times like this.

Willie Geddes never arrived in Bridlington but went to Scotland instead. However, he may come down here. I only hope it is soon. I do miss all of them so much – the Squadron is going up to shoot in Scotland on Friday - but I am not going, so I will be left alone here which will be very boring – and I shall be a bit lonely I expect.

I wonder how you are. I am writing in my room – as there is no chair or table I have had to go to bed! The walls are bare and I have to look at rainbow coloured wallpaper peeling off the walls! However, my books and photographs of the family and the horses have, at least improved it!

Can you believe it – they are making me wear a beret! The 9th abhor such headwear!

From Bridlington:
22nd January 1944

Most of the Squadron has left for Scotland now, and I am left in charge! So there has been a certain amount to do – seeing that everyone has a job, and settling what job is to be done by whom. But it is all rather fun – and a very good experience for me. I even write Squadron orders out!

I suppose that things are settling down a bit now – anyway life seems much better. I discovered that rather a nice fellow in the Bays who was at Sandhurst with me, called John Lyle, has turned up here – and last night we went to a film together. It was called *King's Rock* – I thought it rather good. I wonder if you have seen it. It was rather a pleasant change getting away from thoughts of the Army anyway.

I had a letter from Ann this morning. So lovely hearing from her. She says that she liked staying at Adwell – that's a good thing. It was lovely having her and we did have fun together in Oxford didn't we? How I value her as a friend. Isn't it odd to think back on a friendship growing up. I suppose that primarily one is attracted to another by looks – not necessarily good looks, but by something that you like. That is the first step – meeting someone. And then we begin to get to know them – to see if we like them. Perhaps then we get fond of them, we find things in common with each other. And so time goes on and with each day the friendship grows until a cement is formed. Then that wonderful gift, loyalty, is set up. Loyalty is so urgently important isn't it?

As can be imagined, my posting to Barnard Castle was surrounded by very strict security. It is for this reason that the letters written from there and from Adwell (I managed to get there for three days embarkation leave) contain very little news. In fact I was very busy getting to know the men for whom I was to be responsible on the voyage to Algiers. They were all very edgy and all were confined to barracks pending embarkation.

Posted to Barnard Castle:
11th February 1944

Things seem to be pretty hectic at the moment! I wonder if you know that I was at Newmarket even! But I expect you will have got my letter by now – Anyhow I am not there any more. I have been told to report up at Barnard Castle tomorrow.

Oh Darling – isn't everything difficult – so now there is no chance of me getting to see you. I'm afraid the time has really come now for you to think about me going abroad - you see Barnard Castle is a posting barracks. Perhaps I shall be getting some leave very soon. Do you think that under any possible wangle you could get the weekend off? I should think that I will report up at the barracks and then probably be sent on leave until there is a draft of men for me to take abroad – so I should be on leave from about Feb 15th. We must just make the best of it and be terribly happy when we are together.

Newmarket was going to be such fun – near to London and lots of horses to ride. A fellow called Bill Luddington who is second in command of my squadron knows a good many trainers and owners and was going to introduce me to them. But it just can't be helped.

I wonder whether I shall be on leave for the Queen Charlotte[32] – it is a good thought anyway. What plans have you made for it? I think it's worth chancing it that I will be on leave. Wouldn't that be lovely? I will know by Friday morning anyway I should think – and will send you a telegram then.

The few days that I was at Newmarket were rather fun – we had little to do as all our tanks have been taken away and we are being re-equipped – I went into Cambridge yesterday and brought a few things. It's rather a lovely place – but some people say lovelier than Oxford! I brought a whole sheep's skin – I thought it would be 'useful'! But what am I going to do with it now!

Douglas Bailie (Scots Guards) was Lorna's only brother. He was an outstanding athlete at Eton. Keeper of Rugby and Mixed Wall, President of Pop and Captain of his Tutor's (Kerry). He must have been about 21 when he was killed. This had huge repercussions because Lorna became heiress of Manderston and the very large estate, west of Berwick on Tweed. Her father was broken-hearted and this seriously affected his relationship with Lorna. I was very much in two minds as to whether I should include the letter which follows. It contains some very private thoughts about Doug's death but, in the end, I decided that it would be wrong to omit it.

Death of Douglas Bailie:
18th February 1944

I got your letter this morning. Through my love for you I feel that someone has gone from me - and I can't think clearly to write to you now. But, in our prayers tonight Our Lord will help us to make us strong and make us brave.

Doug's death is not the end, for you will always remember the lovely things he did and thought. I do not believe, I cannot think, that it was His will that he died. But rather do I believe that it is now a test for you to accept that he is now in His hands.

Darling, I know how difficult it is but I believe that, through prayer you will come to see through truth - unburden your heart to Him.

I won't go on writing to you now - you know that I am thinking of you all so constantly.

Douglas Bailie

Adwell:
15th March 1944

Wasn't it rather awful saying goodbye last night – but I am, somehow, sure that all will be well and that you will be able to get off on Monday night. And if we can't do that we will have to make some other plan.

But it is no good just not facing the fact that it is all going to be beastly saying goodbye – we will both have to help each other to be brave about it, not that we can just rely on each other.

I went back to Vincents and simply couldn't go to bed, and just wandered about, picking up the *Tatler*, and then writing to Colin and then thinking about you. I came back to Adwell this morning. Mother is being so wonderful and helps me so much. It is lovely that she knows about us both.

I saw Mrs Holland-Hibbert – D's lovely horse Rocquilla has had to be shot, so she will be feeling pretty low. He was one of Lord Bicester's horses and he was third in the Grand National – I rode him quite a bit at the time, a most wonderfully good ride. She gets so low when things like that happen, poor old thing.

Lavinia has arrived in Algiers – it is lovely as I shall definitely see a good bit of her.

It is a perfect afternoon – they are threshing out in the farm, and George is very busy!

I hope that you got back all right in that funny lorry – and that it wasn't too awful at Poundon.

I must stop now or I shall never get this letter off.

Still at Barnard Castle, preparing for posting abroad:
Undated (about 30th March 1944)

Today has been fairly busy getting everything in order – and seeing that the men I am taking out have everything too. We had a tremendous parade at the square. Colonel Lumley inspected us and gave us all a most unenterprising speech – but I suppose that morale was to be boosted by the Band of the 10th Hussars who marched up and down in their red hats. But it was all rather depressing. I showed signs of it anyway by giving my word of command on the wrong foot!

I have just returned from driving with Christopher Bostock[35]. It was lovely seeing the old boy again. He seems to think that he will be coming out in the next draft. He is so happy too – Joe is a lovely wife for him. He is so completely different from all the others – he knows nothing of the life that I have been brought up in – and it is so refreshing to talk to him.

I had a letter from Mother this morning – she doesn't sound too good. Darling, go out to Adwell to see her – she would so love it. Ros has sent me a lovely pair of sheepskin gloves! Most elegant and equally warm. But you might try and trace the rabbit fur ones!

I am now making myself a cup of Bovril – not particularly because I want it, but because I want to know how well the camp cooker that Father gave me works! At the moment it is making the most comforting purring sound – I hope it continues.

I am reading Francis Brett Young's book called *The Crescent Moon* – it appears rather good.

Tomorrow I hope to ride one of the horses here – I took courage into both my hands and asked rather a pompous looking major if I might. All seems to be well!

Footnotes to Part I

1.   The house, which is now open to the public, was built by Lorna's great uncle and completed in 1908. It is famous for the silver balustrade on the front stairs and the stables which are glorious.

2.   Ann Bewicke (later Price). She was a very great friend of Lorna's for many years. There is a picture of her on page 24. For some reason, which I now forget, there was a parting of the ways after a number of incidents. I saw a lot of her and you will see from her photograph that she was very pretty. She died in 2004.

3.   Dick Fanshawe, Master of the South Oxfordshire Hounds.

4.   Eleanor, Lorna's younger sister, afterwards Mrs Tim Rettalack.

5.   Nicholas Prideaux, Cynthia's eldest son.

6.   I had had a badly poisoned finger.

7.   Cuffie Hubler – the very worldly French proprietor of a finishing school in Oxford. Her 'partner' was Foxy Falk. She was a particularly brilliant teacher.

8.   Jimmy Galbraith – invalided out of the Navy, having lost an arm in the Bismarck (a German warship sunk in the River Plate) action. He became a great friend and later the factor and general adviser to Johnnie Dalkeith.

9.   Tim Laws, a close friend at Oxford.

10.   Colin Balfour – one of my very greatest friends, a regular Naval Officer and my contemporary. His father, Melville, realised that I like pictures and allowed me to bid for him at Christies aged 16!

11.   Carol Gibbons at the Savoy Hotel; a wonderful pianist.

12.   Lord Fairfax of Cameron, a contemporary of mine at Eton.

13. Jeanine, afterwards married, fiirst Alan Scott and then Admiral Josef Bartosik, and Marigold Bridgeman; Juliet Ponsonby, my cousin.

14. Molly Middleton, afterwards Mrs John Boyd, Harry's sister.

15. General Sir Robert Fanshawe, Dick's uncle (see Prologue).

16. Lavinia Holland-Hibbert, married to Peter Orde, Delia's elder sister; a very special girl and extremely intelligent. Mike Leslie Melville was Elizabeth Joicey's brother.

17. Johnny Althorp, afterwards Earl Spencer. I saw a lot of him and liked him very much. He won the Belt of Honour at Sandhurst (I was next!); Princess Diana's father.

18. Kit Egerton, Colonel Christopher MC, later to marry Rosamund. He was probably my best friend; we messed together at Eton for 5 years.

19. Hugh Euston, later Duke of Grafton KG.

20. Jimmy Marriott, Major James, later killed in the Normandy Invasion. He was in the Oxford & Bucks Light Infantry and was killed in his glider on landing. He won the George Medal.

21. The Ross Café, High Street, Oxford; a popular place for breakfast.

22. The annual pay for MPs.

23. Betsy Ponsonby, later Mrs John Clay, my first cousin. Her father was the Rev Canon Maurice Ponsonby. Her brother John, Coldstream Guards, was killed – see later.

24. Rachel Maxwell, my cousin, later Mrs Lambert.

25. The proprietor of the Cockpit at Eton. A famous snob! My fagmaster at Eton, Tony Garton, called himself Lord Drinkwater for years and always got a table!

26. The first mention of David Laurie, Lt. Col. MC. He became a great

friend and, as will be seen, a wonderful Squadron leader. His father was Sir Percy Laurie, Scots Greys, a not attractive man. When David asked him to recommend him for his regiment, the Greys, he refused to do so. He ran the Mounted Police for many years.

27. The 400 was the most famous of all the London night clubs. (See Appendix 10.)

28. Dukie Hussey, later Lord Hussey of North Bradley; very badly wounded; he became Chairman of the B.B.C..

29. Johnnie Dalkeith as will be seen later; a great friend and contemporary. (See picture of Loders Club on page 26.)

30. Angus Rowan-Hamilton - a neighbour of Lorna's in Berwickshire; married Jean Lockett whose parents were very kind to me when I was in Norfolk. His son Guy is a great friend of Thomas B.R.

31. Psalm 27 reads (verse 1) "The Lord is my light and my salvation; whom then shall I fear. The Lord is the strength of my life, of whom then shall I be afraid?"

32. The Queen Charlotte's Ball in aid of Queen Charlotte's Hospital. At this ball, the debutantes curtsied to a huge white cake. It was the great ball of the Season.

33. Sir Thomas Armstrong, organist first at Eton and then at Christ Church. He later ran the Royal Academy of Music. His son, Sir Robert Armstrong, was Secretary to the Cabinet Office, famous for saying that he might have been "somewhat economical with the truth".

34. Lavinia Ponsonby (married Michael Hamilton MP); third daughter of Charles Ponsonby and a great beauty.

35. Christopher Bostock was a great friend and contemporary at Oxford.

Part II
April to August 1944
Regimental Soldiering

Arrival at 9th Lancers, Algiers:
11th April 1944

I have now reached land – at last!

Oh it does seem such ages since I left England – and I miss your letters dreadfully. We haven't arrived yet at our final destination, and I am now writing to you on the train on the way.

But I must begin at the beginning – there seems so much to tell you so I am writing this air mail and will send you an air mail letter as soon as we arrive at the Regiment. I hope that my letter from the ship arrived all right.

It was a lovely voyage. I knew a good many people on the train – Rupert Watson and Tony Meredith Hardy (in the Life Guards), Peter Clifton (Grenadiers), and Major Mike McCullen (10th Hussars). That was a good start.

The first day was really rather rough and Mike and I walked round the boat deck to try and keep going. We kept passing two F.A.N.Ys (who looked even more uncomfortable than we) – and they came up and talked to us in the end. They were quite charming and in a few moments I found that they know hundreds of people that I do – their names are Diana Holden and Ursula Barclay. I wonder whether they hit a note - Diana knows Delia frightfully well - and Ursula was at school with Ros! Wasn't it extraordinary?

Diana is really terribly nice - and we had some tremendously long talks. The extraordinary thing was, Darling, that we talked as if we had known each other for years. I make a rule not to do this generally – as I feel it is rather a pity, but somehow – for some reason – we could talk about things which really seemed to matter in life. She had some very good ideas. I really do owe an awful lot to her for making the voyage such fun. I so dreaded being bored and sad – and I really wasn't ever.

It was the most lovely weather most of the way over – and we lay on the deck and read most of the time. An awfully nice fellow called Martin Abraham in the 12th was there too – and, of course, will be near me when we arrive.

There was rather a nice padre on board – it was particularly lucky as we were there in Holy Week.

Disembarkation was a frightful business – every bit of luggage seemed to get lost, and most of the men too – but all is well now, and I have arrived with all of them intact – much to Reggie Gordon Lennox's[36] surprise!

And now as I write in the train I am looking out on some really lovely country. It is all so much greener than I ever dreamed it would be. The railway is lined with tall trees rather like poplars, and the fields vary from the bright yellow of mustard flowers to the dark green of oats. But the farming appears to be run on rather lax lines and cows and sheep roam about rather aimlessly in the crops, and the Arabs just laze about paying no attention to them except occasionally to throw a stick at them.

We have just stopped at a station – the platform (merely a sandy space with a cottage on it!) was lined with Arabs carrying enormous wicker baskets full of oranges – but as we have no money changed yet I had to give him five cigarettes 'en lieu'! But they are so good!

Actually it isn't very hot – thank goodness. The train is going so slowly – nothing seems to matter in these parts, and no one does anything quickly.

A train has just passed us – some of the Arabs were wearing rather lovely clothes – interwoven gold braid and silk, but most of them are frightfully dirty and poor.

Later: We have just stopped again – for an hour! No apparent reason. We all walked about and looked at the horses – but I haven't seen a really good one yet. They are so narrow with great long legs with no bone in them. There are lots of donkeys and mules too – they use them tremendously here evidently. The flowers are most lovely – and now we are getting into country covered with them. The sky is so clear that the hills climb away right into the distance in greens, then blues, then purples.

And so I could go on writing to you – whenever I look out of the window there is something new to see. Oh Darling I wish that you were here to see these new things with me – it is so exciting but rather frightening too. I wonder how you are feeling - and whether you have seen any of the family or Ann lately. I haven't written to her yet – I must. I'm not allowed to post this yet so I will stop for a moment – terribly thirsty so I shall have to go along the corridor to Mike and collect his mug.

Later: I have now had my lunch – one of the new American pack rations. Really awfully tasteless, but better than nothing! This really is the oddest train journey – people are lying in the sun on the roofs of the carriages and I have been sitting on the steps of my coach looking at the country as we go slowly by. The ground is covered with bright colours – such lovely flowers and flowering shrubs, and there is always something new to see.

We keep stopping at these odd little stations and leap out and buy eggs and oranges from the Arabs – but as we have no French money it all has to be done with cigarettes or American rations! There is such a lovely sunset now – and you are so close.

Saturday morning: Really rather an awful night in the train – trying to sleep on wooden benches – but not very successful! However we have all arrived. You can imagine how hectic it was getting all our luggage off the train – but at last is was complete and we were driving about twenty miles to the camp where I am leaving the chaps and await orders from the Regiment – goodness knows how long I shall stay here doing nothing.

I have just been out to change English money for French francs and have paid the men. Most complicated – 200 to the £1, and I was 15 frs short at the end!

Later: Most marvellous – the 9th sent over a subaltern[37] and collected me, and here I am at last. We drove about fifty miles through most lovely country, planted mostly with vines, and arrived at the Regimental Headquarters at the foot of the hills. It really is most beautiful! I am in B Squadron and the mess is in a large farmhouse surrounded by cypress trees. The garden is filled with flowers – and there is a long avenue of trees (rather like limes) leading from the front door.

I am writing in my bedroom and just out of my window there is a tree with a stork's nest in it! From time to time it gives the oddest gurgles – but no doubt I shall make great friends with it!

Oh how lovely – a letter from you, Darling, and three from Mother and one from Cynthia. And yours only took a week. It made such a tremendous difference – and you made me so happy.

So I will now write an air mail letter as this will not get to you for about three weeks . . . . .

Regimental Life in Algeria: I so well remember arriving at our Regimental H.Q. outside Algiers. After preliminary introductions in the Mess – I felt extremely shy! – I was taken to meet my Troop. Sgt. Edmunds was there to greet me with an extremely smart salute. He then took me round the tanks to meet each crew member. They were all charming and friendly. They had all been at Alamein and here I was, about to command them, aged 20 and with no experience.

Algiers
17th April 1944

This will take an awful long time to get to you and will be very out of date when at last it does arrive – but somehow those air mails are so short with their three pages and I can never get down to 'talking to you' as we used to in letters.

I can't quite make up my mind whether it seems ages or just yesterday that I arrived here – a mixture of both. Anyway I am now pretty well settled in and feel much more at home. It is not much good trying to think that I am in England, for not only is the country here quite different – but somehow people think in other ways out here. Remember most of the chaps have been in battle – they have seen death, they have known fear; and somehow it has changed them. I don't think that they are all very happy – many of them have family troubles in England. And it is not only their wives' fault – I feel that you would hate to know how lax they are morally – but the temptation is very great out here for them without a home to keep them straight – and they do fail so often. As you know, I cannot condemn them for this, however wrong I (and you too) may think they are. But they are causing a great deal of selfish unhappiness which of course they will regret, though perhaps they are never found out.

They are charming fellows, much better than any trooper seen in England today – I talk to them for hours. They have experienced so many things which I have never – and it is so very interesting to hear their point of view. Really there is terribly little to do at the moment. Sometimes I do get rather out of a job, and it always makes me feel a bit depressed (as you know) – but it only lasts a short while. There is, after all, such a great deal to think about.

I have been riding quite a lot – and on Saturday and Sunday I rode over to A Squadron and saw Bill P[38]. He has an enormous grey Arab stallion just about up to his weight which he rides! They have built (with a little of my help) a very good jumping lane with some large obstacles in it which we school the horses over. At the moment I haven't got a horse of my own but I am going over to the Spahi Cavalry Depot in the near future to choose a horse and then it will be much more fun. I never really like riding a borrowed horse for a completely selfish reason. Anything I teach a horse (if ever) is always rather pointless and often in vain. For instance, the horse I ride belongs to John Joicey. He never jumped before but already he is doing quite well – but he isn't mine!

The Regiment are having a gymkhana on the 30th organised by Bill which should be the greatest fun. He has been very nice and kind to me – but he is an unusual sort of fellow isn't he – and needs a bit of knowing I imagine. But by the time you get this I will know him!

I went to Holy Communion yesterday morning. So lovely it was with the sun just up, shining on the dew. The service is held in the 'rectory', a tiny little wooden hut where the padre sleeps, etc – but he takes the service most reverently.

There seem to be lots of F.A.N.Ys in the town[39] – but I don't know any of them and haven't seen Elizabeth Fooks yet. I do like her, but I never know quite where I am with her. Poor thing, she is really very unhappy. I did tell you that she was engaged to a man in the Air

Force who was killed, didn't I? Life is very hard for her as she has little faith now and feels so lost and miserable – quite naturally.

We had a tremendous game of football after tea today in the Squadron. You will be sorry to hear that the officers and sergeants were beaten badly by the corporals! I never know the rules and keep forgetting that I am not playing the Field game – all most tricky!

On Wednesday night we are all dancing in the town – as we did last week. It should be great fun as we will be a large party and no doubt there will be lots of people there that I know – but I will write an air mail and tell you about that.

I wonder how you are my Darling. Perhaps life is by now beginning to feel pretty beastly – but you will keep going and be happy. Try to get away from Poundon as much as you can – and dance in London (however much you may hate the idea at first). I feel that it is so much easier for me with new things to do, new people to know – in fact, with everything new.

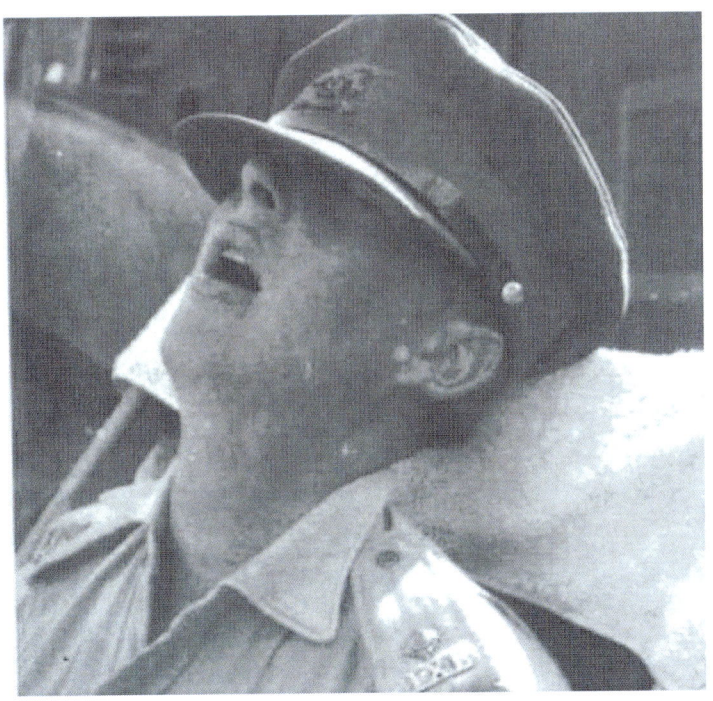

W.B.R. IN ALGIERS
1944

Trip to Morocco and Gibraltar:

I suspect that the reason for the lack of detail in these two letters was that I knew that we were about to go to Italy and, therefore, security was redoubled and censorship stricter.

My diary does, however, give a rather more detailed account. I started off with John Joicey and our servants, drivers, etc, in two 15cwt trucks on 29th April. The first night we stayed at Mascara, the second night at Oudjda (having lunched with the Foreign Legion at Sidi Bel Abbes which was fascinating). We arrived in Fez and stayed in great luxury at the Palais Jamais. On May 4th we continued our journey, stopping at Moulay Idris and visiting the ruins of Volubilis.

On Friday 5th May we drove via Meknes to Rabat, then on to Casablanca. On the way my truck broke down. We were towed back to the local aerodrome, Corporal Emerson driving (he remained my driver during the battles – see later). I managed to 'hitch-hike' by air to Gibraltar in search of a differential, but could not get the right model – so flew back after shopping!

Then on May 10th we received signal (we had a wireless in the truck) to return. I left the truck and flew back via Oran, arriving with the Regiment on the 11th, just in time!

News of Dukie Hussey as prisoner:
13th May 1944

I'm back here once again, having flown from Rabat. I hope you got my letter from Gibraltar all right. It was the most lovely fortnight – but I'm afraid you went much too long without a letter which was bad. When I returned there were two lovely ones from you, nos. 6 and 8.

Oh Darling, how lovely for you all to know that Doug was killed in such bravery – how proud you must be of him. Your news of Dukie was half relief and yet great sorrow too, for I did not know that he was a prisoner. It is something for him to be safe – but his leg being cut off will be terribly hard for him; you know that he was a very good athlete and played rugger for Oxford.

I'm glad Ann was better – but isn't it a bit harsh to say that you can now see through her? If there was something for you to see through she would be deceitful – Ann isn't deceitful. Remember what a friend (a sister!) she is of ours. We have to pay for that and try to be patient with her moods. I had a letter from her which I got when I came back here – but there wasn't much in it.

How lucky that I bought a pen in Gibraltar as a spare one. It hasn't got a v.thick nib, but I have sent it off with a pair of silk stockings and it should arrive in about a month's time. I hope you will like them. There is nothing to buy in the town.

Darling, do go over to Adwell again – they love seeing you, that I can promise. Apparently they had a tremendous christening party at Adwell and now they have gone down to Jimmy – strictly against all rules.

Oh, how I know what you mean – how difficult and almost tiring it is to stay on the right lines – and not run off them. But then it is never easy to do things worthwhile, is it? As Jock Lynam used to say "You can't be a Christian sitting in an armchair."

Gibraltar
19th May 1944

I haven't written to you for ages now. And why? Look where I am! I have been having the most extraordinary time and cannot write fully about it now but will write a sea mail later. To give you a quick idea, I drove away from the Regiment on Sat April 25th with John Joicey and our two servants to go to Morocco. After three days of driving fast through lovely country full of mountains and waterfalls and rivers, we drove up the mountain to Fez, the capital of Morocco. Oh it is a lovely place and the Medina (or native quarter) is absolutely fascinating, full of narrow winding streets lined with Moorish stalls selling every sort of thing. I have bought you a Moorish bag but don't know whether to send it or not in case it is lost. There we stayed surrounded by a galaxy of glamorous French girls for three days.

We then drove on to Rabat to look at the Sultan's famous horses. I have never seen anything like them – hundreds of the most lovely creatures, I wanted them all. Into the car again we jumped and drove to Casablanca – a modern and rather dull town, but we wanted to see it and the port.

Then we had to turn homewards which was sad, but just east of Rabat there was an ugly sound and the truck stopped! To make a short story of it I had to stay with my servant and try to repair it – but there are no spare parts in Rabat and so I flew to Gib. and am here looking for one – but no success here either, so I am flying back again – the next move isn't certain!

Just before I left the Regiment your 4 and 5 arrived. Oh Darling, how I love getting them – I am glad that mine are at last beginning to turn up! And that you are feeling happier with them. What good news about your new job – I am so pleased and I think it is a bit of well deserved encouragement. I wonder whether Judy has arrived yet – I am longing to see her and hear all the news.

Sailing for Italy:
25th May 1944

I am writing to you as we slowly, and possibly rather sadly, sail away from North Africa for a new land. I really loved it – the flowers and trees and the mountains ever in the distance with the silver water falls pouring down in to the green valley below. And wasn't I lucky to see so much of it before I left? It really is so exciting seeing new places – each with its own beauty, each with its own differences – and yet it makes me realise how much I love England – her beauty is so quiet and modest – and Africa hasn't the smell of hay and winding lanes and the little cottages nooked in some age old bank, and the talk, oh the quiet contented gossip as the sun goes down. Yes, England wins – how much I want her back, and you as well. Your two sea mails were so lovely – they came just when we moved off and I had to read them very quickly. They were both written in the days when

Personal Message from the Army Commander

Great events lie ahead of us. All round Hitler's Germany, the Allies are closing in: on the East, the victorious Russians drive on — in the West, the British and American Armies are massed to invade.

— Now in the South, the Eighth and Fifth Armies are about to strike.

Side by side with our French and American Allies, we will break through the enemy's winter line and start our great advance Northwards. Our plan is worked out in every detail — we attack in great strength, with large numbers of tanks and guns, supported by a powerful American Air Force and our own Desert Air Force.

The peoples of the United Nations will be watching the Eighth Army. Let us live up to our great traditions and give them news of fresh achievements — great news such as they expect from this Army.

We welcome gladly to our ranks those Divisions whose first fight this is with the Eighth Army. We send a special message to our Polish Corps, now battling beside us to regain its beloved country.

I say to you all — Into action, with the light of battle in your eyes. Let every man do his duty throughout the fight and the Day is ours!

Good Luck and God Speed to each one of you!

Oliver Leese.
Lieut.-General.

ITALY.
MAY, 1944.

I was still at Barnard Castle – what ages ago that seems now. How much has happened since then.

Just think of the things we will both have to talk about when I come back - oh Darling – it seems so odd to think of not coming back that it is difficult to contemplate it, isn't it? I suppose that we should – and yet we both have the feeling that I will be all right – that is a lovely thing because it is a positive thought – if we thought otherwise it would be negative and destructive. Therefore you cannot prepare for me dying, for if I did you would already be prepared by your positive thinking. Do you understand what I mean? But all will be well, all will be well!

It was such fun dining with Judy[40] the other night – and hearing all about you from someone who had seen you such a comparatively short time ago. We had dinner at a funny little restaurant in the town near which we were camping – she arrived looking very hot, the reason being that she had uniform over her ordinary clothes as apparently she is not allowed out in 'civvies'! So off she went to change in the local gents and arrive back looking so pretty (but still a bit hot!) and we sat down to the most enormous meal given to us by my Squadron Leader, Derek Allhusen, who was also there.

We had a terrific gossip and then at 10.30 she had to go back on night duty – poor thing. I would have been so cross not to have seen her – and I only just managed it. What wonderful news it is – it seems that they will soon be in Rome – perhaps the war hasn't long to go now.

I have just been listening to Jim Weatherby[41] – a fellow who lived next door in the old days – playing the piano. He really does play most awfully well – and I rather stupidly asked him to play the following selection: *Night and Day*, *The Tramp*, *Smoke Gets in Your Eyes* and *Honeysuckle Rose* – and of course got rather depressed!

Music I think reminds me most of things – their smells (I shall always remember my late home by the latter!).

I wonder whether you have been to the 400– what lovely happy times were had there – just you and me together.

I wonder how Ann is – I haven't heard from her lately which is a pity. Perhaps her ideas on being in love do appear rather odd to us but on the other hand she is a very lovable person, and her love goes out to many people and I have no doubt that she at least has thought herself to be in love with many people. When one really loves a person, one loves with three different capacities – physical, mental and spiritual. But often one loves a person physically and sometimes mentally and you think you are in love. Not till one loves wholly can one know one's mistake – and that whole love comes so seldom; then one is in love.

It is important to remember that all letters were censored and one was forbidden to give details of places and troop movements, etc.

I almost lived at the San Carlo Opera House which, notwithstanding the fact that there was a war on, was in full production! My constant companion was Otto Thwaites (later to be recommended for a V.C.). He was mostly German by breeding and was educated there. His uncle commanded the Panzer brigade which we were to fight in three months' time! His knowledge of opera was encyclopaedic and I learnt a great deal from him. This, of course, was to colour the rest of my life!

Although the Germans had not long been out of Naples, the quality of the productions and singing was unbelievable. We heard Gianne Bechi, Maria Caniglia, Renato Tebaldi, Gigli and Tito Gobbi – just to name a few! (The next time that I was to hear Tito Gobbi was with Callas in Tosca at Covent Garden, I think in 1962. The date might be inaccurate but I'll never forget the night!)

I once asked Otto why it was he joined the British and not the German Army. His answer was immediate, "because it was the better army, of course". Wars suited him – and he was at a loss when peace came. He looked around, after the War, for somewhere to fight.

In the end he joined the forces of one of the Trucial States (I forget which) and was involved in a duel, fought in the desert. He was killed in this escapade – but a fitting end to his life.

In Naples; Operas at San Carlo: 3rd June 1944

I am afraid that this letter will be quite unreadable as I am writing it in a very bumpy, very slow train as I cross a new country inside a cattle truck! I haven't written to you since I arrived from North Africa because I have been pretty busy and any little time that I have had to spare I have spent hearing operas – *Aida, Tosca, Mme Butterfly*, and *l'Elisir d'Amore*. Oh Darling you just have no idea how lovely they were and in such a perfect opera house – there I saw simply hundreds of people who I haven't seen for years – John Synge, Tommy St Aubyn, Simon Codrington, Colin Lindsey, Mark Gilbey, Simon Worsthorne, oh lots more! I simply loved it and we had a tremendous gossip! Then one afternoon we went to see some very famous ruins quite near – with the most beautiful murals – I also saw the cathedral which is so famous for its lovely painted ceiling – what fun it is seeing all these new places. I dined one night with Lavinia H-H who was in very good form and had lots of news.

The next letters cover the period from June to September (three months) we were going slowly north, but much of the time was also spent training – though there were also opportunities to visit Bari and Rome, arrange entertainments for the soldiers, etc.

I don't think that we were in any way apprehensive about the future though we were well aware that, quite soon, we would be fighting. There were visits from the Army Commander (Oliver Leese), the Divisional Commander (Dick Hull) and the Brigadier (Richard Goodbody), all of whom addressed us about our future. My diary quotes the latter as saying "We will go on and on, on and on, day and night until we are too exhausted to see the target." (He was dead right!)

On July 17th the Regiment arrived at Porto Civitanova (due west of Perugia), having driven through Ortona and Francolino. Here we concentrated on gunnery. Finally, on 31st August, we were told to be ready to move that evening. In the event we didn't move till September 2nd. My diary states "Stayed in Leaguer till 5.30 pm. Drove all night through awful dust. Early on Sunday morning John Goldsmid's tank broke down and, later, mine went too. Fitters arrived at 4.30 am. Moved out at 6.30 am."

This was a really gruelling approach march through appalling country with high mountains on the left and a precipice on the right! No-one had any sleep for 38 hours. There was a two hour pause, but then we were ordered on again. It was fifty hours after we started that we halted by the River Foglia. My diary states "Sleep till 2.30. Move off towards Coriano. Long stop for lunch. Move to attack at 5.30 pm. Nothing came of it. My first battle was at San Savino on 5th September. Moved out of Leaguer at 7.30 towards San Clemente. North east attack, B Squadron leading 4th troop (mine) on right, 3rd troop on left. After 20 minutes lost tracks off my tank and Sergeant Hughes's. Sergeant Edmunds O.K.. Heavily shelled. Peter Caro's tank knocked out. Robbie badly wounded. Take objective. 32 prisoners."

So how did I feel? People often ask whether I was frightened. This was a completely new experience which one's brain could not take in. The answer, therefore, is no. Anyway, there was no time to think!

After this battle – and when we had withdrawn to Leaguer, Derek Allhusen ordered a Squadron Parade in uniform with belts and brasses shining! No trouble for us Troop Leaders because we all had soldier servants who had everything ready for us – but a bit tough on the soldiers!

Jimmy Marriott's death:
9th June 1944

Two lovely letters from you have arrived (nos 13, 14) which have been simply marvellous. I am so glad that you had a good day at Adwell, they do all love having you – and it is equally lovely for me to know that you are there.

And now the invasion has started. The great and final action to break the Germans. We all listened to the King's speech – a very wonderful one. I know that we will all have to be brave in the future and be ready for great sorrows – but the great thing is to prepare for them. Poor Ros – I suppose that Jimmy was almost the first to go. What a lovely thing it is that she has got Christopher.

I am so glad that Judy gives such a good report of me! I had a letter from her yesterday, and she seemed to be having fun. I must write and tell her not to come over here though as I'm sure that she wouldn't enjoy it so much. I have been having the loveliest time, buzzing all over this rather beautiful country – some of which looks so very like the downland in England.

I had dinner last night with Derek Allhusen (my Squadron Leader who is so very kind) and saw Mike Wheatley, Andrew Caldecott, Martin Rich and Humphrey Leak (I wonder if you remember him at the House – he was a friend of Peter Lothian.) Wasn't it fun for me? But everywhere I go I seem to know hundreds of people! It just makes the whole difference. Father writes that David Laurie and the others (David Wentworth Stanley) will be out here in a few days and with them will come a parcel from Mother. The drought sounds pretty dreadful – what will the poor horses eat?

On Wednesday I went to a rather lovely concert – a good but local orchestra played Beethoven's V, Strauss' *Death and Transfiguration*, Mendelsohn's *Calm Sea* and *The Valkyries*. I felt quite civilized once more and so happy.

I have just sent you a little cameo brooch which I bought for you in Naples (I've just been told I am allowed to say that now!) I hope you will like it – I can't understand why the other things have taken so long, I only hope they haven't been sunk.

You will be sorry to hear that Corporal Stevens[42] now has a bad boil on his arm and walks about the mess (he is Mess Corporal) looking very mis. – but no doubt he will recover very soon!

Now Darling, don't worry about me – I am doing nothing more dangerous than driving a jeep to go and see people. Haven't time (or space!) for more.

In hospital with Malaria
Jimmy Marriott killed
1ˢᵗ July 1944

I expect by now that you will have heard about Jimmy being killed in Normandy. You will know better than I do what this means to Ros, poor darling – but I go on thanking God that she has Christopher to remind her of him – to remind her of his physical love for her and hers for him. We were all so fond of him – you liked him too, didn't you?

Absolutely maddening, I have got malaria and jaundice and so am now in this beastly place and will be, I'm afraid, for at least three weeks which seems ghastly! So do write a lot as it is frightfully boring and I don't feel nearly ill enough!

David L, David Wentworth Stanley, Robert Stuart and Guy

Hannan have all arrived – I just saw them before I went away. They are such good chaps – it is lovely having them again. Mother gave a parcel to David but I haven't got it yet as his luggage hasn't arrived.

A lovely sea mail dated 23rd full of good things: I love Gilbert & Sullivan! Can't think how you can hate them so. Did I never tell you that Dickie and I sang a duet together in *Iolanthe?* It was famous!

It really is pretty hot here now (and I suppose I feel a bit hotter!). We had a heavenly bathe the other day, just outside the big town about 40 miles from the Regiment where there are some F.A.N.Ys (I met one called Pat Lennor).

Still in hospital; visit by David Laurie, Guy Hannen and David Wentworth Stanley:
6th July 1944

Your no 19 came a few days ago – just after I had heard about Jimmy. Thank you for writing to Ros, you know how much I love her and therefore just how much this great sorrow means to me. But Mother writes to say how courageous and good she is being – it is no surprise to me and I can only thank the Almighty that she has such faith that they can still be close together, connected by their unanimous love for each other and their belief in Him.

But my Darling, things seem pretty beastly – that awful catastrophe at the church[43] (Mrs Attenborough was buried for 4 ½ hours, but survived with broken bones) made me very sad. These new bombs sound quite beastly and most demoralising.

I think I told you that I had gone to hospital, absolutely maddening, but no need to worry when I tell you that I was sent in with jaundice and they further diagnosed malaria and slight dysentery! But I am now well on the way to recovery and hope to be out in a week, when I go on sick leave.

As I told you, the Regiment was very busy but that has finished, so I am not really missing much; and everyone has been so kind and not a day has passed without them coming in to see me, bringing fruit and letters. They are all so perfectly charming, and I keep on being thankful that I joined them.

David Laurie and the others arrived a week ago – they brought a parcel from Mother full of the most amazing things, but just the little things one wants. Mr Thomas also sent me a bottle of Royal Yacht which is lovely! You should have your hair done by Mrs T – she is awfully good! All my girlfriends go there! Which reminds me that I had letters from Margaret and Elizabeth so of course I am riding on the crest of the wave!

Judy writes very happily from N. Africa and loves getting your letters – apparently Inky Webber has arrived in Italy and I shall make hectic enquiries where she is as soon as I get out of hospital.

Bill P never had malaria, but a dose of sun stroke which caused much amusement – he has never stopped being ragged!

Apparently Father is in bed at Adwell with his old wound – it is such agony for him and he gets so depressed about it. I only hope he is better now – how are your family, and Puss? Please give them my love. I think of them all so often.

In fact these long days here have given me time to think about things a good deal and to read some interesting books including *Between the Thunder and the Sun* by Vincent Sheean, which you should read if you have not already. It is quite fascinating and I know it would interest you.

You sounded a bit depressed in your last letter – I don't blame you, I know I was. What is civilization? I will give you Herbert Agar's (a modern American philosopher) definition:

"It is a set of rules by which most men abide, of promises to which most men adhere. It is a set of institutions, of homely customs which express the experience of centuries. It has its roots in cultural discipline, religious and humanistic, which give life its meaning. Man creates these disciplines and supports them to foster what is good in his nature and control what is bad. When he begins to break his own rules and ignore his customs, instead of making them ever more subtle and humane with the passing of decades, civilization sickens at the roots."

I would dare to qualify this definition by insisting that we weak humans cannot successfully control what is bad and foster what is good without the help of the Almighty – it would, as I always say, be conceited of us to think otherwise. We must all therefore train ourselves to be worthy of the title of a Christian, and attempt in our small way to set an example, with great humility, to others who do not believe. This is all rather a homily, but you know how I feel about this, and you will understand.

Regimental dance:
19th July 1944

Your nos. 21 and 22nd arrived at the convalescent home yesterday. I am terribly sorry about that gap – but you blame me needlessly! You see we were on training then and very busy and the letters took a long time to get from the Regt. to the A.P.O – therefore, although my dating appeared wrong, it wasn't! And it must have been horrible for you – and I only hope they are coming through better now.

I have at last met Inky Webber – isn't she a nice person? She came and had lunch with me in the town and then we hitched back and bathed and lay in the sun and talked about you and then about England. It was lovely and the time went much too quickly. However, the Regt. are giving a dance on Friday – and I am hoping that she can come with me, though it is going to be a little tricky to get away from this place as I am still, quite unnecessarily, "under observation". But no doubt it will all come out in the wash! I really do like her awfully – and it was so lovely to talk to someone who knows you. I really am perfectly all right now and the medicos are merely fussing!

We had a dance here last night and I was asked if I could produce any F.A.N.Ys for it. As I was going to be given a staff car to collect them in, I said that I probably could! So off Colin Hill (a v.nice fellow here in the Irish Fusiliers) and I went to find Georgina – but she was going on duty and so were all her friends, but she told us to go and knock up someone else at another depot – so off we went. But she was no good, and, in turn sent us to another place! After an hour and a half of this we at last collected two completely unknown girls – but who turned out to be very nice and know lots of people we do. So, in the end, all was well! What odd mad things we do seem to do out here!

But I pity the F.A.N.Ys; I think people behave frightfully badly towards them – and, as they said, they are treated just like machines instead of human beings; and they have begun to loathe going out – though they are asked to parties every night. Although undoubtedly one learns a lot out here, and sees a lot of interesting things, I honestly don't think you would like it abroad – and I don't think that any girl is much the better for it, and unless they are really strong in every way, they are the worse for it.

Preparation for sick leave:
23rd July 1944

Your No 24 came yesterday – most original with its numerous and puzzling pages – it took me hours to find my way round!

I'm glad you liked the brooch and stockings. I forget if I have told you that I have sent some hair grips and nail varnish which my numerous friends out here said were short in England! You must write and tell me what you want and I will send it along.

Your news about Mary P[44] amazed me. As you know, I am fond of her, but I do just wonder if perhaps she is quite the right sort of person for the Princess, who is such a very valuable person to us all. However no doubt it will all come out in the wash.

I really have more or less given up the idea of being a doctor. And now I have absolutely no idea what to do. It is a terrific problem and I have thought an awful lot about it lately – it is so hard to make up one's mind without being in England to ask advice from people who know what they are talking about. I have thought of all sorts of things from farming to working in London (can't you see me!) – but I believe that it will suddenly flash at me, and then I shall begin.

I really am all right now and am going to Rome on Tuesday for a week's sick leave. Won't that be lovely? I want to see St Peters and so many other lovely places – and I believe the country up there is quite lovely.

I let Inky down very badly the other night. The Regiment had a dance and a jeep had been promised me so I arranged to pick her up in it. But at the last moment the jeep had to go out on an important job and I couldn't let her know. Thank goodness she got to the dance all right and seemed to enjoy it which is a good thing. I went to see her yesterday to apologise. She is nice – I hope to see her before I leave. We are very near them (at the Regt.) so I might be able to.

Willie Geddes writes to say that John Althorp is now in Normandy. You do promise to tell me if anyone I know gets killed or is missing and not keep it from me, as I would far rather know now, instead of hearing when I get back expecting to see him? Don't you agree? You see, we never know out here as there is no way of seeing a casualty list.

There is really awfully little to tell you since I last wrote. Lovely letters keep flowing in from people which make the whole difference. Juliet writes every week – most amazing letters full of gossip. Father is a bit better, but it's been an awful long time hasn't it – and he will be so weak. He hasn't written to me for ages.

The people up at this convalescent home are most weird and varied! There is a communist here in the Oxford & Bucks called Hugh Lee. Really quite astounding ideas he has got – but we have great fun talking and ragging each other! I was reading *The Tatler* the other evening and he came up and said "I am surprised to see you reading that communist paper. My father who is a blasted stick-in-the-mud Conservative won't have it in the house." "*The Tatler*," I said "a communist paper?" "Yes," he said "for it shows the idle rich being really and completely idle!"

I am sure that their ideas are wrong (though not wholly) but it is so difficult to know until one has seen more of life and lived a bit with people who really have to rough it. I believe we all ought to go and live in a slum for a bit – then perhaps we would see a little what they are talking about – and we would probably all turn raving socialists!

Visit to Rome
3rd August 1944

I haven't written to you for ages, but I have been most preoccupied. I suppose that I have just returned from one of the loveliest weeks I have ever spent (or anyway abroad). For I have been up to Rome – it really is the most wonderful place. I rushed round trying to see as much as I could – but a week isn't nearly enough. But Darling, I can't begin to describe the beauty of St Peters, the Sistine Chapel, the Vatican Galleries – and so many lovely places. Just know that I have never seen such concentrated beauty and that I was very happy. I have written a long letter to the family about it which you must read. I flew the aeroplane back myself! It really was tremendous fun – I consider myself the champion Hitch Hiker Par Avion now! (If you want to do something you invariably can!)

And now I am back with the Regiment again which is lovely after being away for so long – and on arrival back I found two sea mails (16,23) and two air mails (25,26). So what could be a better sight to see? And they were full of lovely little bits – I shall answer them 'methodical like'! Subject: Photographs – could you send Ann and your Polyfotos to me. Thank you for sending your HL photographs – that will be really lovely – and thirdly you can't have my identity card photograph because I must have them or I shall be put behind the bars! The pictures of Hugh E. and Felicity W[45]. were most amusing – but H. doesn't think much of F. So the Princess has still got a chance (and I shall then be able to shoot at Sandringham!). The A.I.M.Ls were lovely – thank you Darling. We really are kept frightfully short of them out here.

Footnotes to Part II

36.   Major Reggie Gordon Lennox, Scots Guards; my Instructor at Sandhurst.

37.   Major John Joicey MC. Later Member of Queen's Bodyguard.

38.   Bill Peek, Sir William, Lorna's cousin.

39.   Algiers. We were at Blida, about a ½ hour drive away.

40.   Judy (née Slessor), daughter of Marshal of the Royal Air Force Sir John (Jack) Slessor and my Aunt Iola Ashton's Goddaughter. Later married Jack Price. Lorna was Godmother to James Price, their second son.

41.   James Weatherby: his whole family were great friends of ours. They lived at Stanton St John. Two girls (Peggy and Mary) and three boys (James, Criffie and Roger). Roger was killed in 1940. He was my age.

42.   Hugh Bailie's stud groom. (What a coincidence!)

43.   The Guards Chapel which was almost completely destroyed.

44.   Mary Palmer who had helped with the children at Adwell.

45.   Hugh Euston and Felicity Wavell. There was much talk of Hugh marrying Princess Elizabeth.

Part III
August 1944 to May 1945
On Active Service

Still moving north:
12th August 1944

I wonder if my letters have been getting to you – we really are pretty mobile now and I am afraid that they will be taking an awful long time to arrive. And I haven't written for ages which is awful – and your lovely letters are now flocking in. During the last week I have had 26, 27 and 28. You are so marvellous – and I am **so** awful! But I believe that you understand. Unfortunately you made no mistake in numbering your last three which is infuriating!

Continued 15th: We had to move in a hurry – but all is well again now! I am so glad you enjoyed your day at Adwell – I love to think that you can go out there when you like. How awful Mother having such a horrible thing as a Peke - and a white one which is even worse. She will be just like an old dowager!

I am afraid that you will not get another letter from me for some time – we are on the move the whole time now.

I got a letter from Judy the other day telling me that I can report fully on Jack Price: I wasn't going to tell even you until she said I could, as she made me promise not to. Well, quite honestly, I hardly know him. He is, as you know, the second in command – and therefore a good deal older than her. He does seem to be frightfully nice, and I hope that I shall know him better soon. What is so funny is that he knows I know all about Judy – but hasn't said a word to me about her, except that he had met a girl friend of mine on the boat coming out! But how serious it all is I do not really know. I often get letters from her which is so very kind and nice of her. I actually owe her a letter!

Darling, I don't think that you can quite put the War down to the greed of one country. For a very long time now the Germans, or anyway the Prussians, have been a hostile people; not only because they are greedy but particularly because they are disunited generally

Diana
Birch Reynardson
1891–1962

Henry
Birch Reynardson
1892–1972

and know that war brings unity. Hitler could not possibly have retained his power without a war. And yet, although he had actively been preparing for war since 1930, England and America did nothing about it, because people were too selfish, too unchristian and too idiotic to know what was happening.

I had a letter from Dickie a few days ago – he is going to be Captain of his House and Captain of Games. I have absolutely no doubt that he will make a very good one. But it is a big job for him.

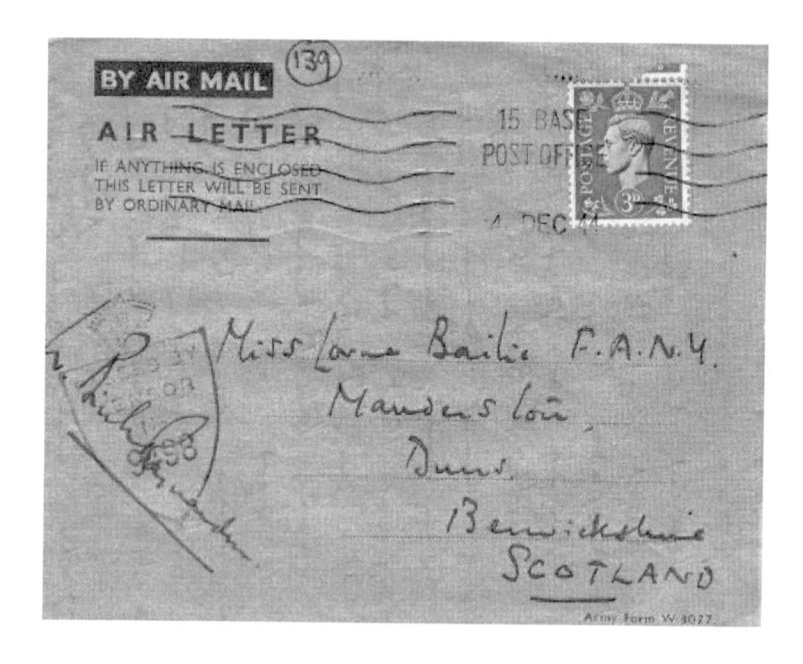

Life with 4th Troop; still travelling north: 19th August 1944

Although I posted a letter to you two days ago, I fear that it will take a good long time to get to you. We have been driving all over southern Italy for the last fortnight or so and there has been really rather little time to write – and there was no way of posting the letter. However Derek (Allhusen) is taking this letter to post this evening. We are now further north than we have ever been before and as I write the sun is going down over the Apennines – it is all rather lovely.

Not only does the country improve as we go northwards – but so do the people. Down in the south they really are awful, very fascist, very dirty, very dishonest. Up here though they are most helpful and today I bought two chickens at 5/- a time for the mess. The Americans haven't been in this part of Italy, and therefore the prices are reasonable, but wherever they are they rocket up, as they are willing to pay anything.

We arrived at this leaguer early this morning and have been bathing all day which has been lovely – I have never had such perfect bathing – how you would love it. We really have had a tremendous lot lately. The sea is as clear as crystal and varies in colour from turquoise green to the brightest blue. But we move on again tomorrow – starting in the dark and driving through the dawn until it gets too hot – then we stop for the rest of the day and bathe. I am so happy seeing so much of this country.

I am – as we all are nowadays – constantly with my Troop. Oh Darling they are the grandest chaps, and I love being with them so much. We laugh so much together. They are quite mad and collect every sort of animal. We have in the Squadron at the moment – and remember we are battle strength – one goose (Arthur), 2 terriers (Loopy and Paddy), 2 hawks (Jane and Sue), 2 chickens (Penelope & May), 1 pigeon (Goosy) and 1 rabbit (Bill)! The females are, of course, named after the owners' girlfriends! They travel on tanks and 3 ton lorries and all seem to enjoy it. The chaps can be seen every evening taking their respective pets out for a walk – oh it is all such fun. So, you see, you have no need to worry about me – I really am so happy. We haven't even seen a German yet – perhaps we never shall. The news seems to be so truly wonderful now.

I am now P.M.C. and therefore have to go round and buy food and drink for the mess – this is really great fun and there is always something amusing cropping up. Last night I interviewed a new mess servant – "Well, Parry, what are your capabilities as a cook?" I asked. "Oh Sir – I fed pigs on the farm before the War, Sir. I'm sure I will suit, Sir". He is now duly installed in the mess!

It's now almost pitch dark – and I'm being eaten up by midges.

We were issued with very lengthy 'Instruction books' (written in American english) when the Shermans were delivered. I decided to summarize them for the members of my Troop. I called Sgt. Hughes (2nd Sergeant) to help me. "Well Sir," he said "I can't read vey well because our Mum always said that reading was bad for our eyes."

**Issued with Sherman tank; going north:
20th August 1944**

We are once again static and near to the sea so once again we can bathe every afternoon which is simply lovely. We are all very busy in the morning on the tanks, getting all the different little, but vitally important, things completely organised (I have a feeling you don't like the expression!) I have got a most impressive looking new tank – of course I can't tell you about it (it is vital to be secretive at all times!) – but it is jolly good. One of the chaps in my Troop has painted a lovely fox on the side which looks too smart for words. What could be better!

Your letters are now beginning to take longer to get to me – rather naturally – and I got no 31 about five days ago. A *Country Life* arrived last night – they are always lovely to read.

I have just come back from having a drink with Malcolm Erskine who used to command a Bn of the Scots Guards. It was fun seeing him again. I forget whether I told you that our new divisional commander[46] knows us all very well which is lovely. He has arrived but I haven't seen him yet – Father gave him some photographs for me. Also my cousin John Ashton is coming out soon and is bringing my gun which will be a great asset.

This is being continued on Sunday and I am sitting outside my tent just before church looking out onto a most beautiful view. This part of Italy is very well watered and therefore very green and English. The whole plain in front of me is highly cultivated and dotted with olive trees. We have done a tremendous lot of map reading lately and it has been simply lovely driving over the country – stopping every now and then at a farm house to buy eggs and the most enormous peaches (for which you pay 5/- in Oxford!). The

Wops round here are really most friendly and invariably produce a glass of white wine just to round off the deal which is excellent!

I forget whether I told you that Oliver FitzRoy[47] (Hugh Euston's brother) was killed in Normandy? He was such a good chap and it is awful Hugh being so far away.

And now I have got to stop – we are all pretty hectic at the moment – but it is all great fun. Please don't worry my Darling – everything is all right, and if you are happy, I am too. I am longing for the photographs to come.

Approaching the enemy:
1 September 1944

I can't even attempt to number this letter as my efficient little letter register which has always been kept so efficiently is now left behind in my kit as I now have to travel light!

We are on the move once again – although I am now writing to you sitting on the sea shore after a lovely bathe as we have been held up on the road for about three hours.

Are my letters arriving to you all right? Yours are taking much longer now – and I am rather worried about mine. But I am frightfully well and happy and we are all in very good form.

How marvellous the news is – and old Monty, a F/M!

Your last letter was written when you had just come back from Manderston. Oh Darling, how lovely that must have been. And long leave starting again too – so it won't be long before you are up there again. I am so glad that you liked the parcel from Rome – but I'm afraid that Berlin will be the next stopping place!

Don't be worried if you don't get letters from me – because in the future there is going to be even less time to write to you. A *Tatler* arrived the other day – with a picture of Judy in it which was fair I thought, and also one of Johnny Kimberley and Julian Mond + girls – I've got to stop now + make a 'brew' (that consists of slinging a filthy old tin full of water onto a petrol fire and making tea!)

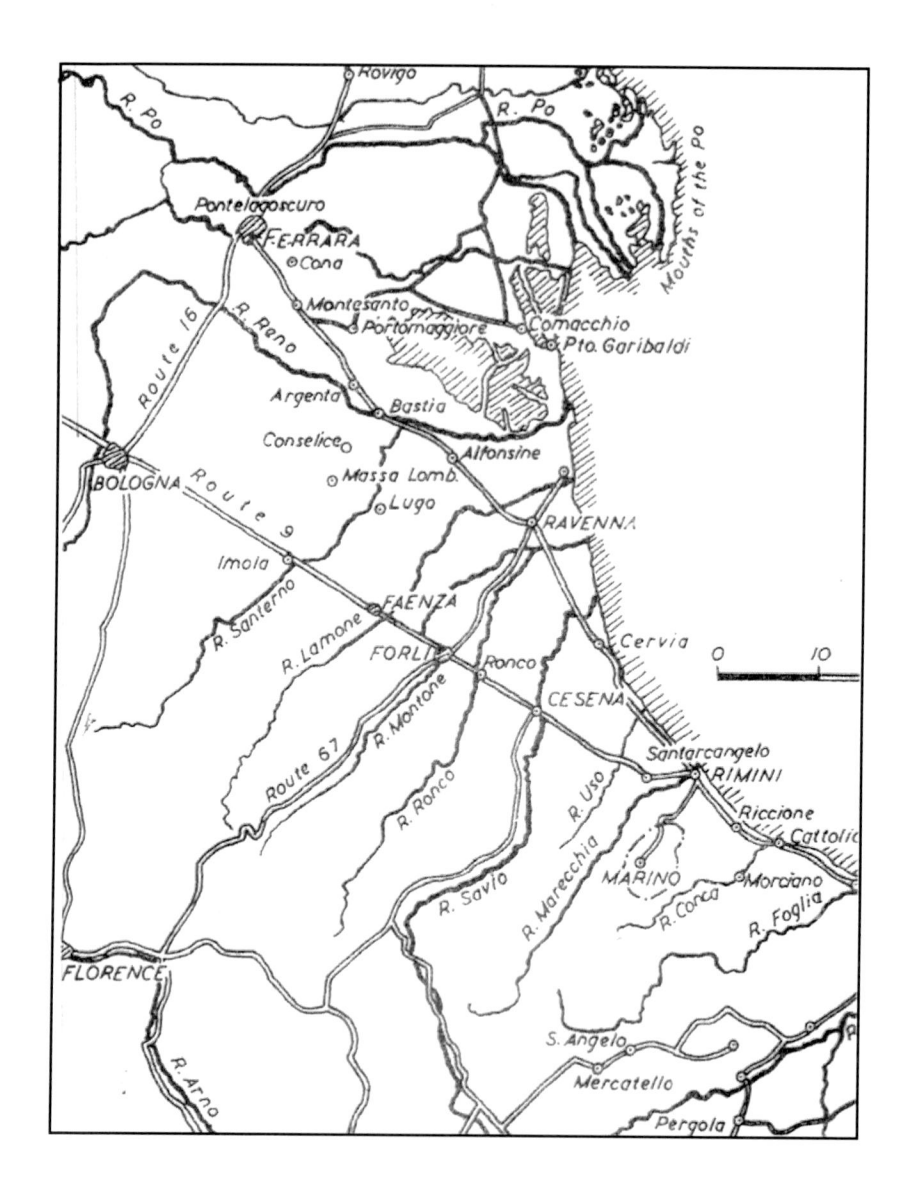

Battle of San Savino:

Even now, after 63 years, I well remember this first battle. There we were, the Squadron in 'line ahead' with my three tanks in the middle. Derek gave the order "B Squadron will advance" and I then said "4th Troop move to the right". There was no question of fear, this (as I've pointed out) was a new experience and of huge excitement. The noise of our guns and the German shelling was unbelievable (no wonder I'm deaf!). Our objective was the small village with a prominent church spire on the high ground in front of us. Life was not made easier by German machine gun fire very close at hand – I saw some soldiers, who had unwisely disembarked from their tank, being mown down, but there was no time to watch. Progress was very slow owing to the deep and rather wide ditches and it was this that caused 2 of my tanks to lose their tracks. As we were 'sitting ducks', I ordered the crew to leave their tanks and get into a trench nearby until things quietened down.

SGT. JACK EDMUNDS M.M.
SAN SAVINO, ITALY.
SEPTEMBER 1944

8*th September 1944*

I am sitting next to David Laurie in the sun – feeling much better after a cup of tea! We have just moved out of battle – after three days' pretty hard battling. How different fighting is to one's first ideas of it. There is so much to think about and I was so excited that there really is not time left to be frightened (otherwise I would have been terrified!). And just as out hunting we don't think of the fox – nor does one think of the Hun.

Actually I had a maddening battle as half way through two tanks of the three in my Troop got stuck and my Troop Sergeant went on. So I and the others were shelled for a day and night and the next morning which was unpleasant. But as luck would have it there was an evacuated Bosh trench just in front of the tanks where we could shelter. It is extraordinary how cunning we became as to the flight of the shells, and in the end we always know when they were coming near. It probably sounds vile, but we laughed most of the time at the incredible things that happened. At one time my Troop (about ten of us) and thirty German prisoners that I had taken were all lying on our tummies in the same trench. It rather shows up the utter stupidity of the War.

I took jolly nice pair of binoculars off one Hun – and gave Sergeant Hughes a watch. They just come in exhausted and wretched – they simply laughed at us when we said that Brussels had fallen. But they fight very hard still I assure you!

It was very sad to get back and hear that Robbie Stuart had been terribly badly wounded – and really there is no hope for him – and that Peter Caro's tank had been knocked out by an 88mm German gun. But of course these sad losses have to be quickly forgotten, or anyway not brooded over – and their deaths are taken in a happy spirit. Considering everything the casualties were very small as things were very 'hot' at times.

But now, as I say, it is all over for the moment and we will not be in again for some time as we have to refit.

Everyone is incredibly well and in first class form. My Troop are a tremendous help and keep me in a continual giggle! It is such an advantage to forget the unpleasant things and hang onto the good things – one of John Joicey's tanks had a huge hole in it. As soon as the tank got back, the crew were out with their brush and painted a large red arrow pointed to the hole with MICE against it - this is the general attitude!

MY TANK AT SAN SAVINO
SEPTEMBER 1944

Now I have purposely told you as much as I am allowed about the battle, because I want to tell you everything – but you are in a position of trust and must not worry because, as we have both decided, there is nothing to worry about! I am v. happy and have never felt better . . . . .

The next engagement was on 12th September when the Regiment was ordered to take Ripa Bianca Ridge overlooking the River Marano, north of San Savino. My diary reads: "Oversleep. David calls me in my deep trench! Spend morning putting maps together. Out on recce with John Goldsmid and Derek. Lead Squadron to 'draw fire'. Get back 8.30. Drink wine."
We then had a few days out of the line.

Battle of Coriano Ridge (Montecieco):

On September 20th we moved out of Leaguer and, after driving for half an hour, getting ever closer to the sound of heavy gunfire, we were halted by Derek. John Joicey and I were told to climb up the hill in front of us and carry out a recce. We (3rd and 4th Troops) were the next to advance over the hill. There was only machine gun fire to be heard as we crawled up the slope. This was rather ominous as we had heard a lot of 88mm gunfire as we approached the ridge. When we poked our heads, very gingerly, over the top we saw 24 tanks of the Bays burning and many soldiers lying dead or wounded on the ground having left their tanks. A long discussion then ensued between us as to whether we should go to the right or the left (obviously we could not go straight over the brow). John thought that we should choose the left flank but then I spotted that there was a bit of a hedge leading away to the right so we agreed that that was the best route.

We returned to our tanks to report to Derek. He looked very white and worried but we said that it was quite O.K. as we we'd found a possible route

BATTLE OF CORIANO RIDGE, 20TH SEPTEMBER 1944.
JOHN JOICEY AND HIS CREW. ON THE BACK OF THIS PHOTOGRAPH HE WROTE "CORIANO RIDGE. WAITING TO GO."
NOTE THE HEDGE ON THE RIGHT, THE FAR SIDE OF THE SLOPE, REFERRED TO IN MY NOTE ON BATTLE OF CORIANO RIDGE (SEE ABOVE).

forward. In the event Derek, who was the 'rear link' radio connection to the Colonel announced that his wireless had "broken down". We never received the order to advance. I always wondered about this mysterious failure of the radio. In Appendix 3 will be found a description of this battle, written by an Italian who sent it to Stug Perry.

The next day we were again in action. My diary entry read: "Went out of Leaguer after breakfast with Sergeant Edmunds. Later on he was hit and Corporal Allan killed. Sergeant Dickinson awful leg wound." I remember crouching behind his tank with our Regimental Doctor Kemp (we called him Kempy – he was an outstandingly good chap). I held him while Kempy amputated what was left of his leg, without any anaesthetic – just a swig of rum. All seemed well but Kempy told me that he would die of shock – which he did. I will never forget, when we had finished, him saying "thank you Sir" with a smile, and then he passed out. He died the next day.

And then, a day or two later my diary reads: "John Joicey and I went out shooting. Bag 1 chicken, 2 rabbits, one pig. Mess arrives." This is what was so extraordinary. When the fighting finished we reverted to living comparatively normal lives (see letter of 30th September).

The procedure after returning from a battle was somewhat as follows: First we Troop Leaders would have an informal parade of the Troop, checking on casualties, talking to the two tank commanders (Sergeants Edmunds and Hughes) for their comments, etc. We then went to our tents, which would have been erected by our soldier servants (every officer of whatever rank had one), where we would wash and change into clean clothes.

Then we went to David Laurie's tent. This was a very special contraption made out of two 'issue' tents. His servant, 'Gunner' Merrick (David's father's groom) would by then have put out the drinks and the Tatler, Country Life, Field and our letters. There we spent an hour relaxing over our drinks, sitting in comfortable chairs and talking calmly about the fighting. We then dispersed to have supper with our Troop (unless the mess lorries had arrived, in which case we would dine in the mess).

On one occasion, when David had been particularly courageous on our behalf (he used to drive his tank up to any one of us in trouble and support us, whatever the danger) I thanked him. "That's all right, but you might go and collect my bedding roll which was blown off my tank." So off I went (my driver, Corporal Emerson, a bit silent but Corporal Nicholls keen at the chance of *having another shot!). We arrived back at the battle field. I remember the extraordinary silence of the place – just numbers of British and German tanks still burning in the twilight. It was obviously a highly dangerous operation, but we got the bed roll! This was of high importance to David as it contained essential items such as a bottle of Mr Thomas' Royal Yacht hair lotion, Mr Trumper's shaving cream, his silk pyjamas and a change of clothes!*

Montecieco; casualties of Queen's Bays; 24th September 1944

Owing to my giving up the efficient numbering I can never remember when I last wrote to you which is most disturbing! The days I lose count of completely – we are either sleeping or doing some other rather more energetic job!

A few days ago the Bays had an awful caning – in fact there was little left of the two Squadrons which went in. Luckily though there were comparatively few casualties in men – and tanks can always be replaced quickly. We were sent up to support them and, but for some enemy resistance to the left, we suffered little except from shelling which, though tiring, is comparatively useless against tanks.

I forget if I told you that the news that we all, in our hearts, expected came four days ago that Robbie Stuart was dead. He had lived with a dreadful wound for some twelve days. Though his ideas were diametrically opposed to mine in many ways, I had become very fond of him and shall miss him terribly. His elder brother was killed in the desert a year ago.

I'm so glad that you did just get a day with Ann at Manderston. I had a letter from her about a fortnight ago which was lovely.

Thank you so much for sending me some more cigarettes – they are the greatest luxury! I can't send you anything at the moment, except grapes and they wouldn't keep! We eat great bunches of them all day which is marvellous!

As you say the Gothic Line is a tough obstacle. The Hun is fighting very hard rear guard actions so that his troops can evacuate out of the Balkans before we arrive there. There is no sign of them weakening in Italy at the moment – and France seems to be getting a tougher spot now. I heard this morning that the Greys caught it a bit, and Ian Dudgeon has been badly wounded.

But what a lot I have written about the War. It is quite monstrous! Yet there really is awfully little else to write about – particularly as we all have been paying quite a lot of thought to the matter lately! I can't fill the letter saying how much I love you, after all! But you are just always there to think about and picture doing something – or wondering how you would think about something, and you know what a help that is.

How long ago it seems now when I came down the stairs of The Mirabelle and saw you – still there after 1 ½ hours! It was January 18th 1943. That was the beginning. We must go there again alone as soon as I get back.

This letter refers to the death of Dickie Pearce. In fact he was killed when walking up to some German soldiers who had surrendered and he was about to take them prisoner.

Withdrawn from battle lines:
30th September 1944

Your letter dated the 20th arrived here today. Poor Darling – it was obviously written on one of those 'bad' days that have, as Mother always says, to be 'crossed off'. But I know so well how it is when things seem to be going wrong. For instance two nights ago the dreaded rain began. At two o'clock in the morning my tent blew down and cold water poured all over me. I decided that the only thing to do was to make for the mess – so I dragged my way over there through rain and mud only to find that the mess also had blown down! I got it up by breakfast time!

After breakfast I went to see how my chaps were and found them soaking, so I went off to find a barn for them to dry in. During my wanderings I fell up to my neck in a sewage pond! I ran back to the Mess to 'dry out' and lit the biggest fire you've ever seen and nearly rounded off the morning by burning the mess down! It was all so ghastly that it became frightfully funny!

The rain has been vile – but we have been out of action for a fortnight now, and the mess has come up – so we have been jolly well off. We moved this morning to a new area so that we can all be under cover; but now, of course, it is simply lovely and I am going to go for a walk soon. We have advanced out of the mountains now and are on the plains, which is a great relief as the ground is a little more possible for tanks.

I know how frightfully hard it is for you to imagine this very odd life that we are leading out here – in fact I know that you will never really understand what it is like. But just remember this: When you joined the F.A.N.Ys everything seemed pretty grim didn't it? But you adapted yourself to the new situation. Humans are very adaptable – therefore slowly one can become adapted to this kind of living.

As to the fighting – well it is really impossible to explain because I don't know what happens – but somehow one's ordinary self disappears and one's emotions are lessened, otherwise battling would be impossible. Please Darling, don't worry about me – nor think that I am hating it. Some of the time it is the greatest fun and the little time that one is battling is quite timeless and so soon forgotten. Tonight, for instance, Derek and John Joicey and I are going out shooting – for we have all got guns now!

I heard from Mrs Egerton today that Kit is all right in France – but that Dickie Pearce who was a great friend of his has been killed – so I must write to him.

Preparing for battle after winter rains:

The rains came soon after the late September fighting and tank movement became impossible for three weeks or so. But on October 7th the enemy counter attacked and "we fired successfully at them and they retired."

26th October 1944

I don't think that I have written since your two lovely letters 44 and 45 – we have been working pretty hard getting the tanks ready for battle again, trying the guns and new ammunition etc – and the weather looked as it was going to be good for a bit longer, but today it is pouring down again, and the wind is now just as awful as ever. This means of course that we will not be able to do a thing for a least a week. It really is rather disappointing as we were absolutely ready. However, we are jolly comfortable here and simply cannot grumble.

The mail to you seems to be awful – your letters always come in about a week; though lately we have had very few except yesterday two *Country Lifes* from you. Thank you so much. I am longing to see your picture in the *Tatler* – Dickie and Kit (whom I heard from two days ago) both report on it, but of course it will be ages before it gets out here.

Darling you are clever becoming a Corporal – that's frightfully good! I was never more than a Private! Please don't come to Italy unless you are certain what your future will be. Honestly I know you wouldn't really enjoy it even if you were with Judy – I think it's a fearful existence for a girl out here, and I would hate to think of you there. But it is for you to make up your mind. After all you are doing a good job in England.

Jack Price has now got jaundice and is in a hospital in Rome where I imagine he will be for some five weeks.

Nothing much happened after this counter attack on 7th October till early November when we moved over the River Ronco (near Grisignano) at night (4th November). My diary (5th November) reads: "Out on reconnaissance with Derek at 10.30. Lovely day, walk for miles. Shelled a bit. Go back to Squadron, see Colonel and David. Start off at 5.15pm and arrive about 6.45. Heavy shelling. Wounded at crossroads." Then (6th November): "Derek and John meet me at Regimental aid post. Taken by quick stages to Cesena, then Rimini. Operated on. Three fingers amputated. David came to see me at Rimini."

Even after all these years I remember this incident very well! What happened was this; we were being heavily shelled by multi-mortars called 'Nebelworthers.' Nevertheless, I simply had to contact our supporting infantry (5th Hampshires) and was almost shot on my way back because the armoured corps type helmet was almost identical with the normal German type! By this time it was dark and, again, I had to contact the infantry which had disappeared. My driver, Corporal Emerson (we called him Daddy because he was 'so old' – he was aged 32 and I 20!) told me not to leave my tank "or you'll be killed". He was nearly right! I was blown into a shell hole and was away from the Regiment for six weeks.

I suppose that, having been blown some yards by the mortars (Nebelwerthers) which practically landed on me, I was 'not quite myself". For this reason I can't remember too much about the incident but I was certainly cared for with great efficiency. The first operation on my fingers was in Rimini. This was rather horrid but I was cheered up by Captain Wakeford V.C. (2/4 Hampshires) who was in the next bed to me. He was constantly having operations and, on one occasion, he returned to the ward full of pentathol (the 'truth drug') and told me exactly how he had won his V.C. – which he certainly would not have done had he not been drugged! (See also letter dated 9th November.)

I then moved to Ancona where I had a room to myself for two or three days until my nurse came in and announced that there had been a nasty battle in Yugoslavia. For this reason, two officers were being moved into my room but they were "very nice gentlemen, one is Captain Randolph Churchill, the other Lieut. Evelyn Waugh." I found myself in the middle of the three beds. They never stopped talking (seldom to me!) and constantly drank whisky, day and night. I was glad to move on. (The only good thing to come out of this rather unenjoyable episode was that when, on my return to Oxford, I became the Chairman of the Chatham Club I got E. Waugh to speak – with David Cecil and John Betjeman - at the Summer Dinner.)

Letter from David Laurie about my wound:
6th November 1944

I have just returned from seeing Bill in hospital who asked me to break the news to you that he had been wounded. It happened last night when he was on his feet with the infantry. He got hit by a piece of shrapnel. He continued walking a considerable time after he had been wounded before he told them he was hurt, so like Bill with such a great sense of duty. Everyone said he put up a great show and was so very brave.

I was so glad I was able to trace where he had been evacuated to, as he was so pleased to see me and I was able to get a first hand report from the sister, and I read the surgeon's report after the operation. He has had the 3rd and 4th (little finger) tip amputated. This will give him no disability at all. I promise you there is no need to worry.

Bill will be away about two months and will be in hospital in Rome, Naples or Bari. I thought he was marvellous as it is of course a bitter disappointment for him, but he is so determined not to let it worry him or get depressed.

Bill is a great loss as he has done so frightfully well and is so highly thought of. Bill and I are the greatest of friends and he has so often mentioned you to me. I will let you know what news I get.

Letter from Mother about being wounded:
8th November 1944

I expect you have heard that Bill has been wounded, but I thought in case he had not been able to get a letter off to you from the hospital I would send you a line. It seems to be a wonderful miracle that he is alive as the shell was so near that the three men that were with him thought it had fallen on him. What it really did was to blow him into the ditch, so the shrapnel spiked his tin hat and broke his fingers, two of which had to be taken off. I had about 24 hours of anxiety, and then his letter arrived. If you have not heard, I will send you on his letters, and the ones from David Laurie, David Wentworth Stanley and Derek Allhusen; they all said he had done **so** well.

Dear me, what a war it is, it seems so wonderful that he should be saved one does not know how to be grateful enough. I should think he will be out of action for perhaps six seeks, anyhow one hopes so. I always think about William that all will be well with him and that God has him in hand. I suppose that the root cause of war being sin, suffering must come. That is the inevitable result, and so when our loved ones are hurt or killed it is as He said in the parable "an enemy hath not done this" but His love, the desire for that person in mind, body and spirit is that He still loves him or her and will make something out of it. Perhaps you think something different.

Description of being wounded:
9th November 1944

    I hope that you have not been worrying about me, as no doubt by now I will have been posted as wounded. I wonder whether David wrote to you and told you what had happened. Oh Darling, it's such a disappointment but I am perfectly all right and already out of bed.

    The Troop was ordered up to support a company of an infantry battn. late one afternoon. I led them up to the position that night. It was terribly exciting – everything was absolutely silent and then suddenly some shells would fall very close, then there was silence again. We arrived in a little village with only a river between us and the Germans. I could see them firing their guns and crawling about in the dark. But my job was to keep absolutely quiet till the dawn.

    When the shelling had died down I dismounted and went to see my opposite number in the infantry. I found him in a house surrounded by his men – they were all very quiet, very tense. We talked out our plans and then I left with three of his chaps as guides to go to the Company Commander about a mile away.

    Just as we were crossing a road the biggest load of shells ever seen (or heard) appeared, sent by express service from those blighters on the other side. I was never very quick at jumping into ditches, particularly when they contain a mixture of mud, manure and water – but I soon had the odd and distinctly unpleasant sensation of being propelled in that direction very quickly (by blast). I landed face first with a small hole in my bottom (negligible) and a rather big one in my left hand. The chaps who I was with were frightfully good and got me to the Regimental Aid Post fairly quickly, where they patched me up and gave me some morphia etc.

    Meanwhile one of the infantry chaps had crawled back to my Troop and told them that I had been wounded – they got hold of Derek on the wireless and he and John Joicey drove miles through the night to see me before I was evacuated further back. It just made the whole difference particularly, seeing those two before I was operated on that night and had three fingers tidied up – I think they have only amputated them at the first joint so that's perfectly all right.

The other fingers are broken. I'm afraid this will depress you a bit – but I am just so lucky. This is my left hand, and I should, by all rules, have been killed!

I am at the moment near Ancona and am being evacuated back to Bari or Barletta in two days time. Oh, why isn't Judy still there! Do get her to write to me soon. Your letters will not arrive with me for ages as they don't know my address. Don't worry.

Further letter from David Laurie:
11th November 1944

As for the moment Bill is obviously not able to write, I thought you would like the latest news on him, which I am able to give you from my batman who saw him two days ago. Having got over the shock, he in himself is delightfully well and really has little pain and everything is going as well as can be expected. My batman caught him up about 150 miles south of Rimini where he will be for a few days and then I think he will move on to Bari, and of course I will let you have his address. I sent all his kit down and he really has everything he could possibly want – masses of cigarettes and plenty of literature.

We were about the first into Forli when it was taken yesterday; it is such an attractive little town with some lovely villas with marvellous gardens which we are now staying in. For the last seven days the weather has been fine, except for a fall of snow this morning. It is essential, if we are to get on, to have fine weather.

I assure you there is no need to worry about Bill.

In hospital ship going south to Bari:
13th November 1944

I am now lying in bed between two Poles in a hospital ship slowly making its way down the Adriatic coast. They are neither of them in the slightest bit glamorous, but rather old and fat – and they chatter unceasingly in their exceedingly unsympathetic lingo across my bed to each other.

I have had one more operation on my hand since I last wrote – and yesterday I saw it for the first time. Darling, it's far better than I thought – the tip of one finger, the first joint of another, and most of the third – but as far as I can seen I shall be as good as new in two months. At the moment all my fingers are broken – but it is quite amazing how little they hurt. I have been up for three days now with my hand in the most enormous bandage surrounded by a quite draconic kind of canary cage!

Col. Coytes, the chap who cut me about, let me come into his operating theatre of Saturday to see him performing. It really was most awfully interesting. They have got a wonderful new anaesthetic called Penterthol which is injected into you and three seconds later you just go to sleep! No smell, no sick feeling – all too simple. It keeps one under for about ½ hour, and then just goes off into a natural sleep for about six hours.

Apparently they heaped Penicillin into my hand – so I am now frightfully valuable!

Your last letter was incredibly rude telling me how vague I am – you will please desist!

So funny, when I was at the last hospital I left a letter addressed to you on my bed, and went out of the ward. On my return I found lying beside it a *Tatler* opened at the page with your photograph on it! Somebody in the ward had just been sent the *Tatler* and happened to see my letter to you – very odd.

I wonder whether Inky W. will still be at Bari – or whether I shall in fact go there at all? I am going to try to wangle my way to Naples so that I will have lots of people like Delia and Diana Holden etc to come and see me and hold my hand!

It will be a very long two months without the Regiment and my Troop won't it? I am already missing them so much.

In Naples; a day spent with Delia:
28th November 1944

I haven't written to you since I arrived here – I've been so busy gadding about! The whole world seems to have congregated here - and it is just the greatest fun. I arrived here four days ago. It's a ghastly hospital, but I'm never in it, except at night and for breakfast. I have got a more or less permanent dressing on my hand now - it is getting on frightfully well, and I should be back with the Regiment by Christmas I think.

I have already seen Delia, Diana Holden, Ursula Barclay, Pamela Stubbs, Susan Rowley, Tim Sergison Brooke, Vivien Naylor Leyland, etc. It is so lovely seeing everyone again. D. is in great form – I spent the day with her on Sunday. First of all we went to the English Church – then I went back to the Wrennery for lunch (100 girls and a boy!) – most embarrassing. We went to *Tosca* after lunch. I love it – though Puccini is not a great admirer of mine usually. *Madame Butterfly* is really very grim!

I haven't heard from you since you last wrote (on 7th Nov) – of course all my letters will take ages to get forwarded on to me. It took a fortnight for letters to get from the front to Bari – and it will take another week for them to get here. Perhaps they will arrive soon. Anyway I was lucky to get those ones that came down from the Regiment by car – I hate not hearing your news, and knowing nothing of how you are etc. And I'm afraid it makes my letters even duller than usual!

It's pouring with rain now – as it is up at the front (so the wireless says). The Regiment is 'busy' again – how beastly for them in the rain etc. And I am in agony to know who is leading my Troop while I am away.

I hope to go out to A.F.H.Q. for a farewell party to General Wilson tomorrow. I wonder how he will like being in Washington. I was so glad that General Alexander is promoted (and is therefore now senior to Monty!); he does deserve all he gets.

This will get to you fairly near Christmas time. Oh Darling, how I long to be with you, particularly then. But I know that we will be very close in spirit. What a wonderful thing it is that we have that. Thank God for it.

I am sending you nothing for Christmas – I really don't think it's worth it at the moment, but I hope that I might be able to get up to Florence on my sick leave – that would be marvellous, and I believe that there are lots of good things to buy there.

At the opera with Delia; lunch with D Holden:
2nd December 1944

Still no letters from you or anyone else which is frightful. It's awful not to know how you are or anything. But I suppose they will arrive soon now. I have been having a perfectly lovely time – and feel almost guilty. But for my fingers (which are healing most wonderfully well) I am able to do everything. Perhaps I will be back by Christmas though – that will be something.

I think I wrote to you last on Tuesday. Since then I have seen *Rigoletto* and *La Boheme*. The Opera here is practically as good as ever – even though just a few of them have now gone to Rome. It is frightening going with Delia – she knows much too much about it! You know music has been rather spoilt for her – if it isn't perfect she gets into an awful state and almost walks out! She is in very good form though and it just makes the whole difference having her here.

I have been out to A.F.H.Q. twice now. There seem to be hundreds of people there I know. Yesterday I lunched with Diana Holden and she walked me up into the hills above the Palace[48]. I can't tell you how wonderful if was looking down the long chestnut avenue leading to Naples. All the trees were a most beautiful red, matching the sky as it set. We had tea at General Airlie's Mess. He is a most charming man and Diana's 'boss'.

I went to see General Wilson after tea – but as he had just arrived back from London he was too busy which was a pity. He has, apparently, been awfully kind and sent hundreds of cables to Mother about me. They can't bear the idea of going to Washington. I think he wanted me to go with him as A.D.C. (or so I gathered from Hermione Ranfurly[49], his Secretary) – I can think of little worse! Of course it would be interesting. But just think of being alone in America without knowing a soul – and doing very little except make polite conversation with local film stars!

I hope that my letters have been arriving all right – oh Darling how I long to hear from you again. I rely on your letters to keep me going far too much, quite obviously!

I'm going into the town now – it's about three miles from the hospital – and lunching with Delia. Then we're going to *Aida*. It's too good – Lavinia may be coming down in time for my birthday.

After arrival in Naples I was unofficially attached, as an A.D.C to Jumbo Wilson, a great friend of my father's.

From General Jumbo Wilson's H.Q., Caserta Palace, Naples: 3rd December 1944

No doubt you will be amazed to see how good the post has suddenly become (just look at the date!). The thing is that I am at the moment writing in General Wilson's office and he is getting this letter sent over by air tomorrow with a very big chief, though I can't tell you who! Look in the papers though!

I have just come back from a most lovely walk above A.F.H.Q. with Bill Cobbold who is the General's A.D.C. – such a good fellow and he has been most awfully kind to me. In fact I have just had a hot bath! Fantastic things – I'm quite new to the art! And it is so difficult to keep clean with only one hand.

No letters from you yet – I'm going to wire all the hospitals and find out where they are getting held up. But David Laurie wrote to say that the Regiment have had a very successful battle – David Wentworth Stanley was wounded, but not badly, I think.

Constant Lambert is here conducting the Opera House Orchestra. I haven't been yet – but am going with Delia tomorrow I hope. We saw him last night - fearful looking bounder - however D. insisted on going over to speak to him! You will know what charming manners he has when I tell you that he never even removed his cigarette from his mouth!

Oh Darling, I'm being shouted at to stop! There seems to be a hurry!

Back with the Regiment after staying in Rome: 22nd December 1944

Of course I'm just so happy that I don't know what to do. Look where I am! Back with the Regiment. Oh yes! It's all very sudden! The fact is that David (Laurie) sent a truck down to the hospital last Sunday and I leapt into it and drove away. Of course being back again is the best cure in the world – and I have simply never felt better.

We stayed at Caserta the first night. General Airlie very kindly asked me to spend the night at his villa which I did in great comfort. I dined with Diana Holden which was lovely and we had a tremendous and very serious talk into the middle of the night – not quite! – mostly about her. I am very fond of her. Also I saw dear cousin John Ashton who gave me a very nice silver cigarette case for my birthday – wasn't it kind of him? He is always putting himself out for me.

We then drove on to Rome, and arrived just in time to go to *La Traviata*. It was the best performance I have ever seen in Italy (or anywhere) – quite perfect. I kept feeling that spider rushing up and down my back like we do in the Rachmaninoff (or N & D!). I came back so happy and dined with two chaps in the 11th H.A.C. who I knew vaguely at the Grand Hotel (can't stop, will go on) . . . . .

Description of Exhibition at Palazzo Vechio: 22nd December 1944

(I have gone straight on!) . . . . . where I was staying in great pomp. One can get absolutely anything to eat – but it costs about 1000 lire (£2.10.0 and no exaggeration!) per head! Well worth it though. I lingered languidly in bed the next morning – and then went off to the Great Picture Exhibition at the Palazzo Venezia.[50]

Oh Darling – they were quite beautiful. From all over Italy these pictures have been searched out – and brought to Rome. I shall write a sea mail and tell you about them – but I shall just say that I saw Memling's *Deposition* – Botticelli's *Venus* – Holbein's *Henry VII* – three Raphaels (*Marriage of the Virgin*, *Deposition* and *Fornarina*) – El Greco's *Nativity and Baptism of Christ* – Rubens' *Romulus and Remus* – and *Pope Innocent X* by Velasquez. I felt very drunk – very small, but supremely happy when I emerged into the sunlight once more. It is an experience that I have very seldom felt before – once when I heard Myra Hess playing the Schumann in the Albert Hall, and once when I saw Joe Dudgeon jumping on Blue Steel (rather an odd mixture I'm afraid!). I had a very amusing lunch with Charlie Toller and Peter Forsyth Forest (both 27th Lancers) (will go straight on!)

Christmas with the Regiment:
31ˢᵗ December 1944

There is only an hour to go before the beginning of a new year – it is somehow rather a great moment. And I feel that so many of the mistakes that I have made this year I may be able to put right next year. I pray God that I, with His help, will be able to achieve that.

I haven't written to you for ages – but I hope that those four that I wrote in a batch have arrived by now. We had a hectic Christmas – in fact it started on Christmas Eve and ended on Boxing Day. It really was great fun – everyone was in tremendous form (a few overdid it a bit). The climax came on Boxing Day after dinner, when the mess waiter took me down to the kitchen and asked me to dance a foursome with my servant, the cook and himself. It was tremendous fun! We finished by singing *John Peel* very lustily with lots of hollering and horn blowing – and went off to bed very happy. Bad for discipline – but well worth it!

I did miss being away from the family most terribly at moments – particularly when we sang all the lovely old Christmas carols in church. But I know how much they were with me, as I was with you, in prayer and it was a tremendous help.

Thank you Darling so much for sending me some books. They haven't actually arrived yet – but they will be a great help when they do. The *Country Lives* arrive absolutely regularly – my Troop love them almost as much as I do! Some cigarettes came the other day too – it is all these little things which make such a difference. Some No 19 lotion arrived from Mr Thomas – I think Ann must have sent it. I haven't written to her for ages.

Just to tell you how well my hand is: The Colonel has collected four horses from the Remount Depot – and I rode with David L this morning. Naturally my fingers are tender but otherwise they could not be better (shall go straight on) . . . . .

In Rome, at the ballet and opera:
16ᵗʰ January 1945

I left the Regiment on Saturday and drove down to Rome via

Ancona, where I went to see Robbie Stuart's grave – and also to put a Regimental Cross on it, which had been beautifully made by the regtl. carpenter. It was rather a depressing place – and it made me feel sad. However as I was passing through the town I saw Perry Fairfax and Mike Bradstock. I had 'a cup o' char and a wad' with them which was great fun – I hadn't seen Perry for ages and heard all his news.

I arrived in Rome in time for dinner – but too late for the opera. It was rather grim – just that night as I didn't know anyone at the hotel and was feeling very depressed about this course. However the next day I went to the lovely art exhibition at the Palazzo Venezia in the morning (I've told you about it, haven't I?) – and to the ballet in the evening. I saw *The Four Seasons* (Vivaldi) and *The Prodigal Son* (Prokofiev). Of course it was simply superb – and up to the opera standard. I then went back and dined with Paddy Leatham (10th Hussars), Micky Hezlett (12th Lancers) and Michael Moule (the Regt) at Marchesa Clarelli's[51] house. It was the greatest fun – and she had asked in three Italian girls who spoke perfect English.

I stayed there the night (she, by the way, is our Wop L/O's mother) in the greatest luxury (b'fast in bed and a hot bath!) I went to see *Il Travatore* in the evening which was marvellous – I had never seen it before – and dined with Peter Walker and Colonel Rodzianco[52] (held as one of the three greatest horsemen in the world – an Anglicised Russian – perhaps you saw him at Olympia). We drove here after dinner, arriving at 1 am. It was a very good weekend!

Of course it is a grim place[53] and very boring – but Mike Woodhead (9th L.) and some other good chaps are here too – so it's not nearly as bad as I thought it would be.

Christmas had been spent peacefully in Pesaro, a largish town on the coast south of Rimini. On January 16th we moved to 'battle stations' near Villanova in the flat Po Valley, separated from the enemy by a canal. It was bitterly cold but fortunately we found a farmhouse which we were able, with hard work, to fortify with barbed wire, sandbags, booby traps, etc.

There was comparatively little action, though one night (21st January) one of the houses (Oxhill) occupied by John Berry's Troop (C Squadron) was attacked and the enemy repulsed. After a time there seemed to have developed an unwritten agreement between the enemy and ourselves that fighting should be postponed until better weather permitted tank movement. It was, therefore, a huge shock when Oxhill (this time occupied by Guy Harman, 4th Troop C Squadron) was heavily shelled on 25th February causing heavy casualties.

This incident enraged the Colonel who ordered the destruction of four houses occupied by the enemy. This ended the truce and shelling was almost constant until 4th March when we were relieved. We had been 'unhorsed' for eight weeks and had not enjoyed the life of an infantry soldier!

Lt. Col. J Price D.S.O.
1945

In Rome with Jack Price and David Laurie: 3rd February 1945

I haven't written to you since I returned from Rome three days ago. It really was the most perfect six days. We did everything that we wanted to do – and seemed to cram a great deal into a comparatively small space of time. Our activities included polo most mornings – riding in the cavalry barracks under Col. Rodzianco, deemed to be one of the three greatest horsemen living – seeing the lovely picture exhibition yet once again, going to *Carmen* and *Rigoletto* at the opera (all quite superb), meeting some very interesting Romans (who care not a jot for Italy, little for Rome, but a very great deal for themselves, etc, etc).

I was with Jack and David all the time – and was therefore able to get to know Jack a little better. I should imagine that it takes a lifetime to know him well. I made the following appreciation of him – probably quite incorrect and unfair! He is a man with the very greatest charm and he knows that with this he can get away with a very great deal. Having no father or mother, he has few people to think of but himself. He is very intelligent and an extremely able soldier. I like him a great deal – but he does have his faults (like most normal people!).

DAVID WENTWORTH STANLEY
FEBRUARY 1945

The weather during the winter of 1945 was appalling – rain almost every day and operations in tanks rendered quite impossible. Nevertheless we had to be on the alert for infantry patrols.

Description of my 'fortress' defending the canal:
14th February 1945

A most amazing envelope was given to me by my Corporal today – it quite embarrassed me! It was such a lovely letter – full, as you say, of the most evil gossip!

I am writing to you in my fortress – or so the formerly very innocent Italian farmhouse has been hastily transformed after a few days of hard work. The whole place is surrounded with barbed wire, mines, trip wires, etc – to the extent that one of my patrols have just arrived back having set off two of our warning flares. Everyone rushed to their stations and, as you can well imagine, there was a bit of a flap. However nobody was shot and all is now well! Quite incredible how stupid some soldiers can be, this patrol commander is a real prize idiot (but so nice!).

A canal separates us from the enemy (thank goodness), so very little occurs except occasional patrols by them. We live very normal lives though – or at least I try to make it fairly normal. It is the mental strain which makes the chaps tired and cross – and therefore less efficient.

I had a letter from Judy on my return from Rome – I haven't written to her for ages.

Oh great news, which I forgot to tell you – C Squadron have been duly rewarded for their big battle (I told you, I think, that the Army Commander had called it the greatest achievement of tanks in the Italian Campaign) and Otto Thwaites, Guy Hannen and Ivor Fitzpatrick have all won MCs. Isn't it good? The battle took place just after I was wounded so I know little about it.

Must stop now and have a walk round the chaps.

I know that it sounds surprising (and unlikely) that 'unmilitary' life could continue nothwithstanding the close proximity of the enemy. But there was a great deal of 'waiting' and we made use of the time! (see in particular my letter of 10th March.)

Still on the canal – waiting for new tanks:
7th March 1945

I've just come back from my Troop to find a letter from you (no 75 – so efficient!). Thank you Darling so much for it.

We are now resting for a few days prior to getting our 'horses' back again. I must say we are all very thankful as the last two months haven't been too pleasant really. I had some rather near misses – though on the whole it wasn't nearly as bad as we thought it was going to be. Shelling is beastly as there is simply nothing that one can do about it – and one just has to sit (head and bottom well down) and hope for the best.

I went for the most lovely ride yesterday afternoon – on Rockaby – who is very nearly my horse (and I further our friendship by surreptitious tit-bits). The sun was shining kindly on me and I was very happy. The actual country round here is very flat and rather dull – but there are lots of green fields and some fences and ditches to jump, so it is perfect for riding.

This is the time that one really loves life – my mind is now free to think of the lovely things.

I have been doing rather badly with letters lately – the 'string' need waking up very badly! Interesting about Nigel K's girlfriend – she got a very good report from Miss Jane. Is he going to marry her? One must be right up with all the gossip!

Rex Hitchcock is now back with us – in very good form. Actually his wedding didn't go down very well – he never asked leave from the Colonel.

Our mess is at least homely: Every evening the cow ascends the stairs on her way to bed. She spends the night with a family consisting of two babies, mother, father and two children. The odd hen also strolls in – so it is all a very varied party. The noise is something draconic!

Oh! the sun is so lovely. I'm sitting outside writing to you – and everything is so peaceful and happy. How absurd it is that a few miles away there is a battle raging.

Race meeting within the sound of guns:
10th March 1945

I think that I got a letter from you on the 8th – anyway it wasn't long ago. But I've lost it, which is maddening as I can't remember whether there were any of those vital questions to answer – and you will be so cross if I forget (but then it is so good for you to be annoyed!).

Nothing much has happened since I last wrote – but no doubt I shall be able to reply through this episode!

I shall now consult my diary: (pause) Oh yes! On Thursday afternoon Otto and I went for our usual ride – but this time I was offered a ride on the Colonel's horse. He is a first class old fellow and we had a lovely time but for one rather tricky moment: We came to a fence which Otto proposed to jump – but I saw a small ditch on the landing side. This I pointed out, but was immediately accused of cowardice! So up I cantered and on landing did a sort of Olympia act in mid-air – needless to say both his front legs had landed in the ditch! However all was well – and after a good deal of brushing nothing could be seen at all.

We went to the Races today! A great gathering. The p'gramme included three steeplechases, two flat races, and a trotting race. 'All the world was there, my dear!' – Giles Gilbey, John Robson, John Middleton, Willie Geddes, etc. It was such fun. And all in the sound of the guns which made it a little more original!

I may not be able to write for a few days.

Within 1,000 yards of Germans; new tank delivered:
22nd March 1945

I am now sitting outside with David and Rex,[54] and we are all wallowing in our laziness. The sun is so lovely – in fact both the others are more or less asleep! And yet the ridiculous thing is that we are within a thousand yards of the Germans. I am reserve Troop for a few days and am therefore back at Squadron Head Quarters. We all make a tremendous effort to make ourselves comfortable – because it is obvious that the more comfortable one is, the more good tempered and therefore more efficient one is. Don't you agree?

Your last letter (dated 15th) arrived three days ago. You were worried about your father. I don't think that it is in the least a dreadful admission that you can't get on with him if it is true. But do remember that it is so easy to think that he thinks you a useless idiotic creature when in fact it is far from the case, and something else that worries him. After all you have proved yourself in the F.A.N.Ys and done jolly well.

Why don't you go and talk it out with him? Ask him what is wrong. You may be able to clear up whatever the difficulty is like that. You say that your father has a very high standard of everything – but so have you, of all people. I'm sure that all will be well. Don't worry – that will be no good.

My old tank has now gone – very sad as I had become almost fond of it. Poor thing though! It had rather a lot of holes in it – and gone an awful long way and was getting very tired. Now I have a new one with a bigger gun which makes me feel a little more secure.

LIEUT.-COLONEL
R. S. G. PERRY, D.S.O.
1944

Did I tell you that the Colonel[55] has got diphtheria? Isn't it bad luck for him? However he had had a very long innings. But this has caused a big change. Derek has now gone as second in command to Jack – so we have lost him; David has come to command us though – so we couldn't have done better than that and, though sorry to no longer have Derek, David is a great friend of all of us.

Adrian writes that he went on the river with Judy the other day – I must write to her or I shan't get a letter from her.

We had only about a week to prepare our tanks for action and we moved off to a staging location near the River Montore on March 10th. The enemy were present in force on the other side of the river. B Squadron was in reserve, relieving A Squadron on March 21st. The next few weeks were spent training for the coming battles. The training finished on 7th April and the next day we moved to a place called Godo, a few miles from Cotingola on the River Senio. (See next letter dated 7th April.)

A few days later we were able to cross the Senio and moved forward into the Santerno bridgehead (the River Santerno runs due south of the River Reno, north-west of Rimini) on April 13th. A & C Squadrons were leading with B Squadron in reserve. Fighting was fierce, David Whately (A Squadron) engaging a 75mm anti tank gun with his machine gun, later to be holed by two rounds of armour piercing shells. C Squadron, meanwhile, were pushing on and Guy Hannen found the main road bridge still intact but, as his Troop approached, it was blown up. Nearby John Berry fired two rounds at a movement on the far bank of a canal and a German officer with two Iron Crosses threw up his hands, waded the canal and surrendered.

We called a halt that night and on the morning of the 14th we reached our objective on the River Reno. Excitement was intense. The Germans were certainly not on the run but they were retreating. Jack Price (who had recently taken over command from Stug Perry) was obviously a brilliant and enthusiastic leader and motored about cheering us on with a broad smile! We were out hunting and the hounds were running!

124

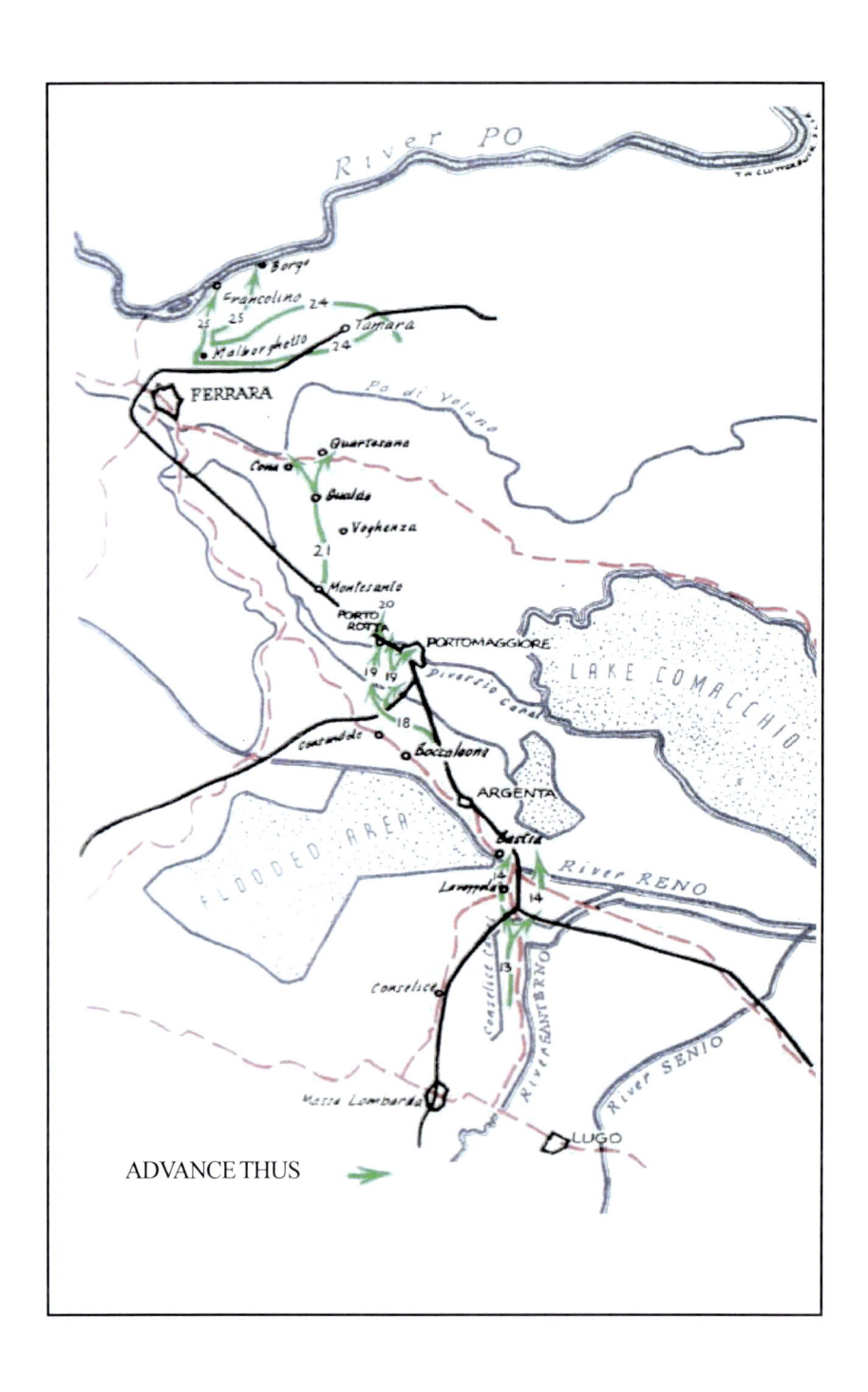

Battle impending:
7th April 1945

Well, our training has now just about finished. It's been jolly hard work – and we are all very glad that it is over. But now there is going to be an even busier time – so I shan't have much time for writing letters. You will know why. Don't worry though – all is well.

Yes, it's just about a year ago now since I left you. Of course we have both changed – living the lives we do it would be odd if we hadn't. And we must be ready – both of us – to expect that change. But, as you say, we may both have grown up together. Out here I do everything with you and I think with you – and at night I pray with you. I can, therefore, never tell you in a letter how I love you.

We are in a big fruit growing district here – and all the fields are a mass of white or pink blossom. Against the blue sky it looks so absolutely beautiful. And I am so happy. David and I went for our usual evening stroll and decided that life, in spite of the present responsibilities, was very good! He is a wonderful Squadron Leader.

Today has been perfect though – we rode before breakfast, then came straight in for Holy Communion full of the lovely fresh morning. So we are strengthened and ready. Jack came in for a drink this evening with Derek. Both in very good form.

Description of battle; knocked out two tanks and three guns:
19th April 1945

Two lovely letters were brought up to me late last night.

But they arrived at a perfect time. We had a very big battle yesterday – and it was so lovely to come into Leaguer and find them waiting for me. I wish so much that I could tell you all about yesterday – it was a tremendous experience. We started off at 4.30 am (with a bully sandwich and a cup of tea in our tummies!) At about eight o'clock we met the forward elements of the enemy – I was leading on the left flank and David Wentworth Stanley was on my right.

By lunch time we had advanced some five miles against very heavy opposition and were held up for a short time by a big water obstacle. Cpl Nicholls (my gunner who one day you will meet –

quite definitely!) was shooting very straight and we had by then knocked out an enemy tank and a self propelled gun. It was intensely exciting and very tiring. John Joicey then came up and took over from David. The big 'charge' then took place. It was terrific. Under a tremendous hail of fire from two squadrons of tanks (ourselves and A) and support from artillery and bombing, we advanced over three miles of very open ground. We knocked out a tank and two guns – and John Joicey got four guns. We took our objective just as night was drawing in. All the farms were blazing and lit the twilight with the setting sun.

This seems to be all about Fourth Troop – they were all so frightfully good though.

Jack Price wrote an account of the fighting immediately afterwards which is reproduced hereunder:

"B Squadron on the left had 4th Troop under Bill Birch Reynardson, supported by S.S.M. Huxford in a 105mm tank, and 3rd Troop under John Joicey, supported by Otto Thwaites in a 105mm tank, leading, with 2nd Troop under John Goldsmid echeloned back to the left rear. All went in together.

In an area of about 800 square yards they overran a battery of 4 88mm anti aircraft guns and a battery of 4 150mm field guns as well as 12 20mm ack ack guns. The German gunners put up a very brave show and all went on firing over open sights right up to the end. Luckily the 88s had been sited primarily for ack ack and were taken completely by surprise. They did manage to load with armour piercing and fired a considerable number of rounds at our tanks but they were so cluttered up with camouflage and branches of trees and so plastered with HE and browning from our tanks that their aim was very erratic and they only hit Michael de Burgh's tank, whose suspension was holed but he was able to continue. David Whately's tank was hit by a 150mm HE shell but was able to continue although the commander's ear drums were broken.

At the same time as this was going on C Squadron and H Company on the right were having a similar party with a battery of 4 105 field guns and a battery of 3 88mm guns which they captured intact. All the time, with all three squadrons, prisoners were streaming in and surprised strong points being routed out by the London Irish. Many enemy vehicles were burning and much equipment, and a large number of houses which had been strong points were on fire, having been set alight by the HE from the tanks.

Just as it was getting dark all squadrons and companies reported that they were on their objectives and were mopping up and consolidating. Further advances were impossible as it was now quite dark and there were still a large number of Germans including many bazooka parties in the area to be dealt with.

R.H.Q. by now had established itself at La Fossa right in the middle the box formed by the 4 squadrons and companies. When I stepped out of my tank the countryside was a most incredible sight. It was quite dark and we were completely surrounded by a ring of fire. There were 21 houses burning with flames roaring through the roofs, innumerable German vehicles burning and 2 ammunition dumps exploding and sending up every sort of firework."

I do not want to go into further detail about the advance to the River Po. Suffice it to say that we were extremely busy with the Germans now in retreat – but by no means on the run. We were constantly in action and we had had to fight every yard of the way. On one occasion 4th Troop was confronted by three German tanks. Sergeant Edmunds got a right and left and then my gunner, Corporal Nicholls, got the third. Later on a Mark IV German tank, which had been causing substantial damage was knocked out, again by the unerring aim of Corporal Nicholls!

After a fortnight of almost continual fighting from the River Santerno to the River Po, Jack Price wrote a message to us at the end of April which ended:

"I feel that the 9th Lancers have probably fired their last shot in Europe, and what a shot!
Tanks: 12 "brewed", 1 captured intact, 11 "self brewed".
Armoured cars: 2 destroyed.
Self propelled: 1 overrun, 6 destroyed, 1 self destroyed.
Guns: 150mm: 4 overrun, 1 destroyed.
        105mm: 2 overrun, 4 destroyed.
        149mm howitzer: 2 overrun.
        88mm: 4 overrun, 7 destroyed.

> *75mm anti tank: 1 destroyed*
> *20mm: 2 overrun, 12 destroyed.*
> *Mortars: 2 (large) destroyed.*
> *Miscellaneous: half-tracks: 1 overrun, 2 destroyed.*
> *Transport (various): 29 destroyed.*
> *Horses: 8 captured.*
> *Ponies & traps: 2 captured.*
> *In addition: 7 officers, 2 medical officers and 870 other ranks were taken prisoner."*

On the evening of 1st May, General Mark Clark, commanding the Allied Troops in Italy, announced that all organised resistance in Italy had ended. And on May 2nd Field Marshal Alexander announced the unconditional surrender of General von Vietinghoff and the German South West Army Group, which numbered a million men.

The firing had ceased and peace had come. I seem to remember (but, please, it was over sixty years ago!) that we had to make an effort to celebrate our victory! There was a special Eighth Army service of thanksgiving in Ferrara. We had all come to thank God for answering our prayer "Defend us, thy humble servants, in all assaults of our enemies that we, surely trusting in Thy defence, may not fear the power of any adversaries." But what of the future?

88mm German gun.
Overrun 18th April 1945 by B Squadron

FROM RIGHT TO LEFT:
SGT. PARIFITT, W.B.R, S.S.M. HUXFORD
'B SQUADRON FIRING INDIRECT'
1945

CAPTURED GERMAN 155MM GUN BEING FIRED BY OTTO THWAITES
ASSISTED BY DAVID WENTWORTH STANLEY
APRIL 1945

Advance to River Po:
28th April 1945

In the last few very hectic days I have lost my book in which I entered all letters to you – thus I have no idea when I last wrote! Most unfortunate! I'm sorry that there has been such a gap – but as you obviously gathered we have been pretty busy.

We have had some land battles and my Troop have knocked out a good deal of enemy equipment – but one day I will tell you all about it. I feel that it wouldn't really interest you now.

We have succeeded – that is the great thing, and Jack has been quite brilliant throughout.

Now we are just off to cross the Po. It is all very exciting as the end draws steadily nearer. We arrived at our present position two nights ago after a rather beastly battle which went on till midnight – so we have all been sleeping since then! Fighting is the most tiring thing in the world – and yet when it is all over one feels rather pleased that one's old body can take it!

Your parcel full of good things arrived about a week ago. Thank you so much for it – you always send just the things that I want.

What ghastly pictures in *The Tatler* of some dance at Oxford! They made us all livid. What a wet crew they all looked. It made me rather sad to think that Oxford has come to this.

I hope I shan't write many more of these things – but I'm in such a hurry now!

Royal Salute on River Po:
5th May 1945

The news is good isn't it! We had a really big party on the night of the 2nd when unconditional surrender was announced – David ordered a Royal Salute from the tank guns. All the chaps were so drunk when the time came that soon every gun in the Squadron was firing – it was far more dangerous than any battle! The Fourth of June simply wasn't in it!

Since then we have all remained with our ears permanently stuck to the wireless! The news is quite fantastic, isn't it?

We have all been wondering what our future is – there appear to be two alternatives, Austria or England. As none of us will be able to leave the army for a year at least, we all want to go to Austria. Leave will obviously be very generous and the idea of soldiering with so many rules and regulations is appalling!

I simply can't make up my mind what to do as soon as my soldiering career is over. I feel that I cannot make up my mind without seeing Father. My goodness, it is a big problem!

I'm afraid I haven't written to you for ages, Darling, and your letters arrive so often. David has now become familiar with that particularly vulgar paper which you will insist on writing to me on! Much too obvious, particularly as David notices far too much! He really has been the most wonderful Squadron Leader. I must admit that I rather feared whether it would work, being such a great friend of his. The only way to deal with the situation has been to separate the Army from normal life (as it always should be anyway!) and our friendship has not been affected!

We are still camping in the same place were we arrived nearly eight days ago. There has been really quite a bit to do – this is the sort of time when one's Troop is liable to become bored and I must say it is rather difficult to know what to do with them. However leave is now beginning for them and parties are now going into Bologna and Ferrara and occasionally to Venice.

I have been riding a good deal in the afternoons with David – we really have got a jolly collection of horses, and of course they make the whole difference to life. David, John Joicey, Rex Hitchcock and I are all going to Venice in about two days – or rather we hope so! Won't it be fun! A full report will come later!

I must stop writing now – this has been a very dull letter. Joicey and David are both making a filthy noise and will not let me write in peace and quiet.

There is one very big question – and that is the subject of the Germans, and particularly over these ghastly concentration camps. I have been thinking a great deal about it, but I will write a letter to you later about my ideas.

GEN-ADM. VON FRIEDENBURG, GERMAN NAVAL C-IN-C IS SEEN SIGNING THE SURRENDER TERMS WHILE FIELD MARSHAL MONTGOMERY LOOKS ON 1945

Commenting on Nazi Atrocities:
6th May 1945

I know so well how much the news of the German atrocities must be appalling to you at this time. I hoped that there could be little truth in the stories I had heard of them – but now the proof is absolute.

Quite obviously it would be impossible for any human being, however cruel and sadistic, to live in such places, let alone help to commit such ghastly acts – I am told that the staff of these prisons are taken away from normal civilized contact with the world when they are young and gradually trained as bullies and sadists. Therefore I believe that they have little conscience about their actions.

Any dictatorship is an idealistic form of government. All opposition is dispelled, and the dictator rules in the manner which he considers best. In this way the government of a country is able to make decisions and accomplish tasks with far greater speed. As an example, the Germans have formed a great and efficient army in a very short time.

Any member of the community who opposes the government is considered to reduce its efficiency – he is a saboteur to his country. If, as in Germany, the country is in the hands of unspeakable sinners, the result has been unspeakable sin.

I blame the Germans on two points: primarily, the leaders of the Nazi Party and their accomplices who have directly caused such horror and fear – and secondly the general German community who have allowed themselves to be drawn down to such filthy depths. The Nazi leaders must be shot, for they have committed crimes against the world which has proved them more than detestable to the world. "It were better for him that a millstone be hung around his neck and that he was drowned in the depth of the sea" – Our Lord would have condemned these men.

And what of the general community? I know comparatively little of the Germans – but I have fought against the German Army. They are, many of them, very good soldiers. And a good soldier – be he of any nation or creed – has many admirable qualities. He must be courageous, he must be unselfish. He must be obedient. They are fighting on the side of sinners – but those qualities still remain. I believe that they can be taught to be useful members of the world society today.

Our Lord tells us to love our enemies, and I know how impossible it sounds! The alternative however is to hate them. And hating is essentially a destructive emotion. Of course we can hate their system and their actions – but is it going to do any good to hate them?

If all our energy is spent in hating how are we going to better them? Hitler rose to power in March 1933 – since then the youth of Germany have been brought up in atmosphere of evil. Those twelve years have first to be obliterated and then they have all to be re-taught – they have to be reborn.

There is a tremendous task ahead of us all. And the glorious fact is that by teaching them to be better men we are being true

Christians – and we are loving them!

To be weak with the Germans would be sinful. It is quite essential that we are firm with them – they must be punished. I took a young Nazi prisoner the other day. "You English have won the war," he said "but, as at the end of the last war, you will lose the Peace." Pray God that we will know better this time.

It is now one o'clock in the morning. I have been listening to Mozart's *Violin Concerto No 7* – what a beautiful piece of music. But the B.B.C. has nothing to say about the end of the War so I'm going to bed!

The paper is, as you see, of a very variable nature! Could you please send me some of a rather more uniform variety!

So, for us, the War in Europe is over and we have been victorious. Anyone reading my letters covering the next year might wonder what on earth was going on! I don't believe that we thought we deserved this extraordinary year of sheer enjoyment, but we were, I suppose, exhausted (though we were all fit and young, so perhaps that word is out of place!) – and, anyway, we wanted to celebrate. Not that we admitted such a thing, but we were still alive, and we certainly celebrated!

First of all we washed off not only the grime of battle (we hadn't seen a bath for weeks!) but also the vision of the wounded and dying – the awful sadness of it all which we had had to shrug off at the time. We wanted to live again in peace. So here is my first sight of Venice!

BACK: W.B.R., JOHN JOICEY, JOHN GOLDSMID, DAVID WENTWORTH STANLEY
FRONT: REX HITCHCOCK, DAVID LAURIE, OTTO THWAITES.
PALMANOVA, ITALY, 1945

CPL NICHOLS (GUNNER), CPL ALLAN (WIRELESS OPERATOR),
L/CPL EMERSON (DRIVER), W.B.R.
LEAVING FOR U.K. ON 'PYTHON RELEASE'
AUGUST 1945

Footnotes to Part III

46.   General (later Field Marshal) Sir Richard Hull, Dick (late 17th/5th Lancers).

47.   He was in India, Lord Wavell's staff.

48.   Caserta, General (later Field Marshal) Wilson's HQ.

49.   Hermione Llewellyn, Later Countess of Ranfurly CBE, was a cousin. She was called 'Secretary' to Jumbo Wilson but I always thought that it was she who told him what to do! She was a most charming but powerful woman! She wrote a lovely book called *To War with Whitaker* (Whitaker was her husband, Dan's, soldier servant). She was very helpful to me as Caserta.

50.   This was a unique exhibition. The pictures shown had been taken from their hiding place (in some salt mines) before going back to their original galleries in Florence, Milan, Venice, etc.

51.   Marchesa Marini Clarelli, the mother of Raymondo who was our Italian Liaison Officer.

52.   Colonel Rodzianco was a fantastic teacher and had a (temporary) riding school in Rome which I attended. He always had a long whip with him with which he was incredibly accurate, hitting one's hand with the lash if you had jabbed your horse in the mouth.

53.   Villanova.

54.   Rex Hitchcock, Major MC (2nd in command of B Squadron).

55.   Stug Perry, Lt Col. DSO. A most charming man and always very kind to me.

Part IV
May 1945 – August 1946
Victory and the Aftermath

First visit to Venice:
10th May 1945

We have just arrived back from Venice. And could it have been a better time to go! We heard the Prime Minister's speech at our hotel overlooking the Grand Canal. But there is comparatively little celebrating – the War came to an end after a tremendous battle and it was obvious that the enemy were beaten as soon as the Invasion of France took place. The war against Japan is not over – and the horrors that we have all heard about it are not forgotten. And lastly the tremendous post-war problems are of great concern to all of us.

Oh! But what a lovely place Venice is! We will go there after the War and sail down the Grand Canal in a gondola! The Canal is flanked on each bank by the most beautiful 15th century buildings of warm red brick and white marble which shines down into the rippling blue water.

And St Marks! The great church standing at the end of the Square like some eastern palace with its domes and pillars and arches of white marble could only be in St Marks Square without being hideous. But here it is beautiful – surrounded on three sides by the most perfect 15th century houses forming a cloister round the square.

After a huge victory lunch we had our photographs taken! Here we are - looking very debauched! Usually we still look a little more normal! A little Wop took us round the lace factory. It was an education just to go there to see such wonderful work. I bought you some lace which I hope will help to smarten up your khaki knickers!

It was a pity we only had forty eight hours there as we really saw very little – and anyway it was so hot that we had little energy for sight seeing! When I got back there were two letters from you waiting for me. Thank you so much for them Darling. You were in very good form.

We are all wondering what our future is going to be! Jim Weatherby's regiment has gone north – but we still sit here doing very little! The horses make just the whole difference – and we now ride in the evenings as it is too hot in the afternoons. Bathing for the keen water-boys has already started!

We all went to church today in Ferrara to thank God for His help and guidance and to pray for a lasting Peace. There was a real atmosphere of sincerity during the service – for He has been so very close to us all – particularly during the last month. I shall always be glad that I have fought in this War. The difference between good and bad shines like a beacon through the darkness of war. It is an experience that I shall never forget.

I hope that Judy is all right after her bathe! How typical of Adrian[56] to capsize her! Do you see him at all nowadays? He writes to me every week, generally enclosing some of his poetry. He has been a very good friend to me.

I really must go to bed now – it's now nearly one o'clock! There always seems to be something on during the day – and consequently I never get to bed!

New headquarters south of Venice; in charge of squadron's horses: 18th May 1945

I know how very guilty I am – and I have very little excuse to offer!

Since I last wrote we have moved from the banks of the Po to a place just south of Venice. I can't tell you what a lovely place it is – a very large comfortable house (with things that pull and gurgle) and a perfect 17th century garden full of lakes and lily ponds. And best of all, a white marble swimming pool full of clear green water! It is all so terribly like England. The place is owned by a charming young Wop who does all he can to make us happy. All his pictures, furniture and silver were taken by the Germans.

I have been working frightfully hard with the horses. David has put me in charge of the stables and my grey and two other horses are now under me. It takes a great deal of time organising food, bedding, grooms, etc – and the difficulties are immense! It is a very useful experience.

David and I have been out all day looking for some more horses. We drove almost to the foot of the Alps. It really was quite lovely – except for the heat which was ghastly! Actually we only saw one really good horse – a thoroughbred standing about 16.2 – but he had a beastly running sore on his off foreleg – so it wasn't worth taking him!

The grey is going on very well – but he is still very green. The snag is that he is really too old to be properly schooled now - however we shall see.

I quite forgot to thank you for the *Esquire* and the cigarettes. I was on my last pot – but all is now well! (It arrived with another parcel of three books from Molly Middleton!)

As you will have gathered the release from the army is not going to be all that quick! I honestly don't think that I will be in 'civvy street' till 1947. I have been thinking a great deal about it lately – particularly as if I decided to be a doctor I could get out fairly quickly. I cannot really make a definite decision before I see Father – and therefore I have decided to wait until I get leave to England which I hope will anyway be within the next six months.

From the point of view of enjoying oneself, staying in the Regiment for the next two years would definitely be the best course! And with Jack as Colonel it will be made all the easier. But when I think of a career and making some money two years seems rather a long time. As far as I can see I shall be broke anyway! I like too many things in life which cost too much money!

Actually I know that in time one can get used to any way of living. I often wonder what the basis of happiness is: I suppose that the more one cuts out self the happier one is, as unhappiness is obviously the unhappiness of oneself. And to annihilate selfishness one has to be a good Christian

The ability to love one's fellow men, to love beauty (in music, in art, in literature, in nature) – Oh! But I can't think now! Something has gone wrong with me – I'm even odder than usual! We are all still acclimatising ourselves to peacetime – and yet there still seems to be a lot of trouble. I wonder what will happen about Trieste – it is rather too near here to be pleasant!

I have just had the most amazing letter from Kit. He wants to marry Ros – and thinks that he will. As you know he has always been very fond of her – as she is of him. But I could never have believed that he thought of such a thing. And anyway I think that it is far too near Jimmy's death to talk about marriage to her (which he has). Obviously Ros has been frightened of hurting him – but he will be all the worse later on. Of course I have written off to her immediately explaining the whole situation. He is my very greatest friend and I should hate him to be sad about Ros (of all people). He seems to have got the most incredible marriage complex (at the age of 21!). I wonder whether he has changed very much.

Did the lace arrive all right? There was very little I'm afraid.

I must go to bed – it's nearly one and I'm riding at 6 tomorrow morning with David. The start of the day is perfect. We ride from 6.30 to eight – then bathe and have an enormous breakfast! David, as usual, is here talking the most amazing nonsense and stopping me writing to you – quite impossible! "You can't still be writing to the border country"..... Later: (2.30 am)! I gave way to D and have since then been having a very deep (and constructive) conversation with him about the rather over discussed question of sex. We know each other well enough at least not to be hypocritical which makes things easier.

I am supposed to ride at six!

Resignation of Prime Minister; soldiers will vote left at next General Election:
23rd May 1945

The most appalling rocket arrived two days ago on that yellow peril! I suppose that I deserved it – very bad of me. But Judy mustn't be so tactless!

The letter situation does seem to be very odd though; you certainly should have had some from me; I am cursed by my family as well, so there is obviously something wrong.

We have now moved from the place near Venice – it was much too good to last – and now we are all living in a ghastly Italian cavalry barracks surrounded by little except dust and a rather high tension with Tito's chaps fairly near at hand! I can only think that nothing will occur in the end. Of course it would be a catastrophe if we did have to fight them – the Yugoslavs will probably get Trieste at the Peace Conference – but quite obviously this grabbing method is too reminiscent of Czechoslovakia and Poland to be permissible. Perhaps Tito thought that we are as weak now as we were then. He couldn't be more wrong!

There is no chance anyway of my flirting with a Tyrolean girl – and the local females are hard to distinguish from males! I should hate to fight them . . . . .

John Joicey and I drove over to the XII Lancers last night and had a most amusing dinner party there. They are the nicest chaps – and I know most of them so well. Giles Gilbey I expect you remember at Oxford – quite mad. I think he made me laugh in those days more than anyone else. John Middleton and John Robson were at Cambridge – a great mistake! But they are little the worse for it. We talked far into the night, and nearly overdid the drink. I often wonder whether I have got into a bad habit – I know that you will notice that I drink much more now.

Bill (Peek) left us yesterday bound for a course in England. Perhaps you will see him. He seems to get more and more odd – and is considered the biggest joke. He has a cousin out here who works in the Catholic Women's League – can't remember her name – but obviously there is far more keenness shown than with normal cousins! Do you know who I mean?

So glad your dotty cousin has died! As Mother would say, I'm sure he's happier now!

I am going down to Venice tomorrow with David – and then on to collect the horses which are at our last location. It will make an enormous difference having them here.

I had a letter from Jimmy G.[57] yesterday – raving about this girl! What a perfect husband he will make. He sent me a book by old Talboys[58] about Wellington. It is illustrated by Mr Huntley (the husband of the Ch. Ch. nurse). It looks a very good sort of book.

Could you possibly send me a book called *Other Men's Flowers* by Lord Wavell? – Father gave it to me but I lost it. I should love to have it.

I give up all hope of ever hearing from Ann again – it really is about six months (and I don't exaggerate!) since she last wrote to me.

The Prime Minister's resignation and the thought of a general election has caused much discussion. The normal soldier out here is definitely voting left – but is extremely ignorant of the facts. They blame the Conservatives for keeping the term of service out here up to 4 ½ years – never thinking that there might be some cause for it – and this fact alone influences the majority of them against the government (which they forget is a coalition and not Conservative).

But why, on the other hand, should they know the policies of the parties? Nobody ever tells them. Like the Irish, they are all for voting 'agin the government'. Oh! If they would only understand what a Labour government would mean for them. Freedom? With everything under the sun under state control? It's all very worrying. I think it only a 50:50 chance that the Conservatives will remain in power.

Is there anything that you would like me to send you from Venice? Lipstick, nail varnish, etc, appears easy.

Collecting horses in Austria: Refugees fleeing from Russian Army: 3rd June 1945

I have been having the most lovely time since I last wrote – and yet I'm afraid that I have written too long ago!

Intelligence reported large numbers of German horses in Southern Austria on Thursday night – and David said that I had got to go up and see what they were like. So on Friday morning I started off in his jeep and drove very fast towards the Alps. For miles we drove up and up through the deep gorges into the mountains, the sides covered with dark fir trees and grass and the peaks snow-covered. We crossed the frontier at 12 o'clock. The change in the whole countryside is amazing. Austria is wholly rolling grass fields and fir trees with clean white little farmhouses tucked into the valleys.

We drove through Villach and Klagenfurt (where there is an

enormous lake – complete with yachts and bathers) and on to St Viet where I met John Joicey and Rex at three o'clock. They had been sent on an advance party to find out exactly where the horses were. They discovered that they had moved 75 miles northwards towards the Russian lines. It was a terrific race as the horses, having mostly been captured from 'Jo' (as the soldiers say) were on their way back to him! But we meant to get there first – and by dint of fast driving through the most lovely Alpine country we arrived (at 6) to find over 4,000 horses waiting for our choice. You can imagine the excitement! But also the difficulties were supreme. David said that I had to be back by the next morning and so we only had two hours to choose in! As the horses were moving about the fields in completely disorganized groups, things were made no easier – however we picked out three medium horses which is anyway better than nothing.

That night we all stayed in a little Austrian farmhouse and drank cider – the old farmer was charming, and really put himself out to make us comfortable. Of course the whole situation is becoming more and more tricky. No soldier is allowed to fraternise with them – while they are only too willing to help us. They are all terrified of the Russians – and our soldiers absolutely loathe them and already there have been some very difficult incidents. The Russians either get drunk or rape the local inhabitants – therefore Austrians are flocking over to our lines, and then having to be taken back into Russian Territory as soon as it is discovered. So the normal soldier is becoming increasingly anti-Russian and pro-Austrian.

At the moment at San Francisco a conference is sitting. The decisions formed there will affect the whole course of the world. And Russia is a main power there. We are, in fact, allowing a country whose ideas of government and of living we have always considered wrong to give counsel. When Germany invaded Russia she automatically became an ally. But this cannot logically mean that we approve of her ideas. She was merely fighting the common enemy. It is a very worrying outlook for the future of the world.

I motored down from Austria – starting at 5.30 – and arrived at 11.30. Then David declared that we were going to Venice! So I packed quickly and we drove slowly down, arriving for tea. As usual an enormous party had been organised. It was held in the most beautiful house on the Grand Canal. Everything was so English – even the old mothers sat gossiping madly round the room.

More or less the same people were there – they all seem to move about altogether. It really was tremendous fun – except that we couldn't get a gondola at 5.30 in the morning and had to walk back through a mass of tiny little alleyways.

We had a big lunch party the next day at the Black Market Restaurant – three very English girls came. It's amazing how they all seem to speak – and they really are very nice (and so plain!). Their mothers are infuriating and insist on coming along too – however we have found a very nice chap[59] who is a brother of a charming girl called Memina Roi and so he acts as chaperone! We went and listened to some music after lunch at one of their houses. So lovely – *The Emperor* and one of the Beet. Piano sonatas (A minor) – but dinner was definitely off – not even the brother was allowed! So we had dinner together and went to bed (jolly tired).

We drove back at great speed at 5 am and arrived here for breakfast. It really was a good weekend.

That evening we all (or those who qualified!) sallied forth to the 4th of June Dinner in Trieste. You can imagine how we all enjoyed ourselves. And of course we gossiped for ages and didn't get home till 2. Ashley Ponsonby, Bobby Chaworth-Musters[60,] Walter Prideaux (Humphrey's brother), etc, were there. We see a lot of the Coldstream who are near here – Ash[61] and David Carr Wilson came to dinner the other night. A's in great form – so lovely seeing him again.

The horses really do take up the most tremendous amount of time – and food is tricky for them. But it just makes the whole difference having them.

Later: Great news: The awards have come through. The Colonel's got a D.S.O.; David Whately, Ribton Crampton and David Steel MCs; my Sgt Edmunds M.M., and Sgt Major Huxford D.C.M.; John Joicey's Tp. Sgt M.M., also David Wentworth Stanley's. We are all so terribly pleased.

David and I are driving down to Montegaldo after lunch to stay with the Rois for a night. Object is to see the Tiepello murals in their house and to hear their music. It really should be great fun – and they are so nice.

Thank you Darling for no. 96. How lovely being at Manderston – your poor Mama seems to be as busy as ever (like most mothers). I must stop now and get ready.

I will have to write again tomorrow to tell you about Rois, etc. Also things I have forgotten now.

Staying at Montegaldo with Boso and Memina Roi: 20th June 1945

The days seem to go by so quickly now that one can't remember when I last wrote to you. I'm afraid it was too long ago.

David, John Joicey and I went down to stay with the Rois near Padua (south of Venice). It really was just like being in England again! The two children – Memina (girl, 23) and Boso (boy, 21) both had an English governess and they speak perfect English. Their parents have both lived quite a long time in England. And the result is a frightfully English family! They won't have a word said against us!

We arrived on Friday afternoon for tea – and found a lovely rather Regency looking house in a perfect Italian garden, surrounded by hills.[62] We very quickly got down to the gramophone records! I should think they have five hundred (at least) of classical music and about two hundred and fifty English dance music. And the most lovely radiogram. I can't remember what we played during the weekend – but it did include Rach. II – *The Emperor* – the Schumann *Piano Concerts.*, the 1st Tchaikovsky – *The Matthew Passion* – Beet. 7, 8 and 9, etc!

However on Friday night a dance had been organised – two South Africans were added to the male contingent and various dark, husky voiced glams arrived for dinner. It was the greatest fun – though hearing all the old tunes was sometimes rather awful. *N & D*[63] by Carol Gibbons …… etc. We couldn't make it after two, but the others went on without stopping till 4.30. They really are fantastic.

We were taken to see their horses by Boso the next morning (not very early) – and then we rode in their manège. It was one of the best mornings I've ever had – for they were two perfect horses. I've never jumped such obstacles before in cold blood! Boso rode really well – the Italian forward seat which, when properly performed, looks superb.

Music began in earnest after lunch – and we played solidly till we went out to tea at a nearby villa; rather like West Wycombe but about 10 times as big! Italian tea parties are most intriguing! Everyone sits down under a tree and conversations in English, French and Italian begin until the lackeys (of which there seems to be no shortage) appear conveying plates of SAMWIDGES, cream buns, tea, coffee, wine, etc. Thence conversation stops for ¼ hour and eating takes its place. By then it is six o'clock and therefore time to dance. And we all danced till 8!

As usual there was an enormous crowd for dinner – but mostly rather ancient bridge players for Father and Mother Roi – and we were fairly free to do what we wanted after dinner. The first thing was to sit down after the enormous dinner. Don't ever think that the rich Italians are – or ever were – short of food. It is only the poor ones: (and then they wonder (a) why there was such a thing as Fascism and (b) why there is such as thing as Communism in Italy). Never have I had such food. And on such china, on exquisite Venetian lace cloths.

There were two really lovely pictures in the house – a Sargent and an Ingre. But otherwise the pictures were disappointing.

The last night we played music till quarter to four! We started away at seven o'clock (breakfast in our rooms before going & hot baths!) and arrived back here at 10.30 . . . . .

. . . . . to find that I should have been orderly officer! Most unfortunate. And as a result I got a medium rocket and three extra duties. But I do hate doing that sort of thing – it could so easily have been avoided. I hope I'm not getting casual. The main thing now is the gymkhana on Friday. Riding school has stopped in the mornings now – and instead we train our horses over the hunter trial course.

My Bagatelle is too green to enter – but I was frightfully lucky and picked up a first class big bay gelding the other day who jumps like a stag. Actually he's not really schooled yet and therefore is not really quite up to hunter trial standard – but I shall have fun!

We spend most of our time with horses now – Colonel Jack is running the Regiment like the old days! Riding School 7 – 8.30. Breakfast. Work with our Troops till 11. Lecture at Veterinary Wing 11 – 12.30. Free afternoon (never is!) and riding from 6 – 8 in the evenings. Could anything be better! I wonder how long it will last.

Don't be too optimistic about me getting back early. I don't think that there is a chance till Christmas. But it will go very quickly. I am terribly depressed when I see the old faces already leaving us – and the knowledge that in a year my Troop will have three old people in it. I shall miss them – as you know – so dreadfully.

Vienna Horse Show; shooting with Alec Simpson:
9th July 1945

The Austrian trip was simply perfect as I thought it would be. We took four horses up for the show (Lancer[64] – the R.S.M's, Monkey, Mistake and a horse that Boso Roi lent us). They went ahead in the horse box (a converted 3 ton lorry) and by the time that David and I arrived, at about six in the evening, they were well settled in their stables. We went down to see the fences immediately. A beautifully laid out course with regulation military jumping fences was shown to us – they looked very formidable!

We then drove on to the 16th/5th lancers where we were met by Alec Simpson. He gave us a very good dinner (champagne straight from France!) and we went to bed fairly early. We were up before breakfast, having spent the night in a lovely little chalet on the banks of one of the little lakes there, and rode over a few practice fences.

The show started at 9.30. The whole world was there! Just like Lords! I rode Mistake and then Monkey in the open jumping. They went fairly well – but neither they nor I are up to the really rather high standard of show jumping. The great thing was that Lancer did a clear round in the eliminating jumps and excitement was intense in the finals. Mr Hardwidge[65] rode magnificently and beat 81 horses to win the event. Of course we were all overjoyed.

We went back to the chalet afterwards and bathed in the lake and then dressed for dinner. We were asked to the Derbyshire Yeomanry farewell party before they left the Division – and we arrived at their mess at nine o'clock. It is right on the banks of a large lake surrounded by pine trees and above them snow topped mountains. I cannot describe the beauty as the sun went down, its red rays catching the mountains and reflecting them into the shimmering silent water below. When it became dark the opposite shore was floodlit and I went right down the lake in a speedboat.

All the good chaps who had been at the show seemed to have been asked and I saw heaps of people I hadn't seen for ages. And the food! – quite fantastic! We gossiped till two in the morning and I just managed to go to bed for an hour before going out roe-buck shooting with Alec[66] at four.

I met him and an ancient old Austrian keeper (who might, so well, have come from England – grooms and keepers all seem to be the same whatever nationality) in the dark and we drove up into the mountains as the sun began to rise. It would have been enough to have simply seen the fir trees and the mountains at that time, but we were led out of one of the woods into an open field by the old keeper – and there – a thousand yards away – stood a really good buck. Excitement was intense as the old boy beckoned us round to the right. When we next saw him he was only 400 yards away – walking towards us. But soon the trees and bracken got in our line of sight – so we had to wait to see him again. I expected him to appear to our left. It was a pity as suddenly he jumped into the wood a hundred yards to the right. He stood stock still for a moment, and then as I brought my rifle over to fire at him he saw us and swung round and galloped off. We never saw him again – it was a pity, but it didn't matter. They are such lovely things.

We spent a lazy morning bathing and started back after lunch. There was nearly a mishap when our off side tyre burst going at 60 mph down the autostrada from Klagenfurt. Luckily Sgt Philpotts was driving and he very skilfully avoided a crash. We were all rather frightened!

The 12th Lancers had a gymkhana yesterday which was great fun

– though not on the same scale as the 16th, so it wasn't taken so seriously! Actually I never jumped as the horses have been having quite enough as it is. There was one hurdle race which David won riding Mistake, which was splendid. I saw Perry Fairfax there (Tom's brother) whom I hadn't seen for ages – and Ashley too. They are a good lot in the 12th. John Brooke[67] came up from Caserta (where he is as A.D.C. to the Field Marshal) and he gave me all the news of Delia, Lavinia and Diana. They all seem to be flourishing, which is good.

Scala Opera singing on banks of River Isonzo; Offered to be John Harding's A.D.C.: 15th July 1945

I really do feel ashamed of myself now – I haven't written to you for absolutely ages. And now you are on strike! I fully deserve it. Where do I begin? There is so much to tell you.

I went up to Austria with David on the 4th for the Sixth Armoured Division Races. It was the most lovely weekend and I shall always remember it. We drove up (that lovely drive through the mountains) and arrived just as the sun was beginning to set over the lake (photograph enclosed!).

As we had no servant with us – and therefore I had to cook – we decided to go out for dinner! The Derbyshire Yeomanry were nearby and we had a very good evening with them. They are such nice chaps.

The races the next day were really first class. The racecourse[68] is built in a bowl of the mountains – all covered with silver firs. And the turf is like an English lawn. All round the course the Regiments in the Division have their luncheon tents (and very good things inside too!). So the setting was good.

The racing was well up to standard. Really good horses – far better than those down here – and there were some very good races. We saw masses of friends – including John and Charles Ashton[69] which was great fun. Charles won a very good race on his horse – but now he has had to go back to England.

I cooked the dinner that evening! The two very nice Austrian couples who own the house joined us. They were extremely well mannered in their praise of English food but it really was amazing! Mostly out of tins anyway – but even so it all seemed to taste very odd. We came back slowly the next day after a late start.

As most of the Squadron are due to leave for England soon we decided to have a farewell party for them. This needed quite a lot of organisation – I produced a sort of record of the Squadron – comprising a short history of the Squadron during the War, names of those who had died, etc. It was well printed by the Italian printers in Trieste, complete with a regimental badge. It really was rather a success – and now the other Squadrons are following suit which is very satisfying.

The party (on the 7th) developed into a tremendous bun fight – but we all got rather drunk in the end which was duly regretted the next morning (particularly by John Joicey who was thrown complete into the swimming pool!). It was a very sad evening in a way. The Sergeant Major made a really moving speech, completely sincere – ending by proposing the toast "of the man who, when he was only a boy, took over the command of the Squadron in battle – and who has brought us from El Alamein to the River Po."[70]

The Scala Opera Company is now singing at Gradisca on the banks of the River Isonzo in an open air opera season. We went twice this week – once to *Cavaliera Rusticana* and last night to *Traviata*. Oh Darling, how you would love it – I long for you to be here to listen to them with me. I am beginning to know Italian opera pretty well now – and love it more and more.

The Colonel asked me whether I would like to go to General Harding as A.D.C. last week. I gave it a lot of thought and asked David and Derek their advice. In a month's time I shall have almost a new troop to train which will be a great experience. I know that I have made mistakes with my present troop – and I am longing to put them right. It will be an invaluable experience. The idea of leaving the Regiment horrifies me.

Therefore I decided to turn the offer down. John Joicey was then offered it – and he accepted. Today he arrived to say that he was flying to England tomorrow for a fortnight!! I'm livid – but still I think I did the right thing.

I had a letter from Judy today. Not much news in it. I wonder when Jack will get back on leave. He came into the mess this evening after riding. I think that he is pretty bored. The serious thing is that he quite obviously does not get on with Derek (who is now his second in command). They are both so different but it is a frightful pity.

Oh! Quite forgot to say that Kit is off to Australia for six months on a tank demonstration. The whole thing is almost too obvious! But I know that it's a good thing.

What a dull letter. I shall turn over a new leaf.

Take 4th Troop to Austria; Sgt Edmunds & Cpl Nicholls leave for England:
21st August 1945

I have been away from the Regiment since last Friday so I have had no letters from you or anyone else. Now I am up in Austria for a week with my troop. Oh Darling, I wish you knew this lovely country and then you would know how happy I am.

We live on the banks of a lake (the Ossiacher See) and after a fairly late breakfast spend the day reading and bathing and walking up in the mountains which surround the lake. It is a lovely existence.

The idea of coming up here was that we should all be together before so many left the troop – but yesterday a dispatch rider turned up to order all those due for England to report back immediately. So Sgt Edmunds, Cpl Nicholls, L/Cpls Jones and Roberts left after lunch yesterday. It was a terribly sad moment – you know what I think of them all. I only hope that I shall see them often in England when all is over and done with. So now we are a very reduced party – and most of them are new to the troop and very different. But at least I am getting to know them all well.

I came up to Austria with David on Friday to go to the 6th Armoured Division Races. We stayed at our usual little wooden schloss on the lake. It was as lovely as ever – and on Friday evening we walked right up in to the mountains to one of those little churches standing in a clearing in the fir trees. Whitewashed, it was, with a tall pinewood steeple. The view from it surely confirmed the church goers on entering the church. We looked down through the clearing in the trees to the green grass below and onto the lake. And coming back we collected mushrooms and talked of England. I was ordered to cook the dinner!

Most of it came from blessed tins – but the chef d'oeuvre, a mushroom omelette, had a misfortune! I put a little too much water with the eggs so that when the omelette was cooked, some water remained in the frying pan. I was slowly and carefully pouring it into the sink when, like a landslide, off slid the omelette! An unfortunate incident which has jeopardised, if not ruined, my cooking reputation!

The races the next day were as much fun as ever. The best thing was that Lavinia Holland-Hibbert was there. We had a tremendous gossip covering every subject (and person!).

We arrived down here late on Saturday evening and David went back on Sunday morning. I must admit that, though I think he is one of the best friends I shall ever have, it is a rest to be away from him.

I go back to the Regiment on Friday to ride in the races on Saturday. It will be the greatest fun – but I fear that I shall be just about last in my race as poor Quicksilver is anyway not up to it and now has to carry an extra stone, go a furlong further and gallop against superior quadrupeds!

After that we get ready for the tattoo. It is being held in Trieste on September 9th, 10th and 11th. The Regiment, under David, are performing in the 'steeplechase' act. This entails jumping four fences under searchlight. The 2nd Armoured Brigade are doing an act called 'The Subaltern's Dream', consisting of first a hunt (by the Bays) and then our do – and lastly a trick ride (by the 10th). It should be great fun. We have had one practice and the horses don't seem to mind jumping in the dark.

But hard work looms ahead. A very good thing really. It will take some getting used to again! Sept 1st seems to be the beginning of things – though David wrote to me saying that all Python[71] chaps will have gone by the 20th (that is 75% of the Squadron) and no reinforcements have arrived yet to take their place.

R.S.M. Hardwidge and Lancer with Tpr Gilmour

Trieste Tattoo:
11th September 1945

It is ages since I have written! There seems to have been such a lot to do in the last ten days that I have completely lost count of everything!

The main item has been the Tattoo. For the last ten nights and often in the afternoon, we have driven into Trieste to practice – and we started performing on the 9th. I really think that it has gone off very well – and so far there have been no blunders. Field Marshal Alex and Admiral Cunningham came the first night with the Corps Commander. What a great person he is.

John Joicey returned from England on the 8th. I went to see him that evening. Poor chap – he never has a moment to himself. And he is so bad at that sort of job. As far as I can see he is a sort of fag-cum-bottle-washer to Sir John Harding. Ghastly. I miss him so much in the Squadron.

But now the idea of driving into Trieste rather appals me – thank goodness this is the last night. We nearly had a crash last night when Desmond McInnes Skinner hit the last fence just in front of me and only just managed to keep going. I shouldn't much like falling off at night as the horses would never see you on the ground.

David Whately has left the Regiment temporarily – so I now have to look after education. As you can imagine, when all the old chaps who used to instruct have left us, the whole system has got to be reorganised and it is a very big job.

My new chaps in the troop are really quite good – better, anyway, than I expected. But I long for the old ones – I never had to bother about even wondering whether they would do as I ordered. I like them though – and training them up to a high standard is a great job.

Did I tell you that we are leaving this area in a week's time – and moving south, nearer to Venice? It's a fearful business moving – finding billets etc. But it will be for the best as this place would be quite unbearable in the winter time. I have been down once to settle up the billets etc – and I think that we shall be much better off there.

Two days ago the telephone rang and a girl's voice asked for me! It was Delia's. She appeared to be on leave and staying with General Harding at his headquarters. I went over to see her and found that she was in fact on leave with a chap called Bill Cunningham (11th Hussars).

I haven't yet sympathised with you about your complaint. It sounds most odd and unpleasant. I do hope it is getting better. Poor Darling. Still, it's giving you more leave which is something. I suppose that the work at Sig. Hill is beginning to be a bit pointless now, isn't it?

Bad about Angus'[72] views on Denis and Ann. Can't you get hold of Denis and find out what he really thinks?

Father wants me to go to General Paget as A.D.C. I don't want to. Partly, I admit, because I love being here – but equally important, because I have a great deal of work to do here which would pay a little of the debt that I owe the Regiment. And in doing that work (my troop, education and second in command to David) I don't consider that I am being in the least bit idle and I know that I will learn a great deal. One day I should like to do a job of that sort – but after only 18 months with the Regiment I don't think my time has quite come yet. Do you agree?

W.B.R.
on Quicksilver
1945

W.B.R. with
Jack Price
and Quicksilver

Pending posting to U.K:
4th November 1945

I'm coming home – any moment! You can expect to hear my voice and hundreds of telegrams any time after the 6th Nov! It's all too good to be true. I have been away in Vienna with Pat Dudding and David for the last five days – and was only told this on my return this evening.

I am going on a course at Old Sarum (Salisbury area) on the 11th for a fortnight and then have a month's leave. Just can't believe it!

A lovely letter from you was waiting for me when I got back (I can't even describe Vienna – it was so lovely – and will be able to tell you about it so soon). You are having fun Darling. I suppose I shall have to ring up all England before I find you. Look, ring up Mother and tell where you will be – that's best.

Do you know anyone who lives near Old Sarum? If so, you must stay there 11th – 23rd or anyway part of the time! It's miles from London.

Must get this letter off or you won't know I'm coming!

I arrived back in England on, I think, November 7th. There is no letter to Lorna for the next three weeks, presumably because I was seeing her regularly during that period. It is frustrating that there is no record of our feelings on my seeing her again after eighteen months of absence - and I can't remember!

At Adwell; hunting:
28th November 1945

We had rather a good party last night - Dick and Ruth Fanshawe, Delia and Rachel Brown and all of us (including Father who is miles better and was cheered up by Dick a great deal). It was such fun and we gossiped till midnight. We are very lucky to have such a good Master. It is almost definite now that he is giving up and that Alastair Miller[73] is taking over – it is very sad, but Alastair will be an Oxfordshire man which is a great thing, as all the farmers know and like him.

D. is in very good form – and I think will quite soon ask to break off her engagement with me. (We became betrothed at the Pony Club Christmas Party exactly 10 years ago.) She goes up to Scotland on Monday week to Bill Cunningham's home in Lanarkshire to try to decide. She's a bit worried I think – poor old thing.

Lavinia Lascelles is going to announce her engagement next week and is getting married in the middle of March.

Nothing from the Millbank Hospital[74] yet – I do hope that they let me know soon or I shall begin to get worried. David hasn't gone back to Italy yet – and now does not return till the 8th. I get letters from him every morning now – meant in all kindness – telling me how (a) to get into hospital, (b) how to get out, (c) who to be operated on by etc, etc – and I am now beginning to get a bit tired of it. Which is v. ungrateful of me.

I forget if I told you that Jean and Ronnie Wallace are at the moment living apart. I am so sad about this. They are both great friends of mine – though I knew that Jean was marrying a very selfish and difficult man. I hope to be able to go and see her as she lives in north Oxon now, near Woodleys.

We had quite a good day on Saturday from Delia's home – lots of nice people were out.

Later, much (!): Went and dined with the Glyns at Attington last night. A very good party – Dick and Ruth, Delia, John and Elizabeth Thompson[75], Johnnie Milne (who talked a lot about Doug), Judy Hutchinson, Pam Stubbs and Audrie and John Glyn. We are a happy county and hunting has done so much to keep us together.

From Millbank Hospital, pending operation:
27th December 1945:

I'm afraid that this won't be very legible – and the paper doesn't help! (It comes out of the little green book which at least gives an air of efficiency!) I miss you terribly although there has been a lot to do since you went.

We had the Estate Party on Christmas Eve – and Dick and I were both shooting at Scotsgrove all day which made things rather hurried for the party, but everything went off all right in the end – like most things! I made a very touching little speech as Father Christmas, and everyone felt very emotional which made them happy!

Christmas Day was great fun – and went very quickly, ending with a large dinner and Rachmaninoff (minus the first record) and hectic boot polishing and button cleaning for the Boxing Day meet at Thame. It really was great fun – and I should think that there were 300 people at the meet and 100 of them mounted – it just shows that foxhunting isn't quite as unpopular as people like to think.

Delia was out on her feet as her horse is lame – she seemed to be in very good form and is coming to dinner tonight with Dick and Ruth Fanshawe. We really had a very good day – hounds ran from Thame to Waterperry Wood (a five mile point) very fast over some fair country – but the wind is pretty ghastly, and sometimes I get a bit depressed. Both Charles Ashton and his wife fell off in the brook which added to the entertainment! It was such fun, so many of us being together.

Cynthia and Hum and I went down to Attington last night and had a drink with the Glyns and Pam Stubbs which was fun – which brings me up to the moment – sitting in Millbank Hospital waiting for an interview with the doctor. Mowlem wrote to me yesterday to say that he can't operate on me till later and that I must get a further extension of leave (which I intended to do anyway!) and this seems to be the place where one applies – but it's an awful bore having to come up to London.

Adwell. Just returned – with a category for a month. It is really rather 'tricky' – you know the type of person who comes back on leave and then never returns! Hope Jack won't think that I'm one of them.

I don't know the date of the operation yet but don't think it will be till after the 11th now – so shall I come up to Manderston if possible before the 11th – I forget when you are going back.

Mad letter from you too. So glad that you had a good journey – very vague, nearly catching the train to Wales! Give my love to Ann.

So, we have reached 1946 and the letters which follow describe the quite extraordinary life which I lived for the next eight months. Was it a reward for our efforts of the previous months of war? I suppose so. Anyway, we had a wonderful time – but it had to end. I went back to England at the end of August and returned to Oxford in October.

I can't resist quoting, though it is rather immodest of me, an extract from a letter which Delia Cunningham (Holland-Hibbert) wrote to me quite recently. 'I have been writing a record of my life for the children and grandchildren and so I am delving into any diaries I kept. Just found an entry for Jan. 3rd 1946 which was just after I got back from Italy. [It read] Bill B.R. came for p.m. and tea. He's a darling boy and I adore him. He will make a perfect husband for someone.'

Children at 141 Banbury Road:
2nd January 1946

So lovely hearing your voice on the telephone. It really is maddening not knowing anything definite and still worse that I might be able to come up. Oh! How I loathe the War Office – but I have been badgering them on the telephone and I hope that it will have some effect on them soon.

Jolly good of me to write so soon – such a strain! But your letter arrived today with those photographs. They are awfully good – but the Trio aren't flattering; Ann looks amazing, and we all look very debauched!

This frost is MADDENING – no hunting today of course, and obviously no lawn meet for you yesterday. But still, it's the first time we've been stopped which isn't bad.

I haven't been doing much the last two days – recovering from letting Jeannine[76] slip out of my hands like that. She didn't even come and have a fatherly talk with me, which I at least expected. But I am going to have one with D. tomorrow before she goes up to Scotland to stay with Bill Cunningham!

Father, Mother and I went over to Winchendon for tea yesterday with Evie Barnard. Such a lovely (I mean it!) house. But poor old Evie has got almost bedridden with rheumatics and can hardly get about now, having hunted three days a week before the War. Awful to see her like that. Needless to say, the car ran out of petrol half way there – and I had to run back to Scotsgrove in the ice cold to collect some! But all was well, and we were soon on our way again. The car is now in Oxford having an overhaul – to prepare for your next visit.

Mother was in Oxford almost all day today. I think that she spent most of the time with the children at 141[77]. Poor darling, she does miss them so much – they had almost become her own children. I wish, for their own sake, though, that they weren't so near in Oxford. They are treated rather like museum pieces by the many well-wishers in the precincts of Oxford, and it is so bad for them not fending for themselves – which, after all, they will have to in 6 years' time. They are asked to stay away by Lady Buxton, Mrs Abel-Smith and Rita Grafton, etc, etc, which is so bad for them. But Mother – who has no ideas of class distinctions (which will always remain, however odious they may be) cannot quite understand my point of view – and it rather upsets her.

I am hearing a lovely concert as I write – Mozart: *E Minor, A Minor* and *Schubert Trout Quintet* (the loveliest of them all).

I must remember to write to you for your birthday! Must stop – it's very late.

**Delia's uncertainty about Bill;
Lorna about to be 21:
6th January 1946**

Your letter arrived this morning. Poor old thing, the morale doesn't seem to be too high – mine's not either!

I'm nearly going mad waiting for this b. War Office to notify me. I could have come on Thursday – and I could be with you now. I have pulled every string through Father, Humphrey and Mowlem – but none of them seem to have any success. The only hope is that I might hear on Monday and I might be able to get up by the 9th. Of course I understand you getting a bit worried about the party. It is important to know exactly what you are going to say to them – and I suggest that you write out word for word exactly what you would like to say. You won't say it – but at least you won't get tongue-tied. (It's always worked very well with me – but the bore is that nobody can ever hear my words of wisdom!)

I can't quite understand about the letter – promise I sent it off before Jan 1st. But I was very good and wrote a note to you the day before yesterday.

I got a lovely book from David today called *Royal Newmarket* with pictures by Lionel Edwards – so perhaps he isn't so annoyed with me as I thought! He is a kind person – but sometimes so difficult! Sometimes I rather wish that I wasn't in his squadron – he is so 'possessive' and is almost hurt when I do something with anyone except him. He doesn't really get on very well with people - he is so stupid.

I expect that it was a most lovely dance – did you find a man? I thought of you last night, and wondered so much how were enjoying yourself. I tried to ring you up this evening – but there was an hour's delay, and it would have made it too late for you. But I will get through tomorrow instead.[78]

I went over to Delia's home yesterday and had a lovely long gossip to her. She simply can't make up her mind about Bill Cunningham. She seems to be quite certain that she loves him enough – but she is frightened by the thought that she would have to live a different sort of life when she is married as he doesn't cope much with horses, etc. It was difficult for me to advise her much – but I told her that if she felt absolutely certain about her love for him and his for her, the differences in living would sort themselves out very quickly. I don't think that marriage is ever a particularly easy undertaking and always needs a lot of fighting for. She is now on her way up to Scotland to stay at his home, which is a good thing.

It is thawing hard now – but not quite hard enough for us to hunt today. So I went over to Chipping Norton with Father (who had some business there) and lunched with Jean Wallace and Peggy Stuart and their father[79] who lives at Addlestrop. I think I told you that Jean was living away from Ronnie. They are both such friends of mine – and it was awful seeing her today, and in such distress. He is now down in Shropshire hunting his hounds four days a week – and not caring a bit. I knew he was selfish – but I never thought that he could go quite mad in this way. She has a sweet little son (exactly like him) whom he has hardly set eyes on. It is all very sad. I think that I can help by praying for them both. But, oh dear, it is so difficult.

I don't think that I shall catch your birthday if I write tomorrow – Scotland seems very behind-hand in the Post Office organisation. Bless you my Darling – I hope that I haven't been too bad an influence during the three years leading up to your coming of age. Will you please tell me what you would like me to give you for your birthday. Would you like any records? – I don't know what you have got. Please tell me.

It's getting very late and I must stop.

Waiting for operation

Hill End Hospital[80], *St Albans:*
17th January 1946

Bless you for ringing up – it has made such a difference. When I heard that someone had rung up I thought that it must be Mother, but I forgot that there is now someone who cares for me like her.

I got so bored this morning that I went into St Albans for no particular reason. It was bitterly cold – but a lovely morning. I wandered very aimlessly round the shops buying Brasso, boot polish and Thawpit. It was too cold to look at the Abbey – so I went into the local café and had a filthy lunch, served by a girl who I was interested to see made no habit of removing her lipstick at night and therefore had an ever thickening layer covering her increasingly ugly lips.

I arrived back here in a bad way! This hospital somehow seems to retain some of the depression of its pre-war use as a lunatic asylum – though the nurses seem to be very nice and try to be helpful. But why is one awakened at six o'clock? I wasn't! The night nurse gave up the struggle of waking me and left it to the day nurse who came on at 7.45!

If you keep what you write strictly true and fair, I should send a letter to Ann pointing out that she is making a prize fool of herself. I really think that it is your duty to do so. You were a great friend of hers – it is never right to stop being friends without trying to give a helping hand. And I'm sure that you could – though it may seem difficult. Don't forget that she is living in very difficult circumstances. Her friends are giving her up – and life begins to become pretty intolerable then.

Ribton[81] had heard nothing about Jack and Judy – and is most intrigued, to the extent that he demanded her address from me and is going to visit her!

Rather a nice picture of Delia and David Fanshawe in *The Tatler* this week, but rather blurred as it was taken by the cameraman from the Oxford Times! I wonder whether you have seen it.

I hope that you realise that this is the second letter I have written today; it puts up my average considerably! Oh Darling, I wish you were here – or rather that I was there.

MANDERSTON

DUNS

BERWICKSHIRE

DUNS 38

Going south in night sleeper after two days at Manderston: 29 January 1946

The train is late – so I'm writing to you from the waiting room in Berwick. A very nice policeman helped me with my luggage. He talked incessantly, but I could understand practically nothing that he said!

It was such a simply lovely 2 days – really perfect. Thank you Darling so much. I do feel so utterly happy (though this waiting room does seem to lower my morale a bit – I wish you were here). I've got a 3rd sleeper – which is a pity, but marvellous of your father to get one at all. However it now doesn't matter where my pyjamas are in my case! I think I shall go and have a bath with Cynthia and then go down to St Albans after breakfast. I wonder whether I should take my trousers off in the sleeper – and my tunic. I obviously will have to make a big decision.

Rather efficient of me to remember this paper don't you think? I shall post it in London first thing in the morning.

Your Grandfather must be absolutely mystified by the proceedings of the last two days – I wonder what he thought we were doing in his sitting room! Your mother is quite remarkable for her capability to be understanding. She was so frightfully kind throughout the pow-wow[82] and afterwards.

Later: Just going into the sleeper. Time 11.50. Obviously something wrong with the engine. I am very comfortably ensconced in the bottom right hand bunk (is there any advantage). Very stuffy smell on entering – but now have got quite used to it and am now rather soothed by the fug! No drugs will be needed tonight.

I have made a lightening decision and have taken off my tunic but not my trousers as I think my knees will get cold (pants rather on the short side).

Later, 6.30 am: Frightfully good night. Never woke up till the tea was brought in five minutes ago. The train is over an hour late which is rather a bore but it doesn't really matter (what does?). I have just noticed that my sleeping partner opposite has taken off his trousers – and now feel that perhaps I was wrong after all! He is a sailor lance corporal (I forget what they call themselves) but I haven't yet discussed his political views. Great excitement, now passed. He has just heaved his case onto his bunk and I saw Gillingham on the label – but it's the Kent one so Di wouldn't know him after all!

I wonder what you will do today – and what the dance will be like this evening.

Later, 8.30: Train very late – so went to sleep again. I am now in the taxi going to Cynthia. I hope that there is a train down to St Albans, otherwise I shall have to go by that very complicated way – by tube to Barnet and bus from there to St Albans.

My trousers now look exactly like your red dress.

I must stop now as we're getting near.

***Back with Regiment;
talked to David L till 3 am;
rode my horse, Titus:
19th February 1946***

The first day back at the Regiment – and a letter from you. Oh Darling, I can't tell you how I loved seeing my Troop again, and David and John and everyone – and the horses.

The day has gone so quickly and now it's past twelve and I've only just got into bed as Tom Toller and Tommy St Aubyn have both been to dinner.

I arrived here last night for dinner – David having sent a jeep into Milan for me. I then spoke to him till 3 am about everything, including my job in The Sudan[83]. It doesn't look as if I'm going to be able to go – or anyway not at the moment – as so many officers have been forced away from the regiments on other jobs. David, as I said he would be, is dead against the whole thing! But I haven't been able to talk to Jack about it as he is away in Trieste till Monday or Tuesday. So I won't know anything till then.

I went for a lovely ride this afternoon on Titus – the new horse David got for me. Of course he is absolutely first class – even though I could only ride with one hand. And the country is looking quite lovely – blue sky and snowy mountains catching the sun.

Yours was such a lovely letter – and you seem to be happy. Don't pay a bit of attention to what your father says about you being badly dressed. You know what I think about your dressing, Darling.

***Skiing with the Regiment;
my future in The Sudan:
21st February 1946***

I haven't written to you properly since I got back here – I seem to have been most frightfully occupied with getting 'settled in'. It is a good thing though, or I would have been depressed.

I shall start at the beginning as my last letter was only a note. David's driver met me at half past three in Milan and we drove back, arriving just in time for dinner. It seemed such ages since I had been with the Regiment – and driving back I really wondered what it was going to be like, and I arrived with very mixed feelings. But after I had been in the mess 10 minutes I began to feel very happy. Comradeship within a regiment really is the most extraordinary thing – and I don't think that one realises it until one goes away.

I talked to David till 3 o'clock in the morning, and told him about my idea of going to The Sudan. He took the whole thing comparatively coolly, though he thinks that it is a very bad plan. But since then I have talked to Derek (in the absence of the Colonel). He doesn't think that I can go as there are simply no officers here now – and he was nice enough to say that he thought that I was valuable in the Regiment. However nothing can definitely be decided until Tuesday when the Colonel gets back.

But if I do stay there certainly will be no spare time. Troop training is beginning seriously again next month – and I have a brand new Troop to train, and once more Derek has made me Educational Officer.

It was so wonderful seeing the Troop again – particularly Cpl (now Sgt) Grogan[84] whom I had not seen for six months. He is the only remaining member of my original tank crew – and is now my Second Troop Sergeant. He is in terrific form – they are all very well, but a bit bored just at the moment. It is such fun getting the Troop reorganised again – and seeing all the new people who are raw recruits.

I went up to Asignano in the mountains with David on Wednesday afternoon to be introduced to skiing. I can't describe the sheer loveliness of the mountains against the deep blue sky. Of course I spent most of the afternoon on my bottom, but it was the greatest fun. It is incredible after leaving England so short a time to be skiing with only a thin shirt on in the blazing sun.

All the few remaining officers disappear from the Regiment at the weekends and go skiing at Cortina (about four hours from here) which sounds the most perfect place in the Dolomites. I don't feel that I can quite go this weekend, having just arrived back - so I am driving up to Asignano again on Saturday afternoon with Pat Dudding (who dined here on Wednesday) and will stay there the night.

I rode again this afternoon with David and Peter Thompson-Glover[85] (who is now Second-in-Command of his Squadron, thank goodness). The most lovely sunny afternoon. There are some very good rides around here into the mountains, and lots of little fences and ditches to jump. I turned a complete somersault over one of them, and now have both thumbs sprained (having fallen on one skiing) but am not really too bad; and my fingers are 100%.

What a nice chap Chris Diggle is – though he doesn't talk yet very much in the mess, as he is still a bit frightened! And can't get over the way we all behave!

I quite forgot to say how very concerned David has been over the Valentine card – but he now thinks that it is from you – as you gave yourself away by not printing everything. I was very hurt not to get one too. Quite obviously you don't love me at all. Hypocrite.

You will be amused to hear that there has been a terrific fire in A Sqn. And one whole house (which contained the squadron office and stores) was demolished. Bill Peek is in the most tremendous fuss, needless to say. Nobody knows quite how the fire started but one theory is that it was caused by the tremendous heat given off from his now scarlet face. He is the colour of an over-ripe orange. His mother wrote to him every time she saw us together – and Bill passed it on throughout the Regiment which is slightly annoying!

I am wearing your girth now – I usually do. Every time I breathe it squeaks – and David complains of my corsets!

In hospital with pneumonia:
6th March 1946

Still no letter from you. I am beginning to wonder whether you are all right – but I think that it must be the post which is quite awful, and letters are now taking ten days to get here. I so wonder whether mine are getting to you.

The most extraordinary thing has occurred. I went up to a place called Madonna di Campiglio with Derek and David last Friday feeling absolutely well really, though still a bit heady after the 'flu. Anyway we had the most lovely day skiing on Saturday and got back to the very luxurious hotel for tea. By dinner time I knew that something was wrong with me and went to bed quite early with a pain in my chest. I couldn't get to sleep and the pain got pretty awful so that when David came up to bed I had to get him to find a doctor.

I was in a bad way and never enjoyed the scene of David going into the ballroom in search of the doctor in his red and silver dressing gown and pink pyjamas. There was a dance in progress!

Anyway the doctor said I had pleurisy[86] and David took me down to Verona the next day (a ghastly drive through snow and then wind and rain) and by the time I got there I had pneumonia. I was moved to this hospital just out of Venice on Monday but haven't felt like doing much till today.

David has been here the whole afternoon bringing with him a sort of Christmas stocking full of every kind of comfort. He seems to think of everything. He was full of the dinner party which he had given on Monday night before Colonel Jack went on Tuesday. He is very pleased with himself and says that everything was just right. I wish I had been there to see his 'attention to detail'.

I wonder what the Drax's dance was like? Oh I do hope your letter comes tomorrow. David promised to send in a dispatch driver if there is any mail for me – it's so hard writing to you when I haven't heard from you for such ages. And it is so awfully boring here that there doesn't seem to be anything to tell you.

The other officers in the ward are quite ghastly! One poor Pole without a leg who covers himself in cheap scent, one R.A.F. type suffering from piles, and another chap who is still pretty ill with pneumonia and not able to talk yet!

One big event is that Toscanini is coming out here in April to open the Scala in Milan. I have asked David to book tickets now or we'll never get in. Won't it be a wonderful thing to see? Am looking forward to it already. I never realised that he was 79.

Still in hospital; a visit to the Doge's Palace, Venice:
13th March 1946

I must have a biography of Mozart! Have you got one? He

must have been a supremely happy man, or how could he have written such music that radiates such happiness and sends one away almost crying with joy! I am at the moment listening to the *Haffner* in the hospital electro-therapy department. The odd electrical constructions all over the room have a most aesthetic influence. A funny super-intellectual little private solder is holding a gramophone recital – and he has chosen a very good programme: *Lohengrin*, the *Haffner*, some Sibelius thing (simply can't deal) and the glorious Brahms *No 4* to finish off with.

I went in to Venice this morning to have lunch with Peter Thompson-Glover who is on a course there. It was a filthy rainy day – but I simply couldn't face yet another day of such unqualified boredom!

In the afternoon he had to go back to work, so I went over the Doge's Palace which has long been on my conscience as I have never somehow been there. It really is a remarkable and most beautiful place. The centre of the ancient Venetian Republic, it was almost entirely burnt down in the middle of the sixteenth century. However it was rebuilt on an even more magnificent scale under the guidance of the great Palladio. Most of the enormous rooms are filled with the most beautiful pictures by the great Renaissance artists such as Tintoretto, Titian, Bassano and Paul Veronese. But, like so many places that should be seen in Italy, there is too much to see – and I nearly died of exhaustion!

(Interlude for the beginning of the Brahms – I can't write just for a moment!)

Darling do you want a sponge! – or really anything? The shops seem to be pretty full. Do please write and tell me what you are short of.

I am going out of hospital on Monday morning – and hope to stay at Villa Roi (the Italian family I've told you about) for a few days and play music and read and be pretty idle and then go to Cortina and get into the sun.

Troop training begins on April 1st – and I think that we shall all be very busy then. Needless to say, Sgt Grogan has been sent on a course and I therefore have no Troop Sergeant which makes things rather difficult.

I may still go to the Sudan anyway, as General Paget – according to Father – is pretty annoyed now and says that it is necessary for me to go. But the whole thing has, thank goodness, been taken out of my hands and so I shall just await developments. But things have got to a pretty high level as this Brigadier has written to say that he can't spare me. Obviously the running of the whole Brigade depends on me! (Oh, you're so conceited.)

Has your wedding (!) sorry, dress got lost yet? I wonder whether your Mother's book has arrived at Manderston yet. I sent off a rather cross letter to Ros about it as she has obviously been vague about it.

Jack and Judy married: 1st April 1946

The blue socks and the Mozart biography arrived this evening. Thank you Darling so much. I haven't had time to look at the book yet – but the socks are perfect, and would even be passed by David!

I am not taking it as a hint – but here are the coupons. Why didn't you ask for them? I completely forgot about them, and only by a hectic search managed to find them.

Your last letter was written going south – I wonder what sort of a wedding it was – and where they are now. Of course it's not selfish to hate the idea of Judy not being 'there' any longer. Selfishness is obviously only bad when it affects others – and I know so exactly how you feel, as I did when Ros (particularly) was married. I sometimes get a bit worried though when I think of Judy as Colonel Jack's wife. It will mean such a change for her in every way – and I shan't be able to see her as I should like to, because she is the Colonel's wife. What a maddening and unreasonable institution the Army is!

Was mightily relieved about the book as you might well imagine. Ros's excuse was Christopher being ill. She apologised in a letter which I got yesterday – Christopher has recovered from his original malady but since then found a large bottle of aspirins in his nursery which he proceeded to demolish! The climax was reached when the doctor arrived with an enormous stomach pump (or stirrup pump as Mama would call it in the fire fighting days at Adwell!) and made him swallow yards of rubber tubing. Bill Parker (who is now trying hard to persuade Ros to marry him) was on the scene and apparently did heroic work forcing the tube down!

As to my own health (so important): (a) Fingers - quite recovered; Mowlem's a genius. (b) Pneumonia, consumption etc - 100%. (c) Leg (internal collateral ligament of the left knee) - causing great inconvenience. I can hardly contain myself with fury as Titus won the race. Do so wish I had been riding.

David and John Goldsmid went up to Madonna this weekend to ski – but it was quite pointless me going so I stayed here with Christopher Diggle. We went sightseeing in Vicenza with Mina Roi as conductor. It really was great fun and very interesting. We went to see the Teatro Olympico and the Rotunda, the two best known building of Palladio's. They really are very beautiful; the Rotunda particularly, which is built on a hill from which you can see the land all the way to Venice. I explained quickly the history of the house to my driver who continued to look fantastically bored and replied by saying "Yes – it's not a bad house – but a bit old for me, Sir". It seems such a pity that so many beautiful things pass unnoticed to soldiers – I wonder why.

We went back to tea at Villa Roi. It's well worth it – I knew – and we ate enormous quantities of creamy cakes and chocolates! Tea is a tremendous social 'do' in Italy and takes place at six – after which the girls disappear to rest and dress for dinner at 8.30! However last night we were honoured and resting was put off while we walked all round the garden. The blossom is out here now, and I can't tell you how beautiful it looks and smells. Acres of orchards are in blossom, casting pink and white veils over the fields.

Tomorrow David and I are going down to the scene of the last battle with Derek and the Brigadier to 'draw conclusions' for future training. It will be most interesting and it will bring back some very exciting memories. I happened to tell Cpl Gatiens (who was in my Troop during the battle) that I was driving down. He asked if he could come with me. He said that he wanted to be reminded of those days too. There were good and bad moments, he said, but the good outweighed the bad because one knew that one was doing one's duty well. How I wish that my Troop now had those feelings which all showed in my last Troop.

I meant to write to you last night – but I got talking to Christopher Diggle. What a charming chap he is. And intelligent too. We didn't get to bed till after 12!

Return to Argenta to explain battle:
2nd April 1946

Lorna's social column just isn't in it. Why don't you sign on with *The Tatler*? Whole job question settled – and I could be your social adviser! Darling, thank you so much for the vivid description of the wedding. What a 'do'. I'm so glad you didn't cry during the proceedings – that would have been a 'bit tricky'. How do you find time to write to me on your social visits to the metropolis? Honestly, I still have to have a clear hour before I can sit down to write – however hard I try to be 'spon'. What are we going to do about my letter writing? They're so undemonstrative - but I dare say you're used to them now!

You were obviously a most excellent b'maid (bridesmaid as opposed to barmaid.) On the back of your last but one letter to me was written 'Ring Sue and John – Collect Ju's coat from Huntsman – Responses'. I hope it didn't put you out having posted these notes – and that Ju did have a coat to wear.

I have been jolly busy during the last two days. Yesterday David and I drove down to Argenta (with Cpl Gatiens who was delighted) and there met all the big wigs to explain just how clever we were during the last battle! It was extraordinary seeing the ground again. I discovered that all sense of time and space must have escaped one – as distances were so much shorter than they seemed. An open field during the battle with no cover from view from the enemy seemed a terribly long way to advance over!

It was a fearfully tiring day though as it took a very long time to explain to some of the old boys there exactly what one did do. They wanted to see a particular tank that I knocked out so we all trooped along, W.B.R. leading, to show the way. Of course I took ages to find it – all the ground seemed so different. And then I had to explain what happened. It was frightfully difficult. The situation then was so impossible to reproduce. One's mind was completely cut off from any outside influence – and one only thought of the job in hand. We both arrived back here very late and very tired – and cross!

And today I have been using my brain very hard trying to discover who in the Squadron has stolen some petrol. We have interviewed thousands of soldiers and discovered absolutely nothing. It does seem such a waste of a day, particularly as my Troop does need so much training.

My leg isn't right yet – so David is insisting that I go into Venice tomorrow to have a specialist to look at it. Complete fuss, needless to say – but I shall go to a concert in the evening which will just make it worthwhile.

I am still so cross about Titus – but I put some money on him and won £5 or so which is lucky as I'm broke!

I received a very odd letter from Adrian Head today, asking me some very deep questions on world problems. I hope he isn't getting too intense!

You might tell your Aunt Joan that Bill is at the moment away skiing! I admit he does work hard (almost to boiling point) but nobody knows quite what the old boy achieves.

My bath is ready – Trooper Bayes has just come in and told me so. He is an amazing chap – never says a word – and looks like a naughty spaniel.

Concert in Vicenza with the Rois; very concerned about communist/socialist government: 11th April 1946

Your correspondence is fantastic! But Darling you can't expect me to keep up with it – two letters a week is my limit, unless I'm desperately ill!

I think I last wrote to you on Sunday morning – before I went off to the concert in Vicenza. It really was awfully good – a trio of harp, viola and flute. All of them played beautifully. The music was all 16th century or before – in fact Bach sounded very modern and dashing, and I hardly knew any of it – but I enjoyed it very much. It was held in the perfectly beautiful Palladian theatre there which added considerably to the general effect.

Mina Roi had collected a large gathering of Wops to come with her – and after it we all drove on up to one of their villas where we had dinner and hopped around a bit to some weird Wop tunes after it.

They really are the most extraordinary nation. They are absolutely petrified for their own skins now as the communists and socialists (which combined to form a bloc) have won the elections practically all over Italy and they feel that their future is very uncertain. I should not be at all happy if I was one of them. Having lived in complete luxury throughout the war – not doing a hand's turn to help their country - the working class people are really after their blood and I don't blame them. But the socialists carry it a bit far when they murder whole families and burn down their houses. The Rois don't dare go down to Bologna to visit an estate of theirs nearby.

At the same time they are all wondering what is going to happen to Trieste. Of course it is of tremendous economic value to them – as well as an almost vital port for them to have for importing food etc. There is no large port along the Adriatic coast – and if the Jugoslavs did get hold of Trieste they would make it very unpleasant for the Italians. However I don't think that there is any fear of that – though very likely Tito will try and bluff his way into it. We are all at the moment preparing to move nearer the scene of activity, and on May 2nd there is going to be a Victory Parade in Trieste in which the Regiment is taking part.

Of course the object is really to have an excuse of getting armour into Trieste and showing Tito that we still have some tanks ready to fight him if he tries any of his tricks. But it's pretty annoying as I loathe moving once I've got 'settled in'! But perhaps it won't be for long. The one thing that the Italians want us to do is to remain in

Italy – because they know that as soon as we leave trouble will begin in no uncertain terms for them.

Darling, I was sorry to hear about the Downham job. But your next letter says that you might be going to help old Mother S with her letters (you'll be 100% effic. at that) which sounds a very interesting job. I do hope you get it so much. It sounds perfect.

Oh I wish I was at Adwell – I long to see you, and you just don't know how much. And Adwell in spring is so wonderful and seems to breathe out happiness. Father obviously has a dash of it in him if he walks round the shrubberies with you arm in arm! Most amazing! And then shows you all my letters. (How furious David would be!) I hope you are having a lovely time there – and that the races were fun. I can't ride at Treviso this w/e which is nearly driving me crazy – though my leg is quite well enough to hack about on. Still I suppose that I must be patient.

I shall anyway go to the races and bet with a vengeance! David and I are then staying at Maser[87] on Saturday night. Do you remember me telling you about it? The most perfect Palladian villa quite near Treviso, full of Paul Veronese paintings. I have only just rushed around looking at them – but now I really shall be able to poke my nose into it, which will be lovely.

There really hasn't been much going on this week except a lot of hard work! My Troop, I discover, is pretty badly in need of more training – and this Tito do makes it essential for me to get them up to standard. Therefore I have been with them all the mornings and afternoons and quite often in the evenings. And I try and ride every day and get some form of exercise – so the days go by very quickly and interestingly (to a point!)

The recital was put off till this evening. It really went quite well and I think that everyone enjoyed it – though only about 25 chaps turned up. But I intend to have it every Thursday evening, and perhaps the attendance will increase.

John Goldsmid has been promoted to Captain – and has left the Squadron to go as second-in-command to Tony Cooke in C Squadron. It's very sad – I shall miss him so much. We had a party for him last night – and after dinner went round to the Sergeant's

Mess for him to say goodbye.

I'm afraid that I'm awfully bad at these sorts of parties – but they are fearfully boring! At about midnight the Sergeants are all pretty merry and the singing begins, and continues for hours. And the songs aren't frightfully funny and are judged for their merit on their comparative filth. The old soldiers' repertoire is inexhaustible – I can never understand how their brains can store them when otherwise they are empty!

We got back at 2.30 – feeling rather sick and very tired. I really consider these 'dos' complete duties – and get no pleasure out of them at all. This particular party had unfortunate repercussions as when I arrived at the Squadron this morning I found that Sgt Teale[88] was not on parade. The inevitable had occurred – and he had got so drunk that he had not got up for parade. So he had to be marched up in front of David. As the Sergeants' Mess had entertained us it was all very awkward – particularly as he didn't take D's rocket very well, and things are now a bit strained between us both!

What good news about Eleanor. Craston married, I think, Nancy Cropper[89] about a year and half ago – or is this his father? If so he taught Father to play the piano at Eton when he was there as music master.

Staying at Maser with Volpes; preparing for Victory Parade in Trieste: 14th April 1946

Two letters waiting for me when I got back last night from a really lovely weekend away. Darling, thank you so much for them – you were in such good form when you wrote them, and they made me so happy, and rounded off the weekend so perfectly.

I took the Rois to the races at Treviso on Saturday. Things didn't go too well – just at the beginning I was very late starting off as quite suddenly, just when I was all ready to go, some work cropped up which simply had to be done. So I arrived in Vicenza (where I had said that I would meet them) pretty late. And then the car broke down. It was all very embarrassing, having said that I would take them – but in the end we went in their car which was much smarter and more comfortable! But of course we arrived very late at the races and Valentine won and I had meant to back him with a vengeance. It really was maddening!

It was a very good meeting – but rather a bore having to look after the Rois the whole time, and not look at the horses enough. There seemed to be a good many people around that I knew – and afterwards we all went to a very good cocktail party given by the H.A.C. next door to the race course which was great fun. It is extraordinary the number of wives around now – particularly at this party, and everything seemed much more civilized instead of a lot of dusky Wops!

David and I then motored on to Maser. The house is built at the foot of the Alps not far from Treviso. Here Palladio and Paul Veronese came to live in their summer holidays – and slowly the great house was built and frescoed in a spirit of great happiness by these two men, resulting in I think the most beautiful house I have ever seen. We arrived in the evening. The sun was just going down behind the purpling mountains – and the white house caught the colours of the setting sun. The dark cypress trees behind it stopped swaying in the breeze for a moment to look down in wonder at such beauty.

After dinner we went out in to the garden to look again at the house. By this time the moon had risen above the trees, and the house shone out of the darkness. Down in the plains stretching towards Venice and the sea the crickets had begun to sing. But we were all very quiet. We went back and played Beethoven's *Sixth Symphony* – it was about the only thing we could have done.

And then we went to bed. I slept till nearly ten – I don't seem to have got to sleep till awfully late this week. I was woken up by a very smart footman carrying breakfast into my room.

I spent the whole morning looking at the frescoes. I probably told you about them – and anyway it would be quite impossible to describe them. They are perfectly lovely - but the really perfect thing about them is that the co-operation between Palladio and Veronese shows them in the right light in the most beautiful rooms.

The Volpes have been brilliantly clever in making the house so very liveable. It might be so terribly like a museum. I bought a lovely book in Venice with masses of prints of the frescoes at Maser in it – and now I shall be able to remember them always.

I played some more music in the afternoon and read in the sun, and after tea we started back. Such a beautiful drive all along the foot of the Alps and then out into the plains. The snow is still on the mountains – but the grass has now grown green in the sun, and all the trees are hazy in blossom, and most of the little whitewashed farmhouses are sprawled over with wisteria.

So glad that you had fun at Adwell – Father writes long letters all about you! You've obviously created an amazingly good impression! How do you do it?

I can't quite make out the Bill Parker situation. I am sorry that you don't like him all that much – as Ros is anyway fond of him if nothing else. Bill anyway wants to marry her – but I believe Kit is returning to England very soon – so the whole situation is a bit complex! You must see him this time. I wonder whether he has changed much. I suppose he must have.

David was horrified at your last envelope. He wrote on it CAFONISSIMO which is about the only Italian he knows and means 'Oh, but how common, my dear'. (Translation not literal, but accurate!) He is now P.M.C. and therefore he's to order the meals in the Mess. Every morning the waiter appears and David proceeds to explain what he wants to eat. This takes about ½ hour. People come over from the other sqns to hear it going on. As you can imagine it's quite funny. It always ends by him getting livid with the man who grins rather sheepishly and shuffles out of the room before anything is thrown at him.

We had dinner with the Allhusens last night. Very good and they were both so charming, though Claudia is very domineering and Derek treats her as a complete equal. She often is present at military conferences and is made to take notes for him – and today she has gone on the battlefield tour of San Savino with him dressed in battledress trousers!

Bill Peek lunched at the Squadron today. He has just come back from 10 days leave in Malta where he has been staying with his uncle.

Who is that? Seemed to enjoy himself no end anyway and is most enthusiastic about it all (as usual!).

Easter; skiing at Madonna di Campiglio;
conference in Bologna:
25th April 1946

    Bless you for your last two letters – they arrived before Easter, and I haven't had a moment to answer them since they arrived. The maddening thing is that whenever I have something really to write about I have always been away, and you'll think that I never do any work – but I do, really!

    The whole Regiment packed up on the Thursday before Easter and we all drove up to Madonna di Campiglio (where I caught pneumonia). The sun had thawed most of the snow away and already the spring flowers were coming into bloom and the grass was getting bright green again. Oh it is a glorious place, and such a perfect place to spend Easter. The land looked so happy as if it was giving thanks for the glorious time in the Christian year.

    All the wives turned up with their husbands – Derek and Claudia, Rex and Joyce, George and Ann Meyrick, Charles and Laura Parnell and about ten 'single' officers. We drove Laura up in our car – she really is a nice girl, though so difficult her being an Italian. Everyone forgets – and talks about the bloody Wops, etc, and it's all rather embarrassing for both sides.

    But the thing that really amazed me was Derek's treatment of Claudia. He really bullies her. She was made to ski down places that were too hard for her, made to climb up mountains, etc, etc, and Derek was really rather unpleasant to her and she became almost tearful. I really can't get over it. Of course Derek has got a tremendously strong character – and he tries to make Claudia like himself. She is made to take a real interest in the Regiment, etc, and goes down with Derek to tour the battlefields which can't interest her overmuch. And she, on her side, is pretty domineering – so you can imagine that the combination is difficult to manage!

    I had a letter from Judy yesterday. Wasn't it sweet of her to write? I so often wonder how she will get on with them all – and I hope you are right. She will have to be tactful, to the extreme.

But to go back to Madonna: We did more or less the same thing each day – and they were perfect days. We had breakfast at about nine and then started off on foot with skis on our backs and walked flat out up into the mountains for an hour to the top of the ski run. As we walked up the south face the sun had melted all the snow – and it was too beautiful walking up through the pine trees into the open heathey mountain and looking down into the valleys far below us.

Tony Cooke set the pace. He is very fit and we really did have to walk hard to keep up with him. In the end the climbing always developed into an undeclared race – and we all arrived dead beat at the top, and quite incapable of skiing down for at least an hour! However there is a little mountain hut there with various liquid refreshments which slowly brought us round again.

So at about 11 o'clock we began our journey downwards. I do love skiing – and have improved a bit. But it is fantastic how often and how hard I fell! The exciting thing about it is that you alone are responsible for the success of the trip downwards, and one gets a tremendous feeling of speed – and achievement on reaching the bottom whole!

It takes about twenty minutes to get down (varying on the number of falls) and then after queuing for a short time one is dragged up the mountain again by a ski lift. This is a complicated movement! A revolving cable runs from the top of the ski run to the bottom of the mountain. About twenty 'hooks' are attached to this cable – from which hang 20 foot lengths of wire. An unshaven Wop binds a belt around your middle – and at the correct moment the wire is secured to your belt, and off you go with a ghastly jerk up the practically vertical mountain. Usually one falls on one's behind extremely hard and the whole movement has to be repeated much to the annoyance of the rest of the queue!

Then, having completed a second run, we drove back to the most scrumptious lunch at the hotel. Never have I eaten such food for such a period! As you can imagine, by dinner time we were all very tired.

I couldn't go to church on Easter Day as there wasn't one for 50 miles – so I read the lessons and thought of you all – and I was very happy. What a glorious message of hope Easter brings.

We came down on Monday evening – and drove all along Lake Garda as the sun was setting. I wish I could describe the beauty of the still lake to you. But we'll come and see it together perhaps one day.

That brings me to Tuesday. I was pretty busy here all day with my Troop getting ready for this Parade – and in the evening I drove out to the gallops and rode Titus who went very well. Unfortunately he is out of his class on Saturday at Aiello as there are at least five horses that are very much better than him, but it will be fun having a ride again after so long.

Yesterday Derek, David, George Meyrick, Michael Moule and I drove down to Ferrara for a final reconnaissance of the battlefield and we decided exactly what we were going to say on the exercise – and we then went on to Bologna where we stayed the night and dined altogether at the famous restaurant there (called the Popagallo, which means parrot). Bologna is famous for its food – and it most certainly lived up to its name by last night's performance. Frightfully good – and equally expensive. Rather a waste of money I suppose really – but so good while it lasted!

All today we have been telling about fifty rather bored officers how 'B' Squadron broke the Argenta Gap. But it went off rather better than we thought it would – and we got back here in time for 'drinks' at six with Derek and Claudia.

David Wentworth Stanley is due to get back from Greece tonight, but as it's nearly 12 now I shouldn't think he'll turn up.

I shall be jolly busy after Saturday with this Parade. It should be rather interesting, but we don't as yet know when we are returning. David's main worry at the moment is that he can see no way out of sleeping in his tent on the parade ground in Trieste – and it doesn't suit him a bit! I think we've all become a bit sissy since the end of the War – and it will do us a lot of good.

I had a letter from Cynthia this evening complaining bitterly that she has had another son! He arrived 10 days early and weighed 5 lbs - very true to form. But, of course, they're both very pleased and excited.

I have been thinking so much about my future lately. I have got to make a decision about Oxford pretty soon. I can go up in October and read for any degree. Alternatively I can remain with the Regiment until I am demobilised which will be about 18 months. As I am not going to be a Regular Officer, I feel that really this would be a waste of time (though very much the easiest and most pleasant way out.) But it seems pretty pointless reading for a degree when I don't know what I am going to do. Of course I was incredibly stupid not to do more about it when I was in England. I simply can't get over it.

But Darling, don't be afraid to make suggestions. I quite understand your point of view, but you do know me better than probably anyone else and what you say or suggest would very likely help. (And I need it!!)

Victory Parade in Trieste;
John Joicey & Mina Roi:
3rd May 1946

I'm writing to you from the Squadron office. It's rather like the days when you used to write to me in 'duty hours' from Poundon! But being a busy officer I usually never have time.

I know that I haven't written to you since last Friday – and oh! – today is Friday. This week seems to have galloped past. You are so wonderful about writing – and I am so awful, and seem to be almost getting back into my old ways again! But that spare hour which, as you say, is so essential to any man before he even attempts to put pen to paper is very scarce these days!

We arrived back from Trieste last night after the Victory Parade, having left the Squadron early on Tuesday morning. It really was rather fun and interesting. Trieste is divided into two parties, the Italians and the Jugoslavs. For the last months, the Jugs have been infiltrating over the Morgan Line[90] into Trieste – and during the last few days they have spent all their time marching up and down the streets of Trieste in enormous crowds, singing and carrying banners – while at the same time the Wops have been doing precisely the same thing in a different part of the town.

The whole incident brought out so very well the Italian characteristics of rather underdeveloped undergraduate groups! Never have I seen such crowds – or heard such a noise. I imagine that the idea was to influence the decisions of the foreign ministers sitting in Paris!

The parade itself went off very well. The march past took nearly four hours, during which poor General Harding had to stand on his fractured leg which he had broken a few days ago playing polo. There was a tremendous amount of armour in the parade – and before it was over the pro-Jugoslav papers had published an article saying that the majority of the tanks had been lent to the Allies by Tito! As you can imagine, they are a very difficult nation to handle!

I saw a lot of John Joicey. I wish he would come back to the Regiment, but I rather doubt whether he will. He is in an awful state of mind as he wants to marry Mina Roi[91]. We had terrific talk all about it. I am terribly against it. The snags are legion. She is very Italian – and he is very English with a large estate to look after when he inherits it. She will never understand his friends, or be able to help him with his home. She is a Roman Cath. and he is Church of England. He wants to stay in the Army and yet he won't be able to if he marries her. And so on … But he still insists that it is a good thing! However, he is coming over to have dinner with us on the 9th – and Memina. So I shall have a crack at him again then!

I had an awful bad race at Aiello on Saturday. I rode Titus, but very soon after the flag had gone down both my leathers broke, and I had the greatest difficulty in remaining in place at all, let along riding in a race! I ended up last! Very bad.

Freddie and class distinction;
Riding school at R.H.Q.
13th May 1946

I am so overjoyed that the job is proving a success – and that you are liking it. You deserve all that as I think that you have done very well in sticking to what you think is right. I know what a beastly time it has been for you – and that you must have so many doubtful moments in your heart. It is so terribly difficult when the head begins to fight the heart. I believe that sometimes one has to give in to the heart, but this time your head won the fight – and you were right.

I have had two letters from you which arrived during the week (May 1st and May 5th). Bless you Darling for both of them – I do love them always so much – I wonder if you realise that.

I nearly sent you that cartoon! You got in first – it appears that we have the same weak sense of humour, such a good thing!

Had Colonel Jack arrived when I last wrote? He's here now anyway – and in very good form, always talking about you whenever he sees me! I am so longing to see Judy. I wonder how she'll like living in that house – miles away up in the mountains – 40 minutes' drive from the Regiment. I should say that she will survive there for about a month!

Darling, I believe we are going to disagree here – but I do feel strongly about it, so shall be stubborn! I think that you would be doing harm to Freddie[92] if you took him to Wharf House. Reasons as follows (rather long-winded, slightly pomp.):

Society will always be divided into two main classes – the people who give the orders, and the people who carry them out. And this is not wrong! Any community has to have a spokesman or a leader. In England at the moment the ruling class is not wholly people who have lived like us – but they have attained their position through their own merit. Also right! But they now lunch at The Berkeley – and like it. They have, in fact, altered their society – or class. (Class distinction is a phrase that so many people hate – but in fact it is a perfectly logical necessity.)

All the children at 141 will have a working man's education. They may rise to the top – I'm sure some of them will – but at the moment they are of the working class. If you begin to take Freddie out of that class and show him another way of living to the one which he is naturally in, he must become dissatisfied – and at his age possibly rather unreasonably so. The task is hard enough at 141 as it is – and already Mother tells me they are asking why they did not remain at Adwell.

Please don't encourage Freddie to grow into a long-haired, loud-mouthed communist. It would be so very embarrassing if he began to tub-thump in Hyde Park. And it wouldn't do him or the world any good. I wonder if you see what I mean?

Reference The Sudan – yes, quite off. Colonel Jack def. wants me here. (You must admit I've answered all your questions today.)

I must go on with this this evening as it's time to go and work.

Evening: I have just been down to the riding school at R.H.Q. putting one of the horses down the free lane. Have you ever seen one? It is merely an enclosed lane (with high rails on each side of it) and fixed jumps of various sorts at 30 yard intervals down it. The horse is put in and made to canter down without anyone on his back. It is a lovely sight seeing them jump quite free and naturally like a stag.

There were a lot of people down there – including Colonel Jack. He is odd – you're quite right! But I think you would like him if you knew him well.

We then went to Derek's house and had a drink. I like Claudia but she is a very powerful character! Derek has just been down on a battlefield tour at San Savino (our first and worst battle in Italy). Gen McCreery was taking the tour and had on parade the German generals who were commanding at that time, who told them what they were doing at that time. It must have been frightfully interesting – I wish I could have been there.

I went over to a lovely house on Sunday evening quite close by to see some Tiepolo murals. Mina Roi was there, having just got back from Milan after the opening night at The Scala. Toscanini was apparently absolutely magnificent and all the Wops went quite mad with excitement. He has been away from Italy for 18 years since his refusal (at Bologna) to play the Fascist national anthem. Can you see England treating a great conductor so like a god? People little realise what music means to the Italians – it is like food to them, and without it they starve. The Scala was rebuilt during the War after it's bombing though thousands of Italians were starving and homeless – but they were, all the same, willing that this should be done.[93]

I hope to go to the Beethoven concert on the 23rd which is the next time that he conducts – but it is right in the middle of the week, and I don't know that I shall be allowed away with all this training going on.

I rode Titus again at Treviso on Saturday – and a most vile ride I had. For some unknown reason both my leathers came off the holders in the first hundred yards as they did before. Obviously I push my legs back too much when kicking him off at the start. Anyway, whereas last time I only had 4 ½ furlongs to go, this time I had to gallop for 7 furlongs, and by the end of it I was nearly sick with exhaustion! We were fourth and definitely should have got a place. All rather maddening!

I do so hope that all is still going well.

Judy Price arrives:
May 22nd 1946, at Pordonone Training Camp

I just had time to read your letter about Judy before coming up here yesterday morning. I forget if I told you that Colonel Jack has sent me up to the Brigade Training Area to train all the new tank commanders in the Regiment. I'm rather pleased that he has chosen me. The work is quite obviously going to be very hard – the chaps know next to nothing about it and there is an enormous amount of ground to cover in only ten days. But I am confident that I can do it, which is an asset, even if I can't! Anyway, it's very good having something definite to do and I am more or less my own master – except that I suppose every sort of person will soon begin to turn up and poke their noses into it!

Of course, like all training areas, the country is pretty flat and boring and consists chiefly of disused aerodromes – but the camp is at the foot of some rather beautiful mountains. Unfortunately for the last ten days it has been raining almost continually. This has not added to the atmosphere of the Officers' Lines.

The messing arrangements were very unwisely left by Brigade Head-quarters to the 4th Tank Regt. I wonder why they are so odd! Honestly, you have no idea what it's like. 'Dinner' is at 5 o'clock and consists of 3 enormous bits of bread, a blob of jam, a hunk of cheese and one sardine. All put on one plate.

I spent yesterday evening looking for food like some stray dog. At last I found a filthy wop pub in the village (it's the only one there) and sat down to a plate of spaghetti. I was nearly sick, everything was so dirty. However, I have so far survived. I am longing to see David's face when he is shown the Mess – and general conditions!

Now about Judy: She should arrive at the Regiment this evening – I believe actually that she got to Venice at 9.30 tonight. She will go out to her house tomorrow morning. I have got to drive back tomorrow evening for the goodbye dinner that 'B' Squadron is giving to Brigadier John Coombe before he goes to command 78th Division. But before dinner, R.H.Q. are giving a cocktail party for him – and Judy should be there.

I expect she will be very frightened, and I don't blame her! It's not an easy thing to do to arrive in an Officers' Mess as the Colonel's wife with everyone looking and criticising you – but if anyone can deal with the situation, I think that she can.

I am longing to see her – but it's all just a bit 'tricky'. I don't think that you will quite understand that. But the Army is sometimes so futile – and a subaltern can't forget that Judy is now Mrs Price! I shall be able to have a gossip to her though some time.

I should have remembered to tell you that Brigadier John is leaving. We are all going to miss him a frightful lot. And most of all Col Jack.

Pat Dudding and David Whately came to dinner at 'B' Squadron on Thursday night. They are now both at Brigade – and had some very interesting things to say.

Wed night: Darling, I am sorry that I never finished this off on Sunday night – and I haven't had a moment since then.

The training has gone well – but it really has been hard work. We go out at 8.30 in the mornings and come back at 6 – and then I have to go out again in a jeep to decide where to go and what to do on the following day.

I never went back to the Brigadier's goodbye party as it was far too far to drive, and I didn't have time. However, David came up yesterday evening with a full report. Judy arrived on Sunday night very late – but was at the cocktail party in very good form, though a bit tired – but looking very nice and not too terrified! Rather a big 'do' for her to start with …..

Colonel Jack is going on a battlefield tour this week and she will therefore be left for a night or two to get her house in order – then I believe they are going off to Rapallo for a weekend. I have never been there, but they say that it is absolutely lovely.

I nearly died with laughing when David inspected the Mess, etc. He kept muttering "I've never done anything like this before" quite loud enough for the R.T.R. officers to hear. But the chef d'oevre was when he shouted at some trooper and told him to do something – and he turned round and said "I 'appen to 'old the same rank as you." "Oh, are you" said David, "Well, never have I experienced such a sight as a Field Officer wearing oily dungarees before."

It's now pouring with rain – but so far the tent is keeping it out, but oh, it is so grim camping in the rain! David has now been sitting for ¾ of an hour with a piece of paper in front of him. He says that he is going to write to you – but he must concentrate. It sometimes takes rather a long time for the mood to overtake him!

I wonder so continually how everything is going at Abingdon …

Letter from David Laurie to Lorna;
9th Lancers:
Wednesday May 22nd 1946

My dear Lorna

Bill being occupied in writing to you makes me think it is about time you had another report!

I understand you did not appreciate my comment on your 'flash envelopes'. I am sorry you think I am pompous! You are not the first person to think so! I should welcome some advice on the matter?

Bill and I are together at Pordenone where Bill has been given the job of training the Regiment's tank commanders; a good job for Bill and, in my opinion, there is no one more suitable. From the soldiering point of view, it is everything having Bill in my squadron at this rather important time. He is first class and I assure you I very much appreciate having him. We have a full summer in front of us with camps, etc.

Judy made her first appearance at a cocktail party we gave to Brig. John Coombe who is leaving us. Although Judy had only arrived a few hours before, she was in extremely good form and appeared to be quite at home. It was rather an ordeal for her as, in a Regiment, the Colonel's wife is a big thing! John Coombe dined in 'B' sqn afterwards. We in particular will miss him a great deal as he is a good friend to my squadron.

I was coming home to command 9th detachment in London on June 8th but I have managed to get out of it as it was not worth the long journey home for a few days' leave.

Bill really is in great form, but it is unfortunate he has not got his future decided as undoubtedly it is a worry.

I hear you are now working. England is obviously no place to be in with nothing to do.

Hope to hear from you soon.

Love David

D's wedding;
preparing for horse show in Austria:
26th May 1946

I'm writing to you in bed! But I no longer trust myself with an inkpot as the last time I found that ink had somehow flown freely all over my bed!

I came back to the Regiment from Pordenone last night – hoping to see Judy, but she had gone off with Jack and the Meyricks and John Reid to Madonna for the weekend. Wasn't it a pity? And it has rained the whole time without stopping and so I've played no tennis or ridden – and I did so want some real hard exercise – I got so flabby up there as I was never out of a tank and therefore took no bodily exercise at all.

I go back tomorrow till Wednesday night to take the Troop on the ranges – it should be quite fun, but I am getting just a little bored of this no food habit – and my brother officers there. They are really rather dreadful!

Then a large party pick me up on their way up to Austria for the 16th/5th Lancers Horse Show. I'm longing to see lovely Austria again – and David and I will be staying at the schloss where we used to stay for the Klagenfurt races last summer. It really should be tremendous fun – Derek and Claudia, Pat Stevens, Desmond McInnes Skinner, David and Tony Cooke. We will be back here on Sunday night.

I dread to think what my exhibition will be like in the ring as I have done no practising (having been away working!) and as yet I don't even know what horse I am going to ride! However, no doubt all will be well.

I found a letter from Juliet Ponsonby waiting for me. She seems to have got herself in a bit of a muddle – she has taken a chalet it Switzerland for July and wants me to go up there and stay. It does sound lovely – and a very good party, but I honestly don't think that there is much of a hope of being able to get away – particularly as the Squadron training will be going on then. I wish I could think of some way. Betsy Ponsonby will be there too – I pray that it will do her some good.

Mother said that Delia's wedding was simply lovely. It sounded a great gathering – I wish I had been there. Apparently the New College Choir sang simply beautifully – and D had chosen some lovely music. I thought so much of her on the 11th – I wonder how it all goes. She was far from confident of herself!

I had a long talk to David last night till 2 o'clock. Sometimes I do feel very sorry for him. He is so terribly easily influenced by people – and relies so much on others for advice. He was saying how much he was going to miss me when I left the Regiment. He relies far too much on me, and it's somehow not right that he should at his age and holding the position that he does in the Regiment. But he really hasn't any great friends left now – and sometimes is very lonely. And much more so than the average person who does things off his own bat without being supported by others. Poor old boy. He has been, in so many ways, a great friend of mine – but he is so 'complex'!

I wonder what Judy will think about regimental soldiering! And how she will get on with Jack's varied and odd friends. John Reid is not a great buddy of mine! He is the sort of person who is always quite charming to one's face – and then says the oddest things about you behind your back. I wonder what he thinks he gains by it – surely only a reputation for not being worthy of trust. But that (above) is perhaps rather unnecessary and unpleasant of me. So forget it!

Saw Judy; 16th/5th Lancers Hunter trials;
last days at Pordenone:
3rd June 1946

At last I've seen Judy! She has been here for a fortnight or more – but I have been away the whole time. And this evening she arrived back from her weekend with Colonel Jack, the Meyricks and John Reid. I was watching a squadron football match – and they went past, however we waved madly – and a few minutes later she arrived at the football field. It was lovely to see her again, and we had a little talk walking back to Derek's house where she had left Colonel Jack.

They had had a most ghastly journey back culminating in a burst tyre at 60 miles an hour which must have been really frightening and they just avoided having a very bad smash. But she was in very good form – and just the same as ever. I longed, of course, to gossip with her for ages – but we just couldn't with such masses of people in Derek's house.

Being with her somehow makes you seem so much closer – in some ways you are both so alike (as all great friends should be, giving to and taking from each other). She seems blissfully happy and serene – I wish she didn't live so far away. It takes ½ an hour to get to their house, and it is too far to 'drop in' on them. She asked me to come up after breakfast on Sunday and leave after dinner. Colonel Jack would relish the idea of me being there all day! But it is so sweet of her to ask me.

Oh Darling, I have been having such a happy time during the last week. We had a very good end to the training at Pordenone with three days on the ranges. The chaps seemed to enjoy firing the new gun – and were impressed by its performance.

George Meyrick – who is a great authority on tank gunnery – came up on the Monday, bringing with him the letter that Judy brought out from you. Thank you so much for it Darling. You sound so happy and satisfied (and Judy endorses that) – I think you know how equally happy it makes me feel.

I left Pordenone on Thursday night and met David in Udine – who brought your letter dated the 20th. I couldn't understand about your fainting fit – and it was only last night that your letter dated 15th arrived. Isn't it odd? Poor Darling – please don't overdo it and get ill. It doesn't sound at all good – and I did feel a bit worried.

I have noted the contents about Freddie – and will not go into it all now. But I am soon going to write to you on the whole subject as, quite obviously, it is due now!

We started for Austria on Friday morning, and after a most unusual journey arrived without even a wheel falling off at Klagenfurt for lunch. The change of country on crossing the border always amazes me. Somehow, quite suddenly, the grass gets more green, the people look nicer, the houses are cleaner – and I am happier. Oh how I do love Austria.

We had a quick lunch and then drove out to the 16th Lancers and found the horses which had come up two days before under the R.S.M. (Mr Hardwidge). Poor chap was in an awful state as Lancer (his lovely horse) was dead lame – but all the others were well; and David and I rode around the hunter trial course. It really was a perfect one – all natural fences, just what one might meet out hunting. I had never ridden Warren before (he is an A Squadron horse) – and he went very well for me.

The whole show was very well run (as it was last year) – and the results were satisfactory: Tony Cooke and Desmond Skinner won with 53. Derek and Otto Thwaites scored 58, and David and I 60. If only we had gone a bit faster we might have won it as we did a clear round but gained points on time. But it was enormous fun.

We didn't do much on Saturday morning – but it was quite hot enough to bathe and sit in the sun and think and read. It was very wonderful looking across the lake that morning. The rippling water, stretching far over the lake, matched the great opaque blue breadth of sky – and out of it slowly rose, in a sweeping strip, the bright green grass like an English lawn, of the foothills which surround the

Wörtersee. And gradually the dark green fir trees began to grow on the higher ground, until the whole mountain was covered in fir forests, save where a little farmhouse, white and glistening, had somehow found a place to nestle – secretly and quietly among the trees; or a chapel, with it's wooden steeple burnished by time to a shining silver, showed itself proudly on some small rise. I read a good deal of Shakespeare, and felt very happy.

We went to a cocktail party at Otto's schloss in the evening. He lives with some charming Austrians called Goess. I asked the girl (who spoke very good English) when she was last in England. She told me that she had left in 1938 after staying at Eton! It turned out that she knew everyone there – and had lived with the Marsdens! Wasn't it extraordinary? She took me round the house – rather a lovely one, but ruined like so many out here by too many pictures and too much furniture.

Of course Otto is in just the job that suits him (G2 Equitation at B.T.S. H.Q.) – and has done very well for himself. Amongst other things he has persuaded a very famous horse-master (can't remember his name) to come and live with him and teach him the continental seat. We went to see him giving a demonstration on Sunday morning. It really was most frightfully impressive. He had trained two very mediocre German horses to do anything in that line – and we watched him for ages. Then we started our journey which was sad.

Quite a situation occurred at the frontier as Claudia Allhusen had got no pass and had to be smuggled through. We put her on the floor of the car and covered her with coats, maps, etc – and finally I more or less sat on her – and all was well, and we sailed through. Poor Claudia was quite scarlet when we uncovered her!

We got back last night to find a tremendous flap going on in the Regiment – and it seems quite possible that some Troops will have to move up to the Trieste area to frighten Tito. Of course Ju is very frightened that Jack will have to go. But I rather doubt anything occurring in the end – or anything serious. But it has made a lot of work, and we seem to have been running about in small circles all day!

Don't worry, Darling, about your Mother's letter. She will soon know that you are not unpurposeful and unbusinesslike and that you are doing a really useful and hard job. It is difficult for her generation to see your point of view – as they were brought up with such a different outlook on life. Share your interests with her – and I am certain that gradually she will be convinced that you have done right (and very well).

You must go and see Dorothy Maud when you next go to Wantage. She is one of the most wonderful women I know – and you will love her.

Situation re Trieste;
John Reid & Jack;
visits to Judy:
8th June 1946

As you will possibly have gathered from the papers the Jugoslav situation is now very serious. We are, in fact, pretty certain to move nearer Trieste in case anything should occur. However, I am confident of my Troop and we have been working sometimes till dinner time on the tanks. It will do them (and me!) an enormous amount of good to get back to battle conditions and really do something of practical use. But, of course, it will all be supremely uncomfortable after our rather luxurious life here.

I am so glad you liked the silk – and that you think I've got good taste! What are you going to have them made into? I bought some shirt stuff – but the shirts haven't yet materialised. It would have been far better and equally quick to send them back to Coles.

I really have seen a lovely lot of Judy since I returned from Austria. It does seem so extraordinary her being out here and taking a place in the Regiment. We all went to a friendly little horse show that the Bays organized very quickly on Wed. afternoon. Everyone seemed to be there – and all the wives. It was so lovely to see English girls and their children about instead of Wops.

I jumped Monkey who went badly on the whole in the open – but it was fun. Then everyone joined in the fray – and the fences were lowered. I then saw Judy up on Mr Hardwidge's precious

Lancer! No-one has ever been allowed to ride him, let alone jump him before. He is not an easy horse to ride by any means – and Judy got full marks from everyone for going round – and riding extremely well, with almost a clear round. In fact all the girls did jolly well and put us all to shame.

They both came to dinner on Thursday night with George and Ann Meyrick and Wac. Anderson our new Brigade Major (who is charming and used to command the 24th Lancers when I was there.) David had been running round in small circles ordering the dinner and being too maddeningly exacting for words – but it was a very good one.

We didn't start till very late as Jack and Judy had a puncture on the way. They are not very lucky with their transport! And of course we gossiped on till after one – and poor Judy looked frightfully tired. But she is so good and natural – and of course she has already captured everyone's heart.

Yesterday Jack and David went out on a recce for a new training area (in place of Pordenone) and so I asked Judy down to ride. It was frightfully hot and we just couldn't ride till rather later in the evening – and by that time Peter Thompson-Glover had finished his work and ordered his horse too. Rather a pity as I wanted to gossip to her alone – however it was a lovely ride, and I think she enjoyed it. She asked me to come up to her house tomorrow – but owing to the sudden increase in the flap I won't be able to go – and therefore David and I went up for lunch and stayed till dinner! They are in a much smaller house than the one I originally went to look at – and ten times nicer. It really is quite perfect – with the most heavenly views.

Of course she has changed Jack so much. I was absolutely amazed! He has become a very 'homey' husband, and seems to 'think of others' so much more. It was such fun – we just lay in the sun and read and talked softly while David and Jack slept. Christopher Beckett[94] joined us up there and then came back to dinner. He is an extraordinary person. He has travelled all over the world and lived a very full life. He was telling us all about bull fighting, which he is absolutely dotty about. I must say he was most awfully interesting, but a filthy sport it does sound.

I was most annoyed to see a letter from you to David and not to me. He wouldn't even let me read it! But it made him laugh for hours. What did you say?

Regiment moved towards Trieste;
Jack and Derek never around:
16th June 1946

I only got your letter yesterday, brought by hand from Chiampi – and of course it had taken ages to get to me. I know so well how perfectly ghastly M&B makes you feel, as I was given practically nothing else for the first three days when I had pneumonia. But of course it does do the trick – and bring your temperature down. I wonder what the trouble is – I know how you will hate being in bed – oh Darling, how I wish I could come and try to buck you up.

And I haven't written to you for a week. As I told you, I thought that we would have to move – and the whole Squadron and most of the Regiment moved on Saturday. We are supposed to be battle-worthy – so you can imagine the organisation entailed to get everyone ready, etc, and to get uprooted again after seven months in one place – with no one except very inexperienced N.C.Os to help!

However, with an enormous amount of fussing from David, we moved off at 4.30 AM on Saturday morning and arrived in this new area 20 miles north of Udine for lunch on Saturday. We were all appalled by the thought of going under canvas again – but really it's rather a lovely spot at the foot of the mountains, an hour's drive from the Austrian border. So far it has done little but rain which has not brightened the party up much – but that can't last, and all will soon be well.

We are sharing a mess with C Squadron (Tony Cooke's) which is very pleas. as John Goldsmid and Desmond McInnes Skinner are both here – but the plan seems to be that in a week or so we all move to a Regimental mess – and I can think of nothing worse. I loathe being herded about and not being allowed to do more or less what one likes when off duty – but of course in a Regimental mess everyone wants to know what you are doing and where you are every hour of the day.

But at the moment nobody knows exactly what is going on as all the senior officers are away looking for houses for themselves and their wives.

    I wonder what Judy thinks about it – she must realise the situation only too well. I only saw her for a moment last week owing to the general flap – but she and the Colonel did look in for a drink on Wednesday evening. She wasn't in very good form – the thought of moving appalled her, particularly as it means leaving such a lovely little house – and they have decided not to go back there when (and if) we return in two months' time, which we are supposed to do. It really was too far away from the Regiment. But she didn't look too well either – perhaps the new climate takes a bit of getting used to.

    I got a long letter from Father with yours yest. all about my career. He says go up to Oxford at all costs and get a degree in Law – not necessarily as a career but as a training for any career that I will have decided on by the time I go down. As he says, to stay on in the Army indefinitely is useless. And to 'look for a job' in England would result in me jumping at an unsuitable one in sheer desperation! I don't think that doctoring is really practicable.[95] Oh Darling – you're probably still feeling beastly, but it is difficult to decide what to do with one's life!

> ***Judy as a regimental wife;***
> ***Lorna recovering;***
> ***letter from Sue:***
> ***18th June 1946***

    I wonder so much how you are – better anyway after stopping the M and B. Sue[96] wrote to me all about you and her letter arrived yesterday morning. She told me that the worst was over. I wonder what on earth it could have been. My poor Darling – it all sounds pretty beastly. Sue put a postscript to her letter "did you know that I am now converted to long long hair"! She is funny person – and I laughed a lot at her letter.

    Things are at last settling down a bit after a very hectic and rather trying four days; and life is now a bit more normal. I am writing to you from my tent (which, thank goodness, I have got to myself). It seems to be full of everything, and I am really comfortable – and alone! I went into Udine today and bought a lamp which was really the only thing I was lacking to be really organised – and now I can write to you in peace out of the mess. It's quite impossible to try and sit down to write with all the others talking and asking questions at odd moments.

We have all suddenly started playing cards – none of us having any idea before of the difference between clubs and spades, and hearts and diamonds! But now we play piquet at all odd moments which is quite fun. We are such an uncardy family – I don't think there is a pack at Adwell!

Desmond McInnes Skinner was 21 yesterday and he gave a most excellent dinner party for us all in Udine. It really was terribly generous of him. Practically every officer was there – and Judy and Claudia. Ju was very worried about you and got me into a corner to find out what I know. Now that she is once more 'settled in' she is in better form again and we had a lovely talk before dinner. I wonder whether she gets fearfully bored by these parties – always sitting at the head of the table next to people years older than herself for hours on end. She certainly never shows it – and is awfully good at them. But just sometimes I feel sorry for her.

The General came round yesterday and looked round the camp. He is a Canadian and seemed a nice sort of person. Colonel Jack brought him to my Troop to see us doing a gunnery practice with which he seemed satisfied.

I had worked very hard with my Troop to get the range ready for the Squadron to use. It really was rather a good one. John Reid saw it and told me that it was to be used by the Regiment. Therefore the Squadron will hardly ever be able to go there. In fact I really wasted a whole day. I don't think I look for praise – but I do rather resent it when somebody takes the credit for something that I've done! John Reid has let the Colonel know quite clearly that he is responsible for the whole thing! How frightfully childish it all is – and how petty, but so often army matters are petty!

The horses arrived up from the rear party late last night which caused some chaos as nothing was ready for them – but they are all right now, and this evening Desmond, David and I went out for a short ride before dinner. It really is perfect riding country – I really would far rather be here than at Chiampo, which, but for the Mear, was pretty dull country for riding.

I have written to Dr Russell[97] to find out what he thinks about me coming back to Oxford – and if he thinks it a good plan whether I can leave the army and go up in October.

I must stop now and get to sleep. Bless you my Darling – I think of you so much, and pray that you are better.

John Joicey takes us to Caladon Camp;
Judy loses her clothes;
River Tagliamento rising!
23rd June 1946

Your letter has been one of the few redeeming features of the past three days. You sounded so much better, and I now feel happier again. Poor Darling, you have had a beastly time. It is always so much worse if you are usually never ill. But, as I suspected, you have obviously been working far too hard – and being much too gay! Please take it steady – particularly to begin with.

We are all pretty demoralised by the continual rain. Honestly, you have absolutely no idea what it is like – it rains harder than I have ever seen in my life, and the result is that the whole camp is a swamp and the chaps are miserable. Everything in my tent is damp and revolting.

The most appalling catastrophe occurred the other day. During dinner all the H.Q. mess tents were robbed. Colonel Jack had left a trunk of Judy's in John Reid's tent, containing practically all her clothes. When he came to his tent after dinner he found that it had gone and a great deal of his own kit – and George Meyrick lost most of his. I haven't seen her since this happened – but of course she is frightfully distressed as it is totally irreplaceable. Poor thing, she really has had a rather tricky time since she arrived – what with the move from such a lovely house to a pretty mediocre one, and now losing all her clothes. A terrific search is going on, of course, but the chances of getting it back are pretty remote.

We were all sitting rather miserably in the pouring rain in our leaky mess tent yesterday afternoon, deciding what to do, when Joicey suddenly walked in, having driven from Corps Head Quarters in his opulent Mercedes Benz. He insisted on us getting out of the quagmire for the night – so we packed our clothes and drove back to Trieste with him where we had a most excellent dinner and gossip and laugh. We saw Bobby Chaworth Musters and Simon Bland[98] there and chatted to them before dinner.

Of course John works jolly hard and is away from all of us in the Regiment – but my goodness it is an interesting job, and he does live in tremendous comfort. I sometimes wonder whether I didn't make a mistake in not taking the job.

I am writing to you from the garden at Caladon Camp, where we have lunched with John. It is not a camp any longer – but the most charming Italian villa not far from Duino[90] Castle (Corps Head Quarters) where General Harding's guests stay. Field Marshal Alexander originally started the camp in the desert – and in those days it was made up of a number of supremely luxurious caravans – and named it Caladon after his home in Ireland.

We have spent a perfect Sunday afternoon here. John walked us round the farm and we looked at the horses all standing under the shade of the chestnut trees, and then we saw the cattle (including the most enormous bull which prompted David to produce his red silk handkerchief which he proceeded to shake at it shouting "I am a toreador – boo!" – of course he's got a distinctive cink!) ending up with the pigs which we poked with the odd stick we found lying about. And now we are all lying out in the sun before tea.

Rather an unusual situation occurred the other day which I must report to you! David decided to fire the guns into a cliff face not far from the camp. This meant that the tanks were lined up on one side of the River Tagliamento and shot over it into the cliff the other side some 1,200 yards away. Usually the river is very shallow and it is quite possible to get a tank over it; and David told me to drive over to the other side so that I could get near to the targets as observation tank. But, of course, we hadn't taken the rain into account – and very soon the water became most alarmingly deep. I just managed to get to a tiny island in the middle of the river, and there I halted.

Then the black clouds began to roll down the sides of the mountains, and in five minutes the rain had started with bags of thunder and lightning. The water began to rise all too quickly – and after half an hour the river had risen four (no exaggeration) feet! The others on the other side considered the whole situation immensely funny. There was nothing for it but to wade back and leave the tank locked up on the now even smaller island!

I admit it must have looked quite funny as I came across battling against the current, but I really was quite frightened! I was followed by the Sgt Major who was washed right off his feet and swept fifty yards down the river, and arrived on the other bank a very shaken man!

And still the river rose! We decided that the remaining survivors would not manage the crossing without aid – so after many attempts we shot a rope across to them and with six chaps on the other end we pulled them across. The tank still remains in the river – with my watch and field glasses inside it. When I shall get them back depends on the rain stopping, if ever![100]

We are trying again tomorrow morning, all being well. Then I start for Milan in a scout car and drive for eight hours to hear Toscanini. David has given me leave to go on condition that I get back on Tuesday for lunch! He is playing *Beethoven's 1st and 9th*. It couldn't be a more perfect programme could it? The Roi family have a very smart box in The Scala and I am meeting them for dinner in Milan before the concert at 9. Can you imagine anything lovelier – and so well worth the long drive. They say that he goes to Paris very soon, and will be in London by July. So you will hear him there. One must never lose the chance to do something like this – and I know that it is worthwhile.

I must stop now as it's tea time, and then we've got to start for camp. What a ghastly thought.

Breakdown en route to Milan;
Concern about officers' wives.
28th June 1946

I never heard Toscanini after all. I set off in a scout car on Monday morning and got about sixty miles when the car broke down – and by the time I had got hold of the right spare part it was no good going as I would have been far too late. You can imagine how furiously disappointed I was. And such a wonderful concert. It was, in fact, an utter waste of an afternoon as I spent five hours driving there and back. But there it is.

Today has been fine for the first time since we arrived, and a good many of the chaps went bathing in the lake. They have had a beastly time and have been wet practically since we arrived up here.

We all went riding this afternoon. The poor horses look pretty grim. The lines are, of course, outside and they have been standing on wet straw and look awful. If only the sun continues they should pick up – but the food is terribly short.

It really is a lovely part of the country to ride in; lots of lanes and all the fields have paths running down the edge of them, and are not wired in – so we can ride practically anywhere we like.

I haven't seen Judy to speak to since we went into camp – but they have got a house of a sort four miles away. I want to see her badly too. I am told that before the War it was the main responsibility of the Colonel's wife to look after the interests of the wives of the soldiers. We have now been here for ten days. All the married officers have their wives with them, but no soldier has – nor has anyone thought of looking for a house for them. Quite rightly, they are very annoyed about it – and I have therefore complained myself for them. Nobody would be better at it than Judy – but nobody has told her that she should do it – and quite obviously she doesn't know the situation.

I haven't even asked you how you are. I expect that you will be at Manderston now. I do hope you are feeling alright, and not too wobbly after being in bed. The spring will do you more good than anything. How lovely everything will be looking. Have you ever read *The Land* by V Sackville West? The poem is divided into four parts – each part for each season of the year. Do read it if you haven't already – it is so lovely, particularly the part about spring.

I had a letter from Ros this morning on her return from Denmark.[101] She seems to have had a lovely time and a good rest. I wish I knew more about this Bill Parker affair. I think she needs watching! She mentioned him all through her letter.

Talking to Judy:
1st July 1946

Most extraordinary – a letter arrived yesterday evening dated June 10th and you hadn't kept it in your bag as it was posted on 12th! Something really is wrong with the mail. It was written on your first day in hospital – thank goodness that it's all over now!

The heat here is now terrific – and only the occasional thunderstorm relieves the tension! I spent a most exhausting afternoon yesterday in Udine where the streets were so hot that the tar was melting away. I saw Ju for a moment – still trying to replace her lost clothes, but I didn't talk for long as I knew that I should be seeing her in the evening.

It really was a very pleas. party. Her house isn't too bad – though miles from here which is a bore as I never see her. The others played bridge – so Ju and I talked in hushed voices most of the time as Col Jack, though he wasn't actually playing bridge, was very busy watching it!

Luckily I came in a separate car and left soon after twelve – but apparently the others went on playing cards till 4.30 am. Judy and Ann went off to bed at 3 o'clock having waited for their husbands in vain!

I drove back and as I approached the camp I realised that one of the storms had descended on our tents! I went and talked to David for a bit – and it was after one o'clock when I got to my tent. The sight was appalling! Just as if a hurricane had gone straight through my tent (I think one had!). The bed was absolutely soaking wet – and, after trying to find a dry blanket, I gave it up in complete fury.

I rather like my servant, Bayes – and he knows me well. The amount of work a servant does is really terribly little. I had been working jolly hard all day and he had done nothing to stop the rain pouring into my tent. So I dragged him out of bed and rubbed his nose in my bed almost literally. I really was very annoyed. In the end, and after I had let off steam thoroughly, I found that Christopher Diggle had not come back from Trieste – so I took the risk and slept in his bed! All was well – and he didn't get back till this morning.

Tomorrow we all go to the show which should be great fun – though very hot. I shan't do any good – it's David's turn to ride Monkey who might win.

To Bodensdorf with Troop;
Aiello show:
13th July 1946

Do you remember last year when I took my Troop up here? That was the old Troop just before they all left for England. I decided to do the same this year – and we arrived up here this afternoon.

Oh my Darling, how much you would love Austria – as I do. I am looking out over the Ossianchensee. It is really more beautiful than the longer and better known Wortersee – because it is so lonely and secret in the hills. And the silence comes with the setting sun – guilding the fir trees on the mountains as it curves down the sky, sad to end such a lovely day.

The chaps are blissfully happy – wandering about with next to nothing on, boating and bathing and eating the rather special rations that I have bought for them.

I don't believe that I have written to you since the Aiello show – which is bad. It really was a very big 'do' for two days. I was very surprised to get into the finals of the novice handy hunters on the Friday – and amazed to win it as I was riding Old Glory who everyone else said was useless! But, quite honestly, it wasn't a very difficult course – though great fun to ride over – and it wasn't hard to complete a clear round. The Regiment did well as Derek was second in the Show Jumping and Tony Cooke placed.

Judy was there on the two days – it was lovely seeing her; I so seldom do now. Poor thing, she looked so hot – I can't tell you what the heat was like – and no shade anywhere on the flat race course. I thought that I would talk to her if I had the chance, but of course I never see her alone – particularly as she shares her house with the Meyricks. I honestly think that I should – but it will be difficult, and I only hope that she will understand.

I drove up to Austria on Tuesday afternoon with Tony Cooke, David, Bill Peek and Pat Stevens to jump in the Allied Show Jumping Contest at Velden. However, when we arrived we were told that the show had been postponed till Thursday because of the rain. It wasn't worth driving back and returning again, so we all had a lovely excuse to spend a lazy day at the Country Club on Wednesday. We played tennis most of the afternoon which was great fun. I am improving slightly! David is amazingly pompous and serious to play with and appallingly bad! Needless to say he arrives on the court dressed as for the Centre Court at Wimbledon!

In the evening we went over to General John Coombe's house and had a drink with him and David Whately and Colonel Denys Smyly (who commands the 16th Lancers). They are all so nice – and it was so lovely sitting down in the cool evening looking down over the Wortersee. We arrived back for dinner to find that the French jumping team had arrived complete with girlfriends – wearing the most amazing kit, much to D's horror. "My dear, what would Mr Huntsman say" was the refrain for the remainder of the evening.

Peek, having consumed large quantities of Austrian gin, grew immensely red and excited and disappeared off to talk to them. Can't you see him, hair on end sprouting from that great moon face, gesticulating like a madman to a rather astonished French officer who failed to hide his ignorance of even a smattering of his attempts at conversational French? It was too much when I arrived in my room to find that I was sharing a double bed with him!!

After a very disturbed night we started off early for the show to find quite the most extraordinary jumps designed by a Romanian colonel called Vichey – the show ground looked like some weird Lilliput – bridges painted bright green, scarlet walls covered in potted flowers (purple), gates with model lodges each side, etc, etc. The hunter trial course was equally unique – and showed only too clearly what a Romanian colonel considered 'fair hunting country'!

We were all rather annoyed – but everything went very well, and not even the French chaps (who we thought would win everything) could beat us. We all got into the finals – and in the jump off Derek was second, and we were all quite well placed.

It was a most exhausting day – we were still riding at seven o'clock, and when I dismounted from Monkey (David rode Old Glory) I found that he had got a bad cut on his foreleg. However, like everything else, it wasn't as bad as I thought and the vet soon had it under control.

General John gave a big party in the evening for the French contingent. I sat next to one of them who spoke not a word of English! Have you ever heard me speak French? I anyway kept the company amused – but I think the little Frog thought I was mad! It's really rather awful, but I cannot make myself clear!

We started back at 8 o'clock on Friday morning and arrived at the Regt at 10.30. A most beautiful drive – everything looked so fresh and cool. I worked hard all day and dressed Monkey's leg when the horses arrived back. It really has kept clean and shouldn't be long job. I only hope he is well enough to go to Vienna on 23rd. I'm simply longing for that. Two days racing and two days show, with Mozart operas every night and a ball at the Schonbrun Palace thrown in! I'm nearly as gay as you.

Pause: Just been persuaded to have a moonlight bathe! It really was lovely and lukewarm. Then I gossiped and drank tea – so the time has flown to midnight already.

We went to a very good cocktail party last night given by Tony Bulkley (SGs) and Sandy Reid-Scott. I wonder whether you know them? Both have their wives out here, who are awfully nice. My dear – the whole world was there, including Sir John Harding + A.D.C. (Joicey) and Lady Harding (who is most impressive). It really was great fun and we stayed for hours and drank too much.

We (David, Christopher Beckett and David Wentworth Stanley) then drove back in to Udine and had a frightfully good dinner at the restaurant (very Black Market) there. Then Beckett suggested that we went dancing. Oh yes – he knew where we could go, frightfully good band, etc, etc. Somehow I thought it might be quite funny and we all drove up to this nightclub in the hills above Udine.

It was quite an interesting experience. I have always wanted to talk to a prostitute and last night I danced with one. I wish I could speak more Italian – because I could then have found out more of her outlook on life – and her feelings towards it. As it was, the whole escapade made me feel very depressed and rather unhappy. It is so perfectly ghastly to even contemplate what their life must be like. We arrived back pretty late – and rather silent.

Reason for my not proposing;
Vienna horse show at Schonbrun;
Corps Commander's inspection:
29th July 1946

Your letter was waiting for me this morning when I got back from Vienna (more about that later!)

These next three years will be impossible unless we both feel free and accept the possibility that one of us might begin to love somebody more than we love each other now. And obviously it would be terribly wrong not to. It would only then be possible to be able to say to each other that we love each other completely and that we are meant to marry.

That is why I've never asked you to marry me! I feel that it is unfair on us both to be bound to each other when we cannot get married for so long – and particularly unfair to you when you could get married tomorrow. Promise me to feel that you are not bound to me.

Oh Darling, how terribly I want to be near you and see you and talk to you – how maddeningly unsatisfactory writing is (particularly these post-war letters!). But you have at least got used to them a bit now – and will understand.

Vienna was absolutely perfect. David, Christopher Beckett and I drove up in the Fiat and stayed with the 16th Lancers last Monday night. They are the most amazing Regiment – they live for gambling and drinking, and yet somehow they manage to be most awfully nice and amusing and hospitable. I got to bed at 6.15 AM!

We drove on the next morning through the most heavenly Austrian country and over the Semmering Pass into the Vienna plain – arriving at about 4.30 for tea at Sachers. From then on there simply wasn't a spare moment. We went racing all day on Wednesday. Crowds of people (the world and his wife) and very good races and food! Pat Stevens won a very good race on Valentine (which I never backed and he paid 13-1!).

The next day we all drove to the Schonbrun Palace for the horse show. I don't suppose that there will ever be another show held in such perfect surroundings. The rather beautiful 18th century Austrian palace at the back and the show ground on the lawns in front, rising up to the Gloria (a long cloistered monument) high up on a lawny hill in the front. The performances were really up to the highest standard – and all the countries taking part won something which was so satisfactory!

But the great achievement on the next day was when Gr. Britain won the team jumping easily – with France second and America 3rd. It really was thrilling to watch them go round such a very big and difficult course.

The hunter trial course was perfect – and our two horses would have done well, I'm sure. It was such a disappointment not to have been able to ride – but there it is. Desmond McInnes Skinner was 2nd to George Rich (in the Bays) for which he deserves full marks. He really does ride well.

We never seemed to get to bed before two, at the earliest! There was a very good dance held by the Racing Committee at the Kingsky Palace. Thousands of people there including all the generals and their hideous wives! Joicey was well to the fore, dancing polkas with Lady Harding. who he calls the kitchen maid practically to her face.

The last day's racing was on Saturday. Again, tremendous fun. How nice people are who love horses! It really was a happy party. The 16th gave a frightfully good dance in the evening. We arrived there very late and the first person I saw was Lavinia Lascelles. We had a tremendous talk – I don't think that her husband is frightfully interesting, but he must be nice. It is amazing how being married changes people. L really seemed rather different and very changed in looks.

It was so sad to go on Sunday morning. We were a great party that night at Velden where we stopped – as most people had the same idea! So once more we didn't go to bed till very late. Do you know Desmond Chichester and his wife Lorna (Twining that was)? Both so very nice; we saw a lot of them.

Back here once again, the work seems to have piled up. I was out all this morning on an air support demonstration. All rather boring except that, as usual, I managed to do something quite funny! I was going pretty fast in my tank and saw that there was a river in front of me – so I ordered my driver to halt. Nothing happened. Of course the wireless communication to him had broken.

The situation was acute as there was now only 25 yards before the river. So I leapt out of the turret to shout at the driver through the hatch. However unfortunately he suddenly saw the river and braked very hard. With no hesitation whatsoever I was thrown straight off the tank head first into the river – and this in front of crowds of people! The whole scheme was halted while I resumed by original position. Most embarrassing!

This afternoon has been ghastly, auditing the Regimental accounts with Derek, who knows even less about it than I do! I do loathe adding things up – particularly as I always do it wrong.

In the spare time (about 2 minutes) I have been rushing round trying to get things ready for the Corps Commander who arrives with Joicey tomorrow morning to inspect us. The Colonel and Judy are in Milan. A D.R. has been sent to try and get them back in time.

I was glad to hear from Mother that Hugh Euston[102] is engaged out of the court circle. I only hope he hasn't done it in desperation!

This is a ghastly place – it's not raining now but vilely hot, and I'm now being eaten by mosquitoes and must stop and go to bed.

Release comes through;
leave Regiment 28th August:
7th August 1946

    I have just heard that my 'B' release has come through – and that I will be leaving the Regiment round about August 22nd, and will be in England at the end of the month anyway. I am still in rather a coma about it. Never did I think that it would come through so quickly, if at all.

    The idea of seeing you so soon dominates everything – and I really can't believe it. Thank goodness there isn't all that rather frightening 'first meeting' to be gone through again! Oh Darling, how perfect it will be. What are your plans? Will you be down in the south or at Manderston?

    I shall miss everyone so terribly – and I'm afraid Oxford won't be at all the same. But more about that when I see you (doesn't that sound amazing?).

    I went to Trieste yesterday and bought you some stuff for a dress and knickers! Also some stockings. Will you write quickly and tell me what else you want. There are lots of lipsticks etc – I must get hold of Judy and ask her.

    We are all very busy preparing for the Regimental Hunter Trial. It starts at 3 o'clock on Wednesday afternoon – and then runs into a cocktail party at 7. Then a dinner party and dance – with b'fast at 5!

    Oh I quite forgot to tell you something that happened last week which pleased me rather a lot. Derek left Laura[103] in my care when he went to England – she is the most wonderful mare, and I am riding her in the Hunter Trials. She very nearly got into the British Jumping Team which is going to Switzerland this month. Wasn't it terribly kind of him – and I'm glad that he thinks enough of my horsemanship to entrust her to me.

    I must stop or I'll miss the post corporal. I can't believe that I'll see you so soon – oh Darling, what a thought.

Visit to Salzburg before leaving Regiment:
August 22nd 1946

It's really rather pointless writing to you as I shall probably be in England before this gets to Manderston – but I have just had such a wonderful week away from the Regiment that I must write and tell you all about it.

But I'll go back to last Wednesday (a week today) when the Regimental Hunter Trials took place. They really were the most tremendous fun – but as you can imagine, it took a lot of organising and hard work. There were over a hundred pairs taking part, in the open and novice courses. The course was big but absolutely fair hunting country – and people seemed to enjoy riding round very much.

I rode on Derek's mare, Laura, with Desmond McInnes Skinner on a rather lazy old brute who let us down by refusing at a fence and therefore put us out of the running. But we had a lovely ride round.

The Hunter Trials finished at about 7.30 and everybody then motored to Buia (where Jack and Judy live) for a cocktail party, developing into a dance and dinner. David and I were in charge of the party! We enlisted the help of the Head Waiter of the Futura Restaurant in Trieste who really organised the whole thing (at enormous cost!) – but it was quite out of the question trying to do it ourselves.

We had a floor outside for people to dance on, and the Bays Band played very well for us. I think that everyone enjoyed themselves to the full. I was in bed by 5.30 am – having spent two weary hours packing everything up after the party was over!

During the evening I had a long talk to Judy. She is a gem – and so unchanged. But, of course, there is masses to tell you about that when I see you (oh, Darling, it does sound so lovely). We talked mostly about the Regiment – and I hinted at the bad state it is in.

Jack is such a charming person – and asked me if there was anything I wanted to do before I left for England. I told him that I wanted to go to Salzburg for the Musical Festival. And so, on Friday at lunch time, David and I started off in the Fiat with the Jeep following with a trailer full of petrol.

We drove over the Austrian frontier and then began to climb up over the great Gross Glockner Pass. I can never describe the beauty of that drive through the mountains. At times we were right up in the snow, and the sun shone through the mountains with a blue light, almost too bright to see. And down the mountain gorges rushed, headlong and uncontrolled, the melted snow from the higher peaks, down into the valleys below the ever-winding road. Sometimes we drove through dark damp fir forests – and then, quite suddenly, we would come out into the open again and see once more the shimmering silver line of the river far below.

We arrived at Salzburg at 7.30, very happy but tired – and, after great arguments with the Americans (who unfortunately control Salzburg), we managed to squeeze into a rather dirty little hotel. They have their last meal at 5.30 so we had nothing to eat at all! And very nearly we both became pretty bad tempered and complaining, which was a pity! However we woke up feeling much better and spent the whole day sight-seeing.

It is a glorious old town, built in the early 15th to late 16th centuries. The whole town is dominated by the huge fortress built on a hill in the centre of the town – looking just like a castle in Hans Anderson's fairy tales, complete with moat, spires and towers. We first saw it on entering the town, all rose-coloured by the setting sun. It was a wonderful sight. We walked up to it, and looked down on Salzburg and into Bavaria. It is so different from the Dolomite country – all the mountains look calmer and quieter with their bright green grass slopes and fir forests.

We went to *Rosenkavalier* in the evening. Not until the very last moment did we get tickets for the opera as the b- Americans wouldn't co-operate in the slightest. However David contacted a brother in law of the Conductor of the Vienna Opera Orchestra (as no-one else in the world would!) and at literally two minutes to six he arrived with them. After all this we arrived at the doors just as they were closing for the first act – and nothing would persuade the little man to open them until the end of the act.

I nearly went mad, but just before I actually threw a fit another little chap came up and said that he would get us in all right. We were then led by devious passages round the back of the Opera House and in the end found ourselves behind the stage! It was with the greatest effort that I prevented David stepping straight onto the stage! It really was great fun watching everything from the wrong end – and hearing such wonderful singing.

Then we managed to get to our perfect seats in the fifth row of the stalls. Oh, it was a wonderful performance – and such a lovely opera. I shall never forget it – or David's face when I told him that we had missed dinner! I must say I was very hungry – but it was tricky avoiding a scene. We went to bed early and woke up with the sun streaming through the windows and all the church bells in Salzburg ringing in Sunday.

We wandered about the town till eleven o'clock and then went to the concert. I couldn't have asked for a better programme. John Barbirolli conducted the Vienna Philharmonic. They played a Rossini Overture, then Elgar's *Introduction* and *Allegro for Strings*, Mozart's Third and Brahms' No 1. The whole performance was quite magnificent and breath-taking and spine-tingling. Never have I heard such an orchestra or seen such a conductor together.

We left straight after the concert and drove away from lovely Salzburg to Berchtesgaden and there we 'did' Hitler's house, etc, just like American tourists! It is the most remarkable place and most interesting. He did choose a glorious site for his house, looking over the Bavarian mountains.

We then drove on to Kitzbuhel and stayed at the French Hotel there. (How very much more helpful they were than the Americans!) It is a perfect little village and we were given a lovely room in the hotel. I should love to take you there one day (so many places we must see together!). The manager came and had a drink with us after dinner. He was most interesting about the Duke of Windsor who always stayed at the hotel (and rather indiscreet!).

The next morning we drove through Innsbruck (a large dull place) and over the Brenner Pass down into the Italian plains and up again into the Dolomites to Cortina, where we stayed the night. It is so different to Bavaria – but so lovely too.

We got back here yesterday for tea and I was told that I would be leaving on Sat 24th – the time is very close. I dined with Jack and Judy last night. Just us three, and such fun. Judy told me that she is having a baby – so you can't tell me first! Delighted! How lovely for her. She assures me that it was all the greatest error!

I got your letter (and photograph, rather a nice one!!) this morning. How lovely if I could come to Manderston. I shall have to ring you up on arrival as I don't know yet where I go to collect my Release Suit! But I suspect Catterick. If so, I could come straight on. But obviously it would really be better to see the family first and then come up. It must be unsatisfactory for you not to know definitely – but I'm not being vague; I simply just don't know how long it takes to be released, etc! We will have to make plans on the telephone!!

The next two days will be pretty vile. This evening the Sqn are giving me a party – 'for he's a jolly good fellow, etc, etc.' You know how dreadfully sad I'll be and just how much I'll hate it. Then Friday night the Officers' Party. You will be thinking of me and knowing how sad I am in one half of me. If it wasn't for you I would be utterly miserable. Already I am saying "this is the last time I will ever do this, or see that."

This book contains coupons authorising the supply of 6 units of motor fuel during each of the first three months.

CONSERVE YOUR PETROL RATION.

1. Co-operate with your friends or neighbours in sharing the use of a car. One car instead of two can often be used for a necessary journey.

2. Driving at high speeds is very wasteful of petrol. 28 to 30 miles per hour is the most economical speed. Do not accelerate violently. Avoid heavy braking.

3. Switch off your engine when the car is standing idle.

4. Remember that the maintenance of correct tyre pressure and regular cleaning of plugs and tuning of your engine will materially increase your mileage per gallon.

This coupon is subject to the conditions that the supply of motor fuel is only made into the tank of the vehicle bearing the number shown on the front of this book and not into any other container, that this book is produced at the time of such supply and that this coupon is detached by the dealer at such time. Motor fuel must only be supplied during the period for which this coupon is expressed to be valid. The particulars below must be filled in by the dealer at the time of such supply.

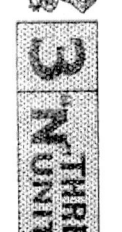

Name and Address of Dealer:

(Quantity supplied if less than the quantity authorised.)
GALLONS

This coupon is subject to the conditions that the supply of motor fuel is only made into the tank of the vehicle bearing the number shown on the front of this book and not into any other container, that this book is produced at the time of such supply and that this coupon is detached by the dealer at such time. Motor fuel must only be supplied during the period for which this coupon is expressed to be valid. The particulars below must be filled in by the dealer at the time of such supply.

Name and Address of Dealer:

(Quantity supplied if less than the quantity authorised.)
GALLONS

PETROL COUPONS

NQ 35992
NOT TRANSFERABLE
This coupon is issued under the authority of the MINISTER of FUEL and POWER

3 THREE UNITS

This coupon is VALID ONLY for the SECOND MONTH

ATTENTION IS DRAWN TO THE PROVISIONS AND CONDITIONS APPEARING OVERLEAF

NQ 35992
Motor Fuel Ration Book
FOR THE FIRST THREE MONTHS
Private Motor Car

14-19 H.P.

This Book is the property of His Majesty's Government

Registered No. of Vehicle: UN 4116

Date and Office of Issue:

The coupons in this book authorise the acquisition of the number of units of motor fuel specified on the coupons. The issue of a ration book does not guarantee to the holder any minimum quantity of motor fuel and the coupons contained in this book may be cancelled at any time. Any person furnishing or acquiring motor fuel otherwise than in accordance with the provisions of the Order for the time being in force under which these coupons are issued or contrary to the conditions appearing thereon will be liable to prosecution.

NQ 35992
NOT TRANSFERABLE
This coupon is issued under the authority of the MINISTER of FUEL and POWER

3 THREE UNITS

This coupon is VALID ONLY for the SECOND MONTH

ATTENTION IS DRAWN TO THE PROVISIONS AND CONDITIONS APPEARING OVERLEAF

Footnotes to Part IV

56. Judge Adrian Head - a great friend at Oxford and thereafter. His elder brother, Henry, was Captain of the School at Eton when I first went there. Adrian was at Dartmouth when he became ill with Polio (then called Infantile Paralysis) and had to leave.

57. Jimmy Galbraith, Lt Commander, James.

58. Talboys, his history Tutor.

59. Boso Roi: We saw a great deal of him (see later). In fact he was a keen Fascist and very unreliable acquaintance!

60. Had been Master of the Beagles at Eton: a good friend.

61. Sir Ashley Ponsonby, Bt, KCVO, MC, later Lord Lieutenant of Oxfordshire.

62. Villa Roi and the gardens were in perfect condition which was surprising considering the state of the neighbouring houses. Later, when I got to know the family better, I asked Marquesa Roi how it was that the house and garden were so well maintained. "Oh, don't be silly Bill. It was a German mess a month ago."

63. *Night & Day*, a favourite dance tune.

64. Lancer was later taken over by Derek Allhusen.

65. Mr Hardwige was our Regimental Sergeant Major. He was a pre-war cavalry 9th Lancer, the most important man after the Colonel! We subalterns were very frightened of him – but he was a charming man: "You call me Sir, and I call you Sir." We young subalterns had to appear before him for a test on Regimental History etc. When he asked me what the Regimental colours were I said 'Red and Yellow.' Oh no, 'Scarlet and Old Gold.' He wore breeches and boots and always looked immaculate. A brilliant horseman.

66. Alec Simpson, 16th/5th Lancers, was a very experienced shot, having stalked before the War in Scotland. We saw a lot of him.

67.   At my Tutor's at Eton (later Lord Brookborough, succeeding his father in Northern Ireland). It was he who had a great argument with Henry Lumsden about the relative merits of N. Ireland over Scotland. This argument developed into a fight. All the Lower boys moved furniture from John's room into the passage. We then formed a ring and the fight began. After some time (when there was much blood flowing) M' Dame (as House Matrons were known) Mrs Peacock, was sent for. The fight was stopped but we were all beaten! My Tutor was furious with us.

68.   At Klagenfürt.

69.   Charles Ashton had won a DSO as a subaltern in France in 1940. He and his twin, Pat, had hunted the Christ Church Beagles before the War.

70.   David Laurie.

71.   Python. Repatriation to U.K.

72.   Angus Rowan-Hamilton.

73.   Lorna's cousin.

74.   Waiting for a further operation on my fingers.

75.   Sir John Thompson of Woodperry, later Lord Lieutenant of Oxfordshire and Chairman of Barclays Bank.

76.   Jeannine Bridgeman, married first Alan Scott and secondly, Admiral Josef Bartosik.

77.   141 Banbury Road, where the evacuees from London lived after moving from Adwell.

78.   To ring up Scotland one had to book a 'long distance' call through the exchange. Often there were long delays. Telegrams were much more reliable.

79.   An old bachelor called Spencer Thornton who adopted Jean and Peggy.

80. Hill End Hospital, St Albans. My plastic surgeon, Mr Mowlem, operated there. He did a great job on my fingers. (Operation Feb 1st.)

81. Ribton Crampton in B Squadron, came from Canada.

82. I think that this pow-wow was when Hugh Bailie asked about "my intentions" regarding Lorna.

83. Offered to go there as ADC.

84. My wireless operator during the fighting, an extremely clever fellow whose technical knowledge was frightening; absolutely cool under all conditions.

85. Major Peter Thompson-Glover, late RHA and transferred to 9th Lancers at the end of the War. He later married Harry Graham-Vivian's sister, Catherine. I was their Trustee.

86. Interesting that my chest troubles started in 1946. My doctors constantly ask this question and now I can tell them – 60 years ago!

87. Owned by the Volpe family; a truly glorious Palladian villa, also a lovely garden.

88. He had replaced Sgt Edmunds as my Troop Sergeant.

89. The Croppers lived near Kendal, not far from Lake Windermere. Their son, Anthony, drove though Africa with my father and mother – and Cynthia and Rosamund. (See *High Street Africa* written by my father.)

90. General Morgan was the architect of this imaginary line.

91. This was a serious drama!

92. Freddie was one of the evacuee children living at 141 Banbury Road. A very attractive little boy (who knew it!).

93. The same thing happened in Vienna.

94. He had a dicey heart and was not with us during the fighting. He had been on a staff job in Gibraltar (later Brigadier Lord Grimthorpe).

95. I had considererd qualifying as a doctor when still at Eton, hence my reading General Science when I went up to Oxford in 1942. But the attraction of this profession faded as I grew older.

96. Sue Mattingley, who married John Berry. She is Adrian Palmer's Godmother.

97. Dr Russell, who taught me at Oxford in 1942; a particularly charming man and a brilliant tutor.

98. Bobby Chaworth Musters hunted the Eton Beagles before I became joint Master with Julien Mond. Simon Bland (Willie Bell's cousin) later became Equerry to the Duke of Gloucester.

99. Duino, a beautiful castle looking out to sea, requisitioned from Prince Thurn and Taxis. (Years later I returned with Colin Harris and had a drink with him. He showed us some damage done, allegedly, by British soldiers. Not very tactful or courteous!)

100. I well remember this episode. Quite apart from the fact that losing a tank (which I thought probable) was a most serious offence, I knew that some of the crew were unable to swim. In fact we recovered the tank the next day.

101. She had made great friends with a Danish girl called Ingrid Riska, who came to Adwell before the War.

102. Hugh Euston (later Duke of Grafton) became engaged to my friend John Smith's sister, Fortune, who was later Mistress of the Robes.

103. Laura, a Hanover mare which I spotted (with John Joicey) when we went up to collect horses belonging to German cavalry regiments. A wonderful horse, the mother of Laurian which Derek rode in the Olympic Games.

Nik Humphreys
Aged 17
1940

221

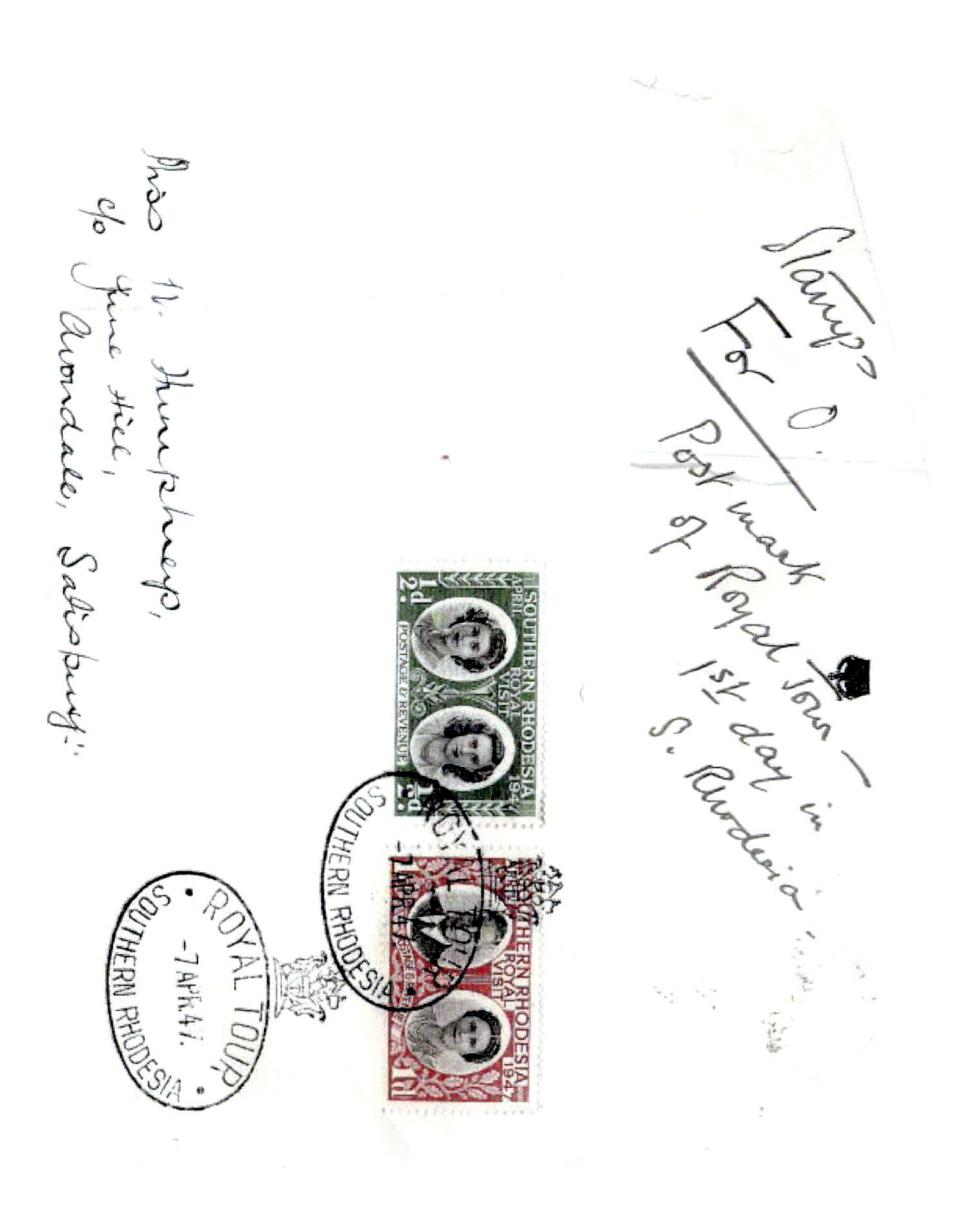

POST MARK OF ROYAL TOUR – 1ST DAY IN SOUTHERN RHODESIA
7 APRIL 1947

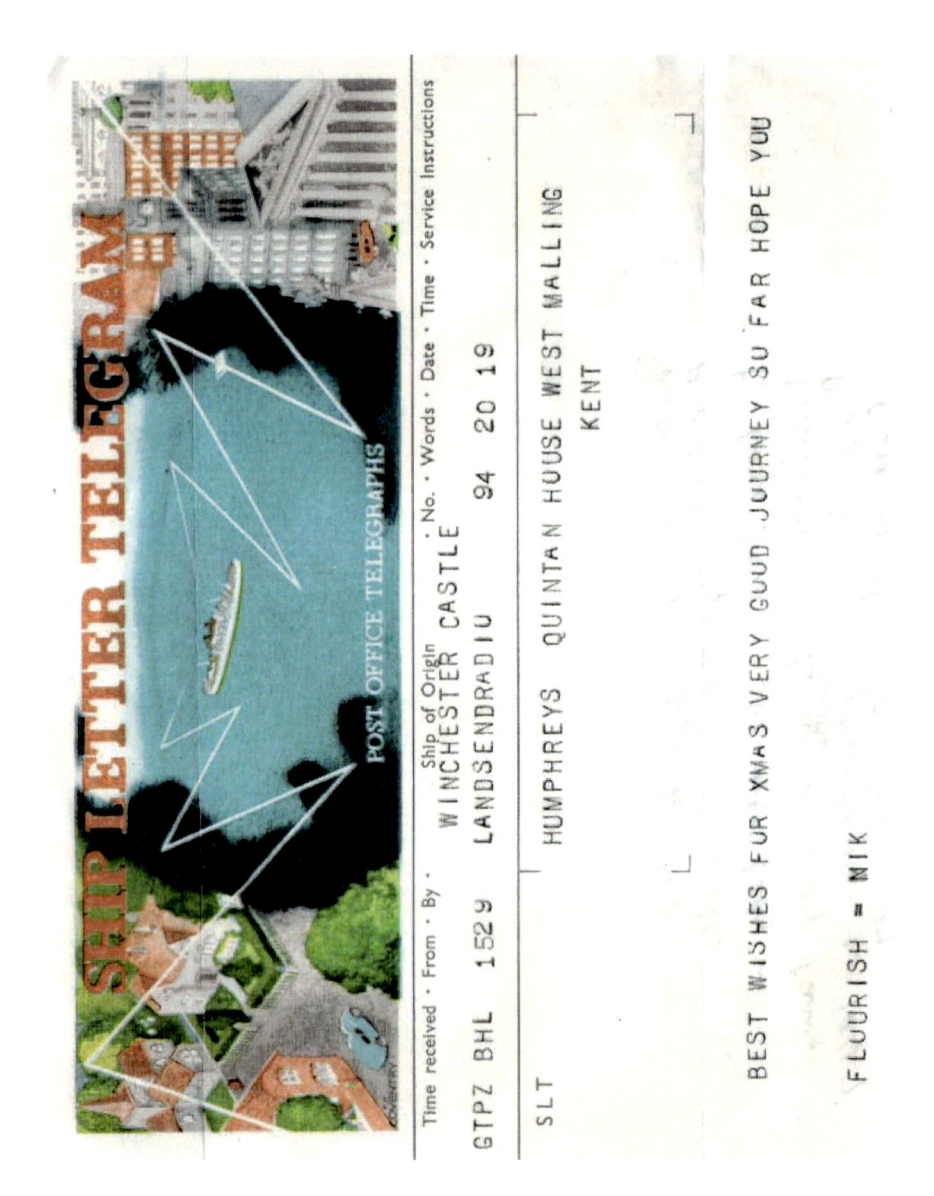

Ship's telegram sent by Nik B.R. (née Humphreys)
en route to Cape Town, 9th December 1946.
She was Lady-in-Waiting to Lady Kennedy, wife of the Governor,
during the Royal Tour of Southern Rhodesia in 1947

Part V
A Civilian again and back at Oxford
September 1946 – April 1948

I left the Regiment at the end of August. I remember how nice and kind everyone was, a whole crowd coming to see me off. Jack Price seemed sad at my going. It was a big break with the past. We had all grown up together over the last year. When you rely on someone for your life you get very close to them!

So, with some trepidation I set forth to England, arriving back in early September 1946, and my letters to Lorna from then till the end of the year were not, inexplicably, among those in the box. So I will have to rely on my memory for those four months.

It was, of course, an important phase in my life. I found getting back into stride in 'civvy street' (as we called civilian life) required a huge effort – talk about having to be adaptable! I found enormous changes. You simply can't imagine what poor London looked like after the bombing – and, for the first time, everyone talked about money. This was a subject which was never mentioned in 'civilized' society and, in our family, the fact that someone was rich was almost despised. The idea that someone should actually want to make money was abhorred. My father was very shocked, if not ashamed, that brother Dickie, on leaving the Army (a gentlemanly profession) became a stockbroker. In this connection I should explain that when I was about fifteen my Ponsonby grandfather took me aside and said "If you ever have any capital, you should invest it in Government bonds - don't go near the Stock Exchange." Economies had to be made at Adwell; writing paper no longer embossed! No footman, for goodness' sake! The garden staff reduced to three men, etc, etc. Food and clothes rationing. Not so many deb. dances.

And then there was Oxford; I returned in October 1946. I was given back my old room in the Old Library which was lovely. I had decided to take my father's advice and read Law; so interviews with my prospective tutor, Steven Grant Baillie, took place. I wondered what on earth I was doing – but I had to do something and a legal training seemed a fairly sensible option – though I'd no idea what it was like to be a barrister! I simply couldn't settle down. I felt completely 'rudderlesss.' Here I was, aged nearly 23, with no idea what I was going to do in life – and longing to be back in the Regiment with my brother officers and an organised army life.

In casting around for a possible job, I had a talk with my Uncle Charles Ponsonby. His wife, my Aunt Winifred, was Walter Aldenham's sister and Charles Ponsonby arranged for me to meet him, the Chairman of the family bank Antony Gibbs & Son. So a few weeks later I duly presented myself at the bank in Bishopsgate. I was met at the door by the Chief Clerk who preceded me up a sort of aisle, with glazed doors on each size. At the 'East end' of the aisle was a huge partner's desk and there sat the Chairman (Lord Aldenham) on one side and, opposite him, his brother Geoffrey Gibbs. I had met both of them before so no introductions were necessary. I sat down and I was told, very briefly, what the job entailed and how much I would be paid (£800 per year)[104]. Without further discussion I was told that I would (not could) start the following month. This was all rather surprising and, I thought, lacked detail! So I asked the Chairman whether it would be possible for him to dictate a letter to his secretary, setting out the main points of the job. "In this office" he said with some firmness "we do not dictate letters, we write them." A silver bell was then rung; in came the secretary who was told to return with the copying machine. In the meantime he started writing the requested letter. Then the secretary returned pushing a massive mahogany trolley which carried, I guessed, the copier. I was right and the letter was handed to the secretary who placed it, face downwards, on a plate containing some form of wax. Then the letter was pressed down onto the waxed plate by a complex screwing mechanism. Then, hey presto, one copy was given to Walter Aldenham and the original to me. It was a very short letter and, having read it, I asked whether I might be allowed a few days to consider the offer. This caused consternation, but he agreed with obvious reluctance. I then started the long walk back, down the aisle. Doors started to open, first Antony Gibbs (Walter's son), David Campbell (cousin) and Dan Ranfurly (married to a cousin). They asked me to lunch at the City Club. "When are you starting?" they asked. I told them that I was almost certainly going to refuse the offer. This was met with incredulity! How lucky I was to be offered a place in the bank, how ungrateful I was and, anyway, what was I going to do instead etc. I wrote back the next day what I hope was an appropriate letter saying that I had decided to read for the Bar.

This is, I know, a rather lengthy deviation from my description of life in post war Oxford, but the episode illustrates the way in which the City of London operated in those days. Here I was, a 'connection' with the Gibbs family, looking *for a job and with typical generosity they offered me employment because they considered me 'one of them.' I suspect that my decision was influenced by this - I wanted to stand on my own feet.*

There were many friends who had returned to Oxford on their demobilisation and some eighteen year olds who had come up for the first time. Tom Quad was full of prams with young wives pushing their babies round Mercury[105] and there were also many wheelchairs whose occupants had lost legs in the War. It was, of course, a male dominated society with ages varying from 27 (for example Ludo Kennedy) to 19 (Willie Gladstone). The President of the J.C.R. (Junior Common Room) was Tony Chevenix-Trench (later Head Master of Eton). He was, I suppose, about 26 and had been a prisoner of the Japanese for nearly 3 years. He organised (having been asked to do so by the Dean, Dr Lowe) a group of us to take on responsibility for certain sectors and I was allocated the Christ Church Boys Club (near the Oval in London). This was a job which I took seriously and you will find further references to it in some of my letters.

The other job was to get the Beagles going again. This was quite a task because there were no hounds at the kennels in Garsington and I had to beg, borrow or steal to get a pack together. Of course Ronnie Wallace was a great help, as were the Eton Beagles (which had not been disbanded during the War). Richard Goodenough[106] was also an enthusiastic, albeit unreliable, supporter. We started again with 9 or 10 couple of hounds with Bob Manners and John Bickersteth whipping in to me – and, of course, Roy and Walter Clinkard as the professionals in the kennels. (See Picture of Walter on page 254.)

I'm afraid (as will become only too clear!) that my legal studies took a very low priority. It certainly didn't help having such an idle and unenthusiastic tutor as Grant Baillie to teach me. I was not the only one to find the situation extremely unsatisfactory. Indeed, early on in the Michaelmas (October) term, I met Michael Joicey who was on his way to my room in the Old Library carrying a load of law books. "These are for you," he said "I simply can't go on with that impossible man a moment longer."

By the time that the letters recommence (in January 1947) I had completed my first term on my return to Oxford. By then things had, I think, settled down. There were horses and beagles to hunt foxes and hares respectively! And old friends to meet again and catch up on our various activities during the last two years of War. My scout, Walters, was kept busy washing up plates and glasses (mostly the latter!) as my room was very often occupied by friends – almost entirely male. (Once I had Caroline Scott, Johnnie's sister, to tea alone. This was considered almost scandalous and certainly very daring!)

W.B.R. HUNTING CHRIST CHURCH BEAGLES
RICHARD GOODENOUGH BEHIND, SEPTEMBER 1947

Agree to be Master of Christ Church Beagles: September 16th 1946

I've spent the last week at Adwell practically alone as Mother and Father went down to Wales last Monday and only returned this evening. Father was pretty groggy all the time they were there – oh, Darling, I sometimes feel so terribly depressed and unhappy about him when I allow myself to remember what he was like before I joined the Regiment. He is, I think, a very ill man – and he takes very little interest in anything.

Poor Mother was absolutely dead beat when she arrived back – she goes to Oxford all day tomorrow, and up to London on Thursday, etc, and so it goes on without a break. Her 'holiday' has, of course, been a constant strain for her, and she now looks more tired than she did before she left for Wales.

I thought at first that I would have to ring you up – however the week has gone very quickly, and I have had great fun – my Oxford plans are now well in hand, and I go up to London on Thursday to see my Tutor (who I am told is not all that pleasant.) I forget if I told you that my rooms are on the first floor of the Old Library at the end of the passage (where Chinless Mitchel lived!) – they really aren't too bad but will need a lot of getting into!

Tommy Hutchinson[107] asked me again to be Master of the Beagles. I told him that I simply couldn't afford the time. So the following plan has been decided upon. I shall hunt the beagles twice a week – and this would be my sole responsibility. Finance, farmers, hounds, etc will be looked after by a Hunt Committee presided over by Hugh Trevor Roper (a young Don I know quite well). This will mean that I give up foxhunting this season – but am willing to do that. I am going to be absolutely firm that I do only hunt hounds and nothing else – as I can't afford the time to mess about with the many other duties. What do you think of all this? I feel that it will work well – but I realise that I shall have to be strong-minded about it. I am going in to see Hugh T. R about it all tomorrow.

I shot with Mr Jim Morrell on Saturday at Culham – and saw St Helen's in the distance. We had a good day, and got 48 brace of partridges and the odd hare. But, oh, I've got so slow! I hope it will come back – but I am afraid that my fingers do hinder me a bit.

I'm also taking Mother, Betsy Ponsonby and Rosemary Hare to the Opera tomorrow evening. I wonder whether you have seen it. I rather doubt whether I shall like it.

I have had masses of letters from the Regiment which is lovely. I do miss them all so much. I quite forgot to say that I haven't got the book (thank goodness) or left my social history at Manderston. I wonder where it has got to. I remember him talking about the man – so he'll hate to lose it.

I had a letter from Galbiati. He is not in Italy! He hopes to see me and my young lady friend soon.

First meeting with my Law Tutor, Grant Bailey: October 1st 1946

Lovely getting a letter from you yesterday. I am so glad that all is well with you. I have had 'pangs' – but nothing more! I search Oxford whenever I go there – but never see even a Vauxhall! I have been fearfully busy (essential) and there is masses to do here.

Father being in bed so much and Mother permanently rushing off somewhere has helped to get Adwell into an appalling state. However it is better now. The great thing is that Father is really better and up and about in this lovely weather. (Thank God that it has come – we have nearly cut all the corn now, and I think the harvest has been saved by stint of a good deal of hard work on all sides.)

I forgot to tell you that I went to a party with Stephanie M.P. at some country club the other day. She said she had seen me somewhere before – with the Bridgemans she thought! I liked her very much.

I went to the *Rape of L.* the other night with Ros, Rosemary Hare, Mother and Mue Dashwood (who also made comments!). I like her too! But odd.

Tomorrow I go to the kennels then on to stay with the Goodenoughs at Filkins to shoot on Wednesday. Back on Thursday for dinner here when the Glyns and Balfours are coming, and shoot here on Saturday. Then I'm static till I go back to Ch. Ch. on the 11th.

Can you come to Oxford one day next week?? (I'm not being weak, please!) and to the theatre and look at my rooms (which are rather grim!). I will ring you up about it.

I haven't even commented on Italy. What a lovely plan. Darling, you will love it so much. But I wish that I was going to show you it first myself. I have still got all the maps and guide books which we will go through together.

I was bored with the sermon on Sunday and 'looking about' when I saw the word San Remo on one of the memorial tablets. It appears that my Great-Grandfather died there (probably in one of the Mattingley hotels!) Small world.

My polyphotos have arrived. Most unfortunate, as throughout my collar is sticking out! You'll hate that. Otherwise they're only fairly awful! You shall have them if you like.

It's now 1.30am and I'm supposed to be reading Law! Oh, must tell you about my Tutor. Having been directed to the top of one of the houses in Greys Inn, I knocked on the door which was soon opened by a somewhat unique looking individual. His dress was sombre. From the top downwards: Long hair nearly to shoulders, unshaved, dirty. Black threadbare coat, striped trousers ending in tatters, carpet slippers. "Is Mr Grant Bailey in?" I asked.

"Are you Birch Reynardson?"

"Yes."

"Well, come in, me boi. I'm your Tutor." Somewhat taken aback, I was led through a room layered thickly in dust and books to his bedroom. "I'll have to see yer in 'ere as there's no room in me study." He threw me a pillow off his bed and I sat on the floor and he 'reclined' on his bed.

His room smelt more than possibly repulsive – and I was hardly surprised when three cats (I do not exaggerate!) jumped out of his bed. "Me cats, dear things" was all he said.

And for the next hour he talked very deeply on the philosophy of Law, ending by handing me six books to be read by the beginning of term! I see him again on the 7th.

Lorna goes to Italy; Hunting at Woodperry: 4th January 1947

I have been thinking of you so much and longing to be with you. I wonder so much how the journey went and how Italy looks now. I know how you will love it – it's the most glorious country. I wonder when your first letter will come.

Life has been more than hectic since you went away – which really has been rather a good thing. I rang up Mother when I got back from Victoria Station – and she said that I wasn't to come home – but was to leave Kit and Ros alone at Adwell! So I had to stay all day in London. Rather the limit. However the time seemed to go very quickly. I went to see the King's pictures and there met David Price and Hubert Miller Stirling and we walked round together which was fun as they are both ultra arty and knew all about them!

I then went and had my hair cut! Mr Thomas was in very good form as he had just cut Prince Michael's hair! He told me all the news of the Regiment!

I went up to Cynthia's for tea and found Humphrey there with his arm in a sling as he had had a badish fall out hunting on Boxing Day and torn his shoulder muscles – awfully painful for the poor old boy. We spent a quiet evening together and I caught the 10.32 down to Adwell on Thursday morning.

Dick and Ruth Fanshawe and Bill and Diana Hesketh (who have just come to live near here) came to dinner in the evening. Dick had a lot to say about me not coming out hunting on Boxing Day, asked where I was, etc. He is very dangerous at dinner parties!

I started for Somerset with Mavis Honey on Friday morning. Well I've learned my lesson. Never again. Honestly Darling, you have no idea what a ghastly dance it was – and it took us four hours to get there! No Tone! I didn't know a soul and was never introduced to anyone. We got in at 3.30 and I started back again at 7.30.

We had a very good hunt at Woodperry but by the end of the day I really felt out! I went fast to sleep having tea at Woodperry and they left me till 7 when I had to change for the Flemings' dance. A very good party of us dined at the Holland-Hibberts and we all trooped to Barton. Really great fun. Pilbeam's band and lots of champagne (I needed it!). I got back here at 4 am.

Read the lessons in church this morning – rather frightened as I hadn't read them through – however Mother seemed to approve of the drawl! I went over to see Sir Donald Somerville with her this afternoon. He was the Attorney General and a most charming and helpful man. I talked to him for ages – he was most instructive and thinks that even if I do not become a barrister, the Law training will be useful in any profession.

Bicester Hunt Ball;
visit to London to Law Tutor:
15 January 1947

Such a lovely long letter from you this morning, but the post is ghastly – the two postcards arrived with the letter. I hope that you got mine all right. Anyway I realised that it was pointless to write to Italy as they seem to take at least ten days to arrive.

Poor Darling – what a ghastly journey you seem to have had – but I knew you would love Venice and Cortina. Oh how I'm longing to hear all about it. I'll ring you up on Friday night and we'll make plans.

Did you have a lovely birthday? I did remember it and thought of you so much (promise!). I haven't bought you a birthday present as I don't know what you want.

Nothing particularly startling has occurred since I last wrote. Kit has now returned to his Regiment which is sad and Humphrey and Cynthia go to London tomorrow. It has been lovely having them here.

Mrs Shuttle has given notice! I'm delighted! But everybody takes a very pessimistic view of getting another cook. Anyway she doesn't leave us until March.

We all went to the Bicester Hunt Ball the other night (Ros and Kit, Humphrey and Cynthia, Bill Heathcote, Diana Houldsworth, Bridget Ransom, Mary Ponsonby and self) which was great fun. There I saw Betty Laurie who says that she thinks that Roddie has turned David down – do you think there is any truth in this amazing theory? I pray it isn't true.

Betsy Ponsonby arrived from Switzerland last night – out of the blue. Nobody knew that she was coming. She doesn't seem to want to do anything – and talks completely vaguely about 'getting a job' in London.

I spent a very dull day in London today. Saw my tutor and sat in the Courts listening to rather dull cases all afternoon – and am now in rather a bad temper.

Oxford in winter;
beagling:
January 1947

I hope you never caught my complaint – I still haven't recovered, and keep getting these maddening headaches every evening. I can't think of anything much worse than beagling tomorrow – but perhaps by then it will have gone.

We had a pretty awful day on Tuesday – but my day was made as Mary Wakefield was out – and came into my room this morning to make arrangements for getting out tomorrow! I only hope Mrs Williams[108] does not hear about it!

I have had three telephone messages from Ann this evening. She wanted me to go up to London to have dinner with them (Verly, etc) tonight. I thought it a bit far. And anyway I have just returned from having dinner with the Holland-Hibberts at Beckley. Lavinia is off to Rome on Wednesday on some government job to deal with the Jugoslavs left in Italy. Lucky thing will be there for 6 months. She will be on FitzRoy Maclean's staff.

I had an immensely depressed letter from David with all the regimental news. David WS, Guy Hannen etc (all those non-regular officers whose time is fairly nearly up) are being left behind and "nobody will be left who I like". It does look a gloomy prospect – and a bit of an anti-climax after Cortina.

I am writing to you in my overcoat – it really is bitterly cold, and my coal has run out. Johnnie Dalkeith has lent me his radiogram – a rather nice one, and I've got some lovely music from Adwell, etc. Glorious Beethoven piano concertos (I'm playing the 3rd now) played by Backhaus most beautifully.

I had a long session with my Tutor this morning, having read the longest essay I've ever written to him. He is an extraordinary man – quite brilliant, but absolutely lacking in any sort of personality. He doesn't help me much – but on the other hand he does know his Law and can always answer any question that is asked.

For the first time in my life I've got a photograph by my bed – I've never had one there because I've never seen one that is like you – and I've always thought it better for me to remember you each night as you are before I go to sleep. But somehow I do love having it there, it is more tangible to look at a photograph and see you with my eyes.

I went to a lecture yesterday morning by David Cecil on the Romantic Poets (Shelley, Keats, Burns, etc). What men they were! At one moment, ecstatically happy and then, having reached such a height of bliss, they crash down into the abyss of depression and wretched sadness. They wrote almost selfishly about their emotions – but most wonderfully. I don't really understand them – and only sometimes glimpse at their minds. I wish I could write – perhaps I will try some day. But somehow everything seems to be pushed aside because 'there is not time' – but somewhere I'm sure there is.

Towcester Races:
April 7th 1947

Rather grim wasn't it – how I loathe this saying goodbye. And for days afterwards I feel so incomplete without you.

I drove on to the Berrys – quite extraordinary – and far odder than anything you can imagine. A dear old Father who speaks with a broad accent straight from the Welsh mountains – no Mother - but John quite unchanged and charming. He has no idea what to do, having been turned down for Oxford – but now talks about going up to London to get trained as a chartered accountant which is, I suppose, quite a good idea – but, of course, it takes ages to qualify.

We all went to Towcester today – it really was great fun, but not, naturally, without incident! Humphrey, Cynthia, Mary and I went in the Rover while Betsy, Ros and Kit went in the little Standard. Our ways parted at Thame as they thought it was quicker to go by Aylesbury – and I thought that Buckingham was the way (and hasten to say that I was right!) However, after climbing the hill out of High Winchendon (just out of Thame) a most curious smell was complained of by the girls sitting behind. We quelled their complaints for some few minutes, but it soon became quite obvious that something 'had gone wrong.'

I opened the bonnet of the car and was practically asphyxiated by the fumes which rose belching from its innards! Naturally I soon found the cause (I was so pleased!). The pipe leading from the radiator was broken! I told Cynthia to switch the engine off, which she did, but it was so hot that it kept on running! After a time it cooled off and stopped. I then approached a house and knocked on the door and out came a beautiful girl who turned out to be a Swede! A great deal of explanation was then needed to get hold of a bucket of water, spanners, etc, - and in three quarters of an hour we were on our way again.

Not till Bicester did the next crisis arrive. Just as we were entering the Market Square the hooter began to sound. Nothing on earth would stop it. In the end we got out, having decided to cut the wire to the horn. After tremendous efforts we managed to cut it, but were surprised that the horn still worked. At the crucial moment a little man arrived, who pointed out that we had cut a pipe in the lubrication system and not one that had anything to do with the horn. This was obviously rather an error!

However in the end we did cut the right wire and we arrived at Towcester only having missed the first race (and, after all, we are used to that!). It is a lovely course and the sun was out. There were masses of people around. But, best of all, Susan Ham and Ashley – we had a great gossip. She was in such good form, but obviously loathed the horses! We all lost money all day – except Humphrey and Cynthia who did back one horse at 12:1 which saved the family fortunes!

I am writing to you from the Library. A most heated discussion is taking place – the following are concerned: Mother, Ros and Mary. Kit is sitting smoking his pipe quite comfortably and serenely. I have been told (by Ros) not to get heated and am therefore furious – but managed not to show it too much. But it does make it rather difficult to try and write to you – particularly as now the subject has got to illegits which is, quite obviously, the subject to be avoided at all costs! If I dared to intervene I should be told that I was narrow-minded, intolerant and pompous. Oh – it is such a pity that I can no longer talk to Ros nowadays. I wonder why it is. I honestly don't think I am entirely to blame.

Later: I went to bed very late last night as Ros insisted on taking

Kit into Oxford to catch the train up to Newcastle – and so Mary and I waited up for her till 12 pm and had a very good talk. She is in my good books at the moment! And now I've just arrived back from London. The Rover went quite beautifully. My Tutor seems satisfied with me which is lucky.

I called in on the Allhusens coming back. They are so nice. He is going as 2 i/c to the Lanarkshire Yeomanry next week – he's rather disappointed not to be with Peter T-G and he will be in a pretty grim place. I shall see him at Cheltenham on Saturday.

I hope that you are having a lovely stay with Sue. I will send this to the Lansdowne as I don't know where you will be in London.

Telephone:
LECHLADE 10.

LANGFORD HOUSE,
LECHLADE,
GLOS.

Cheltenham Races:
14th April 1947

Thank you so much for your lovely letter which arrived this morning. What a bore that you never got my last letter. I wrote it and addressed it to The Lansdowne where I thought you would almost certainly go during your visit. Goodness knows where they will send it. And now I'm in bad books. I am sorry Darling.

Penelope Fairbairn is nearly right about Dick. He is due back for about 3 months on 25th – a week after Father. Won't it be fun? So everything is now done to 'get ready not only for Father but also for Dickie'.

I am so sorry about Sue. I didn't think that she looked to be in very good form (can always sense the situation acutely!). It must be pretty grim for her. The obvious answer is for her to get married – and the equally obvious danger is for her to rush into it in her hurry to get away from the scullery!

I am now back from Langford after a most unusual visit! Each member of the family is, individually, as different from the other as chalk from cheese. Cheltenham was enormous fun. I love the course anyway – but with the wonderful day and masses of nice people, it really was perfect. (Except that I lost money throughout.)

I saw Tone[109] and had a word with him – which was not particularly embarrassing! Also Brigadier and Mrs Brett – both in a foul temper as they had missed the first two races owing to the Brigadier failing to start in time. Zandra,[110] of course, mouth bright red – but looking very nice. Juliet, the Bridgemans, Eliz. Lambart – all staying at Dowdeswell. Ronnie Wallace, poor chap looking pretty lonely – particularly as Jean and Peggy were both there. Ashley and Lavinia, etc, etc.

Lord Grimthorpe[111] won the Gold Cup with Fortina (rhyming with Cortina – and so nearly put some money on it!) and Kit told me about the horse as he saw it when he was staying up there. I went and had a drink out of his gold cup on the way back. He was so excited about it.

After dinner we decided (or it was decided for me) to go back to Cheltenham to dance at the Lillybrook Hotel. So we set off in two cars; June,[112] Winifred,[113] Phinola, Brewis and self in the Rover – Gerald and Richard Sale in his car. There we found Zandra (I can never attempt to dance without seeing her!), David Beaman and Pat what's-her-name (the usual girl!). We got into the most appalling racing crowd including Lorry Gardner who owns Knights Pass who was second in the Foxhunters. He declared that he was a cousin of David L's. He wouldn't have owned him!

We started back at 2, and arrived back at Langford at three. As Gerald had not arrived I decided to wait for him. At 3.30 he had not returned, and I felt that I had to go back and find him. So I started off, very tired and slightly cross. I never found his car till nearly back at Cheltenham. They had had a puncture. The only bright spot was that I for once was not broken down! We got back to Langford at 5.45 – which by double summer time was 6.45. Not particularly happy!

I spent Sunday afternoon with the Goodenoughs[114] – so lovely walking round seeing the horses, etc. I then returned to Langford and had dinner and took June and Gerald into Oxford. I was quite tired when I arrived in last night!

I go up to London on the 17th to see my Tutor at 2.30. Will you be in London that day? Couldn't we make a plan? Mother wants to go down to Southampton alone on 18th so that she can talk to Father coming back.

It terrifies me how much work I have got before May 6th! And it hasn't been going too well this morning. However – I am going over to tea at West Wycombe this afternoon to talk to Lady D about the Hunt Ball. Now that Sarah is married, people who are not Lords are, apparently, suffered in the house. I was seldom asked before but now they continually ring up and ask me over to play tennis! I played the other afternoon with Mary. Frightfully bad – and I was nearly beaten.

How I love this weather. It really is awful having to work indoors. Everything looks so perfectly lovely – and the trees are really beginning to burst with energy, and now the elm avenue[115] is showing its green against the blue sky. I wish you were here so terribly, to share it all with me.

Preparing for Father's return; Hunt Ball to be at West Wycombe: 19th April 1947

A lovely long letter from you arrived last night. I am so sorry that the Lansdowne one has never turned up – but perhaps it will be sent on to you.

I had a slightly better day in London yesterday than usual, as I lunched with Bobby Lacey Thomson. He was in 'our' Regiment and a frightfully nice person. But Oh! How awful it must be living alone in London without a penny and terribly lonely. He was very depressed, poor chap – but I hope he will come down to Adwell soon and get away from the beastly place.

My Tutor was in great form – masses of cats as usual, but unusually chatty! I came out feeling in very good form and went and had tea with Charles Parnell (who works in Jack Barclays amongst the biggest and most expensive cars). He says that there are precious few advantages except that he can drive about in an enormous Bentley and make people look at him! I rather like him – he married an Italian, which you obviously know!

I worked till the early hours this morning frightfully hard. And all today I have been 'tidying things away' before Father's arrival![116] Everyone seemed very busy doing much the same. As Cynthia says, it's a pity he doesn't go away more often, so that something is done every time he comes back!

He arrived with Mother at tea time, looking frightfully well and brown and in good form. It is lovely to have him back again after so long – though sometimes he is a bit of a 'restraining' influence, which is probably a very good thing!

Before I forget – this is most important, I saw Lady Dashwood the other day and she will allow us to have the Hunt Ball at West Wycombe in June. The only day seems to be June 21st which is the Saturday that Oxford comes down. Will you be able to get to it? You really simply must. Please Darling, make a v. big effort as I couldn't bear you not to be there (even if we aren't very good at Hunt Balls!).

Therefore I am working on this and working for my exam and they don't go well together. I am pretty frightened now as I realise that I have taken up a bit too much, and I really know nothing about the subject.

I am so glad you enjoyed being with Pam and at the Malt. I shall see Percy at the Jenkinsons. What fun. He is a very nice person, but rather a pity that Percy and Pam Browne have to be combined!

Toni and Major Morland[117] are coming over to Adwell on Sunday. It will be lovely seeing them. Poor T sounded frightfully depressed when she rang up. I wonder what the situation is.

Bicester pt to pt tomorrow. I shouldn't go but feel that I must as it is Father's first day home. It will be great fun anyway.

I will be thinking of you at the Memorial Service[118] – poor Darling, I'm afraid you will feel very sad.

I mention, for the first time, Francis Dashwood in this letter. He was a great friend of mine and a highly colourful character!

His enthusiasm for life was catching. A great talker - sometimes his stories may have lacked complete accuracy! He once rang me up in great excitement to tell me to come and look at his new pheasant laying pen. So off I went to West Wycombe. A huge pen (Francis never did anything by halves) but I couldn't see any cocks among the large number of hens. "Why are you looking so worried?" he asked. "Francis, I can't see any cocks." "Cocks," he replied. "We don't need any cocks, they don't lay eggs." Francis was, I should stress, the last person for whom biological instruction was necessary; but I had to explain that all the eggs were probably infertile and should, therefore be thrown away. He was very silent about this - he was always very generous but disliked waste!

Anyway that evening he rang me up. "Are you doing anything for lunch tomorrow?" he asked. He explained that Princess Margaret had asked herself to lunch and could I come to "help out?" I found myself sitting next to the Princess. Old Leigh, Francis and Victoria's butler, came in bearing a huge silver bowl full of pheasant eggs! "I hope you like gulls eggs, Ma'am?" asked Francis. The Princess turned to me and said, sotto voce, "Surely they're not gulls eggs." I assured her that they were and we happily ate all of them. When she left she said "I liked talking to you but you LIED."

Written from Christ Church;
(Puss is Eleanor who received a music scholarship in London) visits to Sgt Edmunds, Cpl Nicholls:
27th April 1947

I got back yesterday evening to find two letters waiting for me from you. Bless you for them. How thrilling about Puss. I wonder whether she got the scholarship. I must ring up – and take her out. It really is frightfully good.

There's a lot to report! I drove up from Adwell (in the Rover!) to Nottingham where I visited Sgt Edmunds[119] in hospital. He really is pretty ill – and frightfully depressed about everything. He has to be in bed for at least 18 months in a room open on one side to the icy wind and rain, trying hard to breathe, and too exhausted most of the time to read or write. It really is pretty dreadful for him. I didn't have time to see his doctor, but I shall write to him.

But we had a tremendous gossip about the old days. How I loved them – we were all such tremendous friends, relying on each other entirely, not only for our enjoyment but for our very lives – and that is indeed a bond for friendship, and I have never met it anywhere else.

I then drove down through Newark and Grantham to the Jenkinsons who live near Oakham and arrived in time for late tea. There I found Lavinia and her little sister Clayre and a girl called Bridget Howard.

The first evening I was filled with regret that I had ever been so utterly stupid to say that I would come! Except that we had a frightfully good dinner, we did nothing! And wasted time till about 11.30 pm making conversation (which was immensely difficult!).

But the next day we all set forth to the Cottesmore pt to pt which was fun. David Burghersh[120] rode in two races – and I saw the odd person who I knew. We got back for tea and I then went into Oakham to see Cpl Nicholls who was my old gunner. He was in tremendous form – and we drank gallons of beer together and talked and talked – until I looked at my watch and had to dash back and get dressed before going to a place in Melton Mowbray where a large party congregated to dine and dance.

It really was rather fun. Mrs Baird is a most amusing person. She was a Harcourt from Nuneham and therefore knows all the Oxfordshire people. And she is a most superb horsewoman and won all the lady's classes at Olympia and Richmond before the War. So we had a lot in common! I danced with her most of the evening which was considered odd! Lavinia is really 'a very nice young girl' – but hasn't got an awful lot to say, except about horses (which, after all, is so deadly!).

I went over to the Cottesmore kennels on Friday afternoon by myself as the others had a scavenger hunt. I was shown round by Colonel Heber-Percy, the Master, with the new Master of the North Cotswold. They have got a wonderful pack of hounds. And masses of horses.

The Hunt Ball was great fun. Percy Browne arrived for dinner with Harry Mildmay and David Bingham joined us for dinner. I knew lots of people there including Ashley and Juliet (with John Smith hovering in the background!) Mollie and Andrew Burnaby-

Atkins, the Owen Hugh Smith family, Mark Bonham Carter, etc. But they really are pretty frightful people. They all look completely debauched and unhappy. Everyone seems to be living with someone else quite openly – and they all talk scandal about each other to overcome the boredom!

I left with Percy on Saturday morning and we drove down together to Northampton where we had lunch and I put him on the London train where he was going to meet Pam and her mother. He is a nice person. We talked hard all the way down – and I hardly had time to look at the glorious country we were driving through. They will obviously be very happy together. He has all the low down about you from Pam so that made it very much easier to talk.

And now I'm back here trying to cope with (a) my work, and (b) the dance on 21st! They don't go well together. So lovely that you can come – that's much better. It will be a pretty awful responsibility! I'm afraid it will be a bit pompous as Lady Dashwood is being difficult about asking her 'friends' who are all dukes!

However Francis is being very good and helpful and I think he will do most of the work! Johnnie D is on the committee and very bolshy! He hates any dance! But otherwise he is in good form.

I will now answer your letter!

Ref Ques 4 – Toni: She looks very beautiful now. But oh, so unhappy. I could hardly bear to talk to her. And, of course, as I'm not allowed to know anything about the trouble, I wouldn't say a word. Oh I do hope she gets right again.

What a ghastly bore about the German measles. But you are bound to get it. It's fearfully catching!

I am so glad that that unveiling ceremony was done so beautifully. I thought of you so much that day – I knew how sad you would be.

About the Edinburgh Festival. It really sounds simply lovely. Johnnie wants me to stay with him to shoot. So I could come on after that. I believe it is a most wonderful programme. How very full of initiative Edinburgh is![121]

The Christ Church Ball is on May 28th. I imagined that it was going to be rather grim. But I'm told by even Johnnie that I must come. You will be at The Wharf then – so you will come, won't you? We can go away if it's grim. Will you let me know if there is a hitch and you can't make it?

Dickie sets foot in England on Tuesday. He couldn't arrive at a worse time from my pt of view what with this b. exam so close. Judy is still at Adwell! Father loves her – so I expect she will stay. I go to the Regimental Dinner on May 17th. <u>Such</u> fun. Will see Jack no doubt.

Must stop now. Johnnie, John and Harry are coming out to Adwell with me to play tennis before dinner. And then more work! I honestly don't think I will have a hope of passing. But I suppose it's good practice to see what it is like.

This letter refers to Eleanor's coming out dance. There is a photograph of the family group which includes Michael Joicey. (See also Michael's photograph and my address at his Thanksgiving service in Appendix 4.)

Lorna's row with David;
Easter in Cornwall:
28th April 1947

Thank you so much for your letter – it was so lovely to hear from you.

Of course you are right about the dance – I've never heard such nonsense, and there was never a question of being hurt. (How damn stupid people are!)

Your row with David has grown into most varied stories from all sources! You must write and tell me all about it. I see him on Saturday at our Regimental Dinner! He wrote me just about the most pompous letter I've ever had from anyone this morning, asking me to a c/tail party – just as if I'd never met the chap before in my life!

What's all your news? Can we have lunch when you come south? Please do let's – if you'd like it? It's no good writing. But there is so much to talk about now.

Mike Joicey was over here last weekend with Harry Graham-Vivian – and he told me what a truly wonderful dance it had been (and you in the lovely dress – you are a cad not to let poor Puss wear it!). I've seen a lot of H lately - he's a very nice chap, don't you think?

Sue and Ann Gibbs and I drove down to Cornwall for Easter to stay with Harry. Such fun – and oh, such a heavenly place,[122] and flowers such as I've never seen before in my life. Great trees of rhododendrons and camellia and – oh, what are those glorious white bell-shaped tree-flowers? All quite heavenly.

On the way down we dropped in to see the Portmans – and then stayed for dinner. What a sweet little thing Rosy is. I saw her dancing last night again. She had so loved her stay at Manderston.

I have been here all alone for nearly a month. And it has been quite perfect. Father and Mother are still away in Rome. The poor old boy has not been at all well lately – so I pray that Italy will have done him some good.

Life in Oxford:
2 May 1947

Your lovely letter arrived yesterday morning. I got up early to hear the Magdalen choristers singing from the Tower and returned to find it waiting for me. The singing wasn't much of a success from my point of view as I didn't hear a thing – however I then walked round Addisons Walk which was looking too beautiful in the early morning light. I had forgotten England – and Oxford – at this most wonderful time of the year.

I work flat out till tea time and go for walk for an hour from five to six. Each day I choose a different direction, one day to St Johns, another day up the river, the next to Worcester Gardens. Everything is bursting with life and loveliness. The days have not been fine – in fact it has been pretty beastly, but I have been locked in my rooms most of the time and haven't really taken much notice of it.

I have worked very hard – but I don't really see that I can get through 18 months' work in 6! So you might as well face it that I shall probably fail. I should be disappointed as it would hurt my pride! But as I have to take the same exam again I don't suppose it matters in the least. I have now reached my limit and cannot take in any more, and I go about with a permanent headache as it is!

I will go to London on Monday night and return on Tuesday. What a ghastly day it will be! I wish I could go to Kelso instead!

It was fun seeing Puss and the Aunt. They arrived quite suddenly before lunch and it was such a lovely respite to see them and giggle. How you must be longing to hear the result of the exam – or rather the scholarship. She was so sweet and modest about it all – and needless to say I never got a word out of her about it.

I shall now answer your letter point by point!

Lovely that you can come to Ch. Ch. Ball. I should love to come to Millers' 'do' – lucky that I refused to go to Lavinia Jenkinson's dance – and Rosalind Bruce's – as they are both on the 29th.

Dickie walked into my room on Tuesday – no Wednesday (must be accurate!) in very good form. He has gone down to Wales with Father for the w/e and then goes to Hythe for 3 months' course at some small arms school. It is lovely to have him back – and I don't believe he is pompous!! Johnnie and I had lunch with him – and I asked J afterwards what he thought – and he says that he would pass as a cavalry officer anywhere!

I am now sitting in J's room listening to Tchaikovsky's *Violin Concerto* – I never knew that he had written one before! Rather a lovely thing – but a bit involved with 'squiggly bits' and scales etc (do write and tell me what the technical name is!).

How simply perfect the Festival sounds. I shall stay with Johnnie in August and shoot. The music will be such a lovely contrast – and being with you again after what seems already such a horribly long dreary time.

Night and Day has been on in Oxford all this week! I longed to go – which Puss did with Aunt.

Peter T-G and Catherine get married on Sept 24th. As I am to be Best Man, I must be down by then!

Exam went badly;
stayed in London with the Ponsonbys:
6th May 1947

I am now in the train coming down after the exam. It really was all pretty b! I suppose I might have passed if I'm lucky – but more than that I know I haven't done. And I hate doing things badly. However I shall now have to wait and see. I was fairly confident before I did the paper – I could hardly be less confident now!

Poor Ian Forbes Watson, who shares a Tutor with me at Oxford, is in a desperate state as he seems to think that there's no hope for him – and it is essential for him to have passed.

I had tea with Knooky in the Cavalry Club yesterday which was the greatest fun! He never stopped talking about you! We must get him down to Oxford when you are there – what a chap! Delighted that he broke his leg and is missing all the unpleasantness of Palestine.

I also saw Guy Gardner who left the Regiment during the War. Such a charming person – I will never forget him going – right in the middle of a battle he was sent to the Staff College at Haifa as an instructor. Of course he wanted to stay desperately badly and I believe that he thinks Colonel Jack was responsible for sending him. He told me that he had not seen him since he left the Regiment.

I then went to the Ponsonbys' flat[123] where I had arranged to stay. They took me to a most curious sherry party given by the Mackintoshes in Camden Hill Square – masses of unknown people but also, of all joys, SHEEP!! He was in terrific form. Juliet was standing by me and I said "This is my cousin Juliet Ponsonby" quite clearly. "Oh" he said, "I know somebody called Juliet Ponsonby very well, are you any relation?" I told him that she was Juliet and he then said "How very silly of me – perhaps it's your cousin Lavinia who is marrying Mike Hamilton I know" – and so he continued getting more and more embarrassed!

I also saw Desmond Stratton and 'partner', Charles Stourton, Iain Moncreiffe and Diana Errol etc. (Maddening – my pen has run out!).

You would have been so impressed to have seen me opening Aunt Win's letters, answering the invitation to L's wedding – and filing them most methodically into alphabetical order under Refusals and Acceptances!

Then Uncle Charles came in – pretty depressed with our present system of government. He works very hard – and is, I believe, very good.

Harry,[124] John[125] and I drove out to Woodstock for dinner on Sunday and looked in at Woodleys beforehand. We spent a lovely quiet evening together talking fairly intelligently about Things. I simply don't know what I would do without John. He has become such an enormous friend of mine, by far the greatest at Oxford. We disagree on most things, and learn a lot from each other (or I do from him!). Things are a bit strained after Clare.[126] After months of indecision J told her that he loved her, etc, and Clare told him that she quite definitely didn't love him and didn't think she ever would. However they still seem to do a good deal together! But he is pretty unhappy about it all.

I never said how terribly happy your last letter made me. You are so obviously pulling your weight at Manderston (which I knew you would) and as a result things are sorting out – even if they are only doing so slowly. It makes the whole difference to me to think that this is so – and I know that slowly you will come to realise how much you are wanted there.

I now have to go and face my Tutor and go through the paper which will be such hell - particularly as I really am feeling pretty tired after concentrating flat out this morning. I can't tell you how much I am longing to see you. Is the 28th the very earliest? I suppose so.

I wonder how the races went today. Did Rope Trick win the 5th race? Bet he did – by miles! Wish I had known he was running and I would have told you.

From Christ Church garden:
Dean asks me to take Chair of Boys' Club:
13th May 1947

I am sitting in the House garden. All the borders are bright with tulips and forget-me-nots and all the trees are out in blossom. I can't get over the beauty of Oxford at the moment – and long so much for you to see it with me.

I never used to come into the garden when I was last up, but now I spend hours here whenever the sun is out, reading and writing. It is so perfectly situated and from here I can see Magdalen Tower rising so majestically at the far side of the Meadows – and here, just beside me, is Merton behind a flowering cherry tree – its pinnacles almost silhouetted against the clear blue sky.

I got your letter about four days ago – but haven't got it here and can't answer it properly! I can't remember whether there were any outstanding questions.

I didn't do very much of interest last week. A great crowd of us went off to Adwell on Sunday to play tennis: Mary, John Bickersteth, Jo and Christopher Bostock, Dick Faber, George M-E, Harry, Andrew Mayes and Donald Yates. It was such fun – particularly as we found Andy and Mrs Vi (Martin) there! Lots of messages to you from him. He is so nice and we laughed a lot. We all played appallingly badly. I am worse now then when I was 14! And I'm very frightened that you will beat me when we play.

But it was very depressing in a way as Father was ill – I have never seen anyone so depressed. It really is awful for him and everyone concerned, particularly Mother of course, who was very unhappy about him. It is such a hideous disappointment after South Africa.

Dickie was there, having come all the way from Hythe. I took him to the train at High Wycombe in the evening. Palestine really does seem to be pretty ghastly – and he obviously loathes the place. He intends to stay on in the Army if he can – but his Regiment is very full – and it is far from certain whether he can get in.

I am being kept pretty busy with the arrangements for the Ball (Beagles) – but Harry Graham-Vivian is an efficient secretary and takes a good deal of the work off my shoulders. But if we are not careful we will have far too many people! Masses of people have already applied for tickets. Who would you like to come in our party? Dickie has asked all his 'little friends' (Lascelles, Scott and Fairbairn etc). I haven't even sent Ann an invitation – she has been as if dead since the Ponsonbys' dance in London.

I made Bobbie Manners Master of the Beagles yesterday!! I do feel so sad – but there it is.

Will you come down to Eton with me on 4th? So lovely, I love Eton next to Oxford – and I do want you to be there too.

I go up to Lavinia's[127] wedding on Friday – and in the evening I hope to go to visit the Christ Church Boys Club at Kennington. The Dean has asked me to take on the Chairmanship of the Oxford Committee. It would be frightfully interesting – but I don't know quite how much it will entail and must find out before I accept.

I must now do some Roman Law which is more boring that I can possibly describe!

Lorna helps Ros move house: 19th May 1947

Your letter written en route to Newcastle arrived on Thursday. Pretty awful of them to let you wait like that – I wonder whether they had a good excuse. I am so longing to hear what you did, etc – and how you liked being with them. Ros rang Mother up and told her that she simply couldn't have done without you. It is good of you Darling – and I do so hope that it all went well.[128]

The wedding was a tremendous 'do'. Masses and masses of people there. Sue and I had a great gossip and both longed for you to be there. Saw Sheep yet again! He was thrilled to hear about Christian and we both agreed that it was heavenly news. He is amazing!! The reception was at 45 Pont Street and all three enormous rooms were completely crowded out with people.

I had to come down rather early as my tutor had planned a most inconvenient tutorial at nine pm which was a pity. I am now struggling with Roman law which is hell – and pretty boring – and, oh, so difficult! Please don't think I've passed the exam. I think it will be pretty lucky if I have.

I can't tell you how glad I am to hear that you are going to the Guards B.C. Ball – I am too! And so is Dickie. What fun. I am going with the Whitakers (Marigold) etc.

Will you be able to come to Adwell on the 20th as the South

Oxfordshire Dance is that night? Do try please, Darling, as I must go.

About 28th (May), are you staying at Adwell or at The Wharf? It doesn't matter either way – but I shall have to be in that night so won't be able to sleep at Adwell. I think it would probably be easier for you to be at The Wharf and then we could go up to London from Oxford for the play. But whichever you like.

Details of parties for Hunt Ball: 23rd May 1947

I can't tell you how really impressed I am at your efficiency, and thank you so much for doing that boring job for me so beautifully.[129] Harry can't get over it – and now, instead of grumbling away, he sets to with a will and keeps saying how much it helps him, etc.

Oh, I am so longing to see you – and in so short a time. Nothing much to say now before I see you – and *so* much then. I will ring you up at The Wharf on the afternoon of the 28th – I will get hold of the car and come and fetch you for dinner. But we will arrange that on the telephone.

Our party will consist of Catherine G.V. and Harry, Peter T-G, David Morgan, Diana Lindsey (that was), and Hermione Hastings – Johnnie's party is too big to join up with us for dinner we decided – and anyway, as Catherine is going to the Royal G.P., she won't be down till about 7.30 and we won't therefore dine till much later.

David Whately arrives tomorrow. He is staying at Adwell and masses of people seem to be coming out to play tennis on Sunday which seems rather fun.

I am sorry that I had to send you a telegram but Winifred Ponsonby wanted me to go to the dance on 6th and I wasn't quite sure of the situation! However it now appears that we are going to two dances in separate parties – which might prove quite awful!

We will have such a lovely day on Sunday. Mother and Father are going down to Wales - and so only Cynthia and Humphrey will be at Adwell (just to look after us!). We will take a picnic miles away in the hills.

I am so terribly pleased about the meeting. That is good. Oh how lovely it will be to see you – no more now.

I am rather ashamed, when reading the following letter about Boughton that I hardly mention the wonderful pictures and furniture. Johnnie was an expert art historian and would, I think, have liked to have specialized in that particular sphere. I remember how impressed I was with his knowledge and his love of the pictures. We had a lovely time together there on my first (I think) visit.

TELEPHONE
KETTERING 3248.

BOUGHTON HOUSE,
KETTERING.

Staying at Boughton with Johnnie D:
7th June 1947

This will be a very short letter as I'm in my room supposed to be dressing for dinner. This w/e has been pretty incredible. Never have I seen such wonderfully beautiful things – we have spent practically the whole time going round the house looking at them as it has been raining practically the whole time.

An enormous party are staying here – all very grand, but quite nice. Johnnie hates the whole thing – and makes it quite clear that he does! And keeps away from the rest of the house party whenever he can. I like him so much – but he is so terribly 'within' himself, and nobody knows him here. He loves the pictures and furniture and has spent most of him time re-hanging pictures and moving furniture.

But oh! I do wish it had been fine so that we could have got outside. I really have felt frightfully cooped up with the nobility and haven't liked it awfully!

Thank you Darling so much for your two letters. The policeman was kind and posted the first one all right.

Pretty amazing about Sue! I can't quite understand her. Poor chap - how inconsiderate you girls are!

I seconded Richard[130] for the Chatham Club this morning. I like him so much.

Later: We arrived back late last night and I have been busy all day. This Beagle Ball is getting a bit out of control! Harry G-V is pretty vague at times! So I have been ringing up, etc and trying to work. We have now sold 375 tickets and are well satisfied with that part. But there are so many details to be considered.

Your letter arrived this morning. So glad you like the little dog. We saw it in St Edward's Street in Oxford. You're very vague. Pretty amazing about Carnegy![131] In fact I really didn't know that No 1 knew anything about it! But, as you say, she's been gossiping like the rest of the world.

Tomorrow I am spending most of the day in consultation with the Warden of the United Clubs about this Boys' Camp. I feel it really is rather a responsibility and I am rather frightened. But, on the other hand, I do think that is a good plan to help – and a job worth doing. It will be very hard work but a great experience.

Boat Club Ball in two days' time – I shall have to be careful not to get disorganised over the next three days – but we will talk about that on Wednesday.

The camp for the Boys' Club at Sutton Courtenay (on the river near Abingdon) was quite an affair. I had John Bickersteth, Michael Joicey and John Northcot helping me, with the club Warden (whose name I forget) and a 'head boy', Tommy, of maybe 25. I suppose there were thirty boys there aged between 14 and 17. We slept in bell tents on the banks of the river and ate in an army marquee (the cooking was done by two women volunteers). It was lovely weather and we spent most of the time canoeing and bathing. The vast majority of the boys had never been in the country and were suitably impressed by what they saw. I took them to see Christ Church one day and Adwell another (where they had a huge tea!). It was, I think, a great success and I felt satisfied – the effort had been worthwhile! (John Northcot became a monk and died young.)

I had rather an intriguing conversation with Tommy, who had been a member of the Magdalen College Boys' Club when Edward VIII, then Prince of Wales, had visited them in camp in the 1930s. I explained that I had met him when he came out to South Africa and how much we had liked him, didn't he agree? "No way" he said "he was a complete fraud and visited us lot merely for publicity purposes."

I had reserved two rooms for the Peterborough Show at The Haycock Inn. On arrival I went to the reception desk, gave my name and asked for the keys to our rooms. "But you have a reservation for only one room" declared the receptionist. After some argument she said "Look there's only one vacant room in the hotel, shall we stop wasting time?" It was a large double bed. Walter found a bolster and we spent a perfectly comfortable night – Walter in his long underpants.

Peterborough Hound Show and Camp at Sutton Courtenay: 17th July 1947

I am writing this sitting on Reading station waiting for the train. The last two days have been pretty full!

Yesterday morning I left the camp[132] at 7.30 am and picked up Walter Clinkard and the hounds at 8. We then drove straight up to Peterborough, arriving there without a hitch (which was pretty amazing!) at 12.30. We dropped the hounds off at a very nice pub about 8 miles out of the town and then went to the Show.

The first person I saw was Mrs Baird – so my day was made! Oh – but such lovely hounds. I gaped at them all afternoon. It was quite funny seeing all the very unhorsy wives who had been dragged to the show by their husbands, trying to look interested but talking to their friends whenever they thought that they were unobserved! I thought of you in the same boat – I wonder how you would have borne up!

I saw Dick and Ruth, Hugh Arbothnot, Ronnie Wallace, etc. Such fun. After dinner, Bobbie Manners (the Master!) joined us and we went along to the big hotel in the town where everybody (who was anybody) was staying – or anyway drinking.

It was such fun talking pure horse and hound till one o'clock in the morning! All the wonderful old huntsmen were reminiscing away to each other and telling the most grossly exaggerated stories which nobody gainsayed, such was the goodwill of the party. There simply wasn't a man in the bar who didn't love hunting – Bob Stevens was in great form and asked after you. He won the champion bitch with a most beautiful Middleton hound.

It was all rather difficult talking to Ronnie. He knows how I disapprove of his matrimonial dealings – and I couldn't congratulate him on his engagement, which perhaps I should have done as I think he was rather hurt.

This morning we were up very early grooming hounds and we were at the show by nine. The whole thing was simply thrilling. We won the entered dog hounds, the stallion hounds, the dog hound couples, and the Champion Cup (dog hound). We were second in the unentered bitches and we won the bitch couples. All too satisfactory.

I wonder whether you remember the old butler at the House called Fred Rickets. He died and I went to his funeral on Monday. Rather sad as he was such a good friend of all of us. It was a most moving funeral. Masses of people came along. I think that it is a good way of showing respect to people – and in cases of this sort it does comfort the family, for that sort of person is always a snob at heart and if Mrs Fred sees 'the gentry' at her husband's funeral I believe she is somehow rather proud.

I sent a large party of the boys over to Culham Air Station that morning which they seem to have enjoyed. Rather good of the authorities, sending a troop carrier to fetch them and then take them back again.

I went over to Adwell on Tuesday to collect a few things I wanted for the show – and I also looked in on Miss Jane.[133] Mary was there – she said she had seen you at Lords. She is going up to stay with the Ramsays fairly soon. What a funny girl she is.

This camp is being a great experience for me and I am really enjoying it immensely. As I was driving through Abingdon the other day I saw Ribton Crampton so I stopped and talked to him. He said "I hear you're running a Boys' Club Camp – what a funny thing for you to be doing." It made me think quite a lot. Was I giving up a fortnight of my time in order that others should say "Bill's such a good fellow, giving up 14 whole days of his time to slum boys" or was I really doing it with entirely Christian motives of duty?

I often think about this sort of thing: I don't believe that it really is an awfully good plan either – as it only makes one completely self-centred! But actually I do believe that in this case the bad motive does at least enter into it, and that worries me. Somerset Ward said, when I put the problem to him, "All actions are caused by many motives – good and bad – but if it is a good action then the good motives must outweigh the bad." I think that he is right. And I hope in this case the good motives outweigh the bad. But why should I wish to impress others – when God is all-knowing of my thoughts. It does seem very unchristian and bad.

I simply revelled when Tony Chenevix Trench said goodbye on Tuesday and told me that he thought 101% of me and the camp, etc!! I suppose I am beginning to realise how lacking I am in so much – and praise is a kind of comforter to the soul (like a cup of tea to the body). Never, Darling, let me be satisfied with myself – however much you praise me (and do, occasionally!).

I am now in the slowest train imaginable on my way to Didcot. I hope I can get a taxi from there to the camp as I must be back tonight. Tomorrow is a big day. We are all going into Oxford to visit Ch. Ch. and have tea in the Hall. Then the Dean comes on in the evening for the campfire. As the boys only sing slightly low cockney songs, it's going to be 'a bit tricky'.

I must stop now and read *I Chose Freedom* by Victor Kravchenko. The most illuminating book on Russia which I will send to you.

WALTER CLINKARD,
KENNEL HUNTSMAN,
CHRIST CHURCH BEAGLES.
AFTER PETERBOROUGH
SHOW,
17TH JULY 1947

Thoughts on Boys' Camp:
27th July 1947

I haven't written to you for absolute ages – but I think you know how busy I have been. Now it's all over - I think the camp was a success, and the boys were very grateful and said kind words about it. I can't tell you how glad I am that I did it – I learnt such a lot and enjoyed doing it tremendously. I feel much happier about my 'reasons' for having run the camp – I do believe that it was really a job worth doing, and that an important link has been forged between the Club and Christ Church without the boys feeling that we are patronising them in any way. I have arranged for football matches to take place next term, etc, etc – and I believe that we really will get some constructive work done.

The boys themselves are quite charming, and far easier to handle than I expected. But I was struck – and rather depressed – how frightfully unreliable they are, and how equally lacking they are in a sense of responsibility. Though I did not expect it, they have absolutely no political views: all they mind is that they themselves have enough money (or rather the more the better), enough food – and a house to live in.

I believe implicitly that if people are clothed, fed and housed sufficiently they have a very substantial basis on which to build up happy lives. I would fight any way possible for that – but to 'equalise' the population of this country – I can think of nothing more dangerous or more catastrophic.

Cynthia told me about General R.H.[134] (I haven't looked at a Times for a fortnight!). I am so sorry and must write to Gavin. Please could you let me know his address. I wonder how you enjoyed the Review. Lady Alexandra Howard Johnston was at the Buccleuchs when I stayed at Boughton the other day. Rather nice – but pretty stupid!

I saw quite a lot of Rosemary[135] and Billy Yates at the camp as they were three minutes walk from my tent. They are a nice couple – and such a sweet little cottage. In fact Sutton Courtenay is a very beautiful village - a perfect little Norman church and some very nice houses.

I also went to see the Shepley Shepleys who live in the lovely Queen Anne house at Culham. Nigel was at my Tutors and was killed in Burma (in Hum's regt) the last day that they were in action. He was the only son, and it was pretty awful talking to Mrs S-S about him. We looked at photographs of him for two hours, and I had to think of something to say as each photograph was produced.

The 'debs' are here this w/e. But no Penelope! Caroline[136] (who I like very much) and Fortune Owen Hugh Smith – also nice. A large tennis party this afternoon. Toni Moreland is coming to lunch which will be nice.

We (Cynthia, Humphrey and I) went to the Whitakers cocktail party last night. Frightfully good party in the garden – with a band and masses to drink! Marigold is nice. The Bretts (Rupert and that b. woman) were there – former slightly tight, latter quite nice really! (Mustn't be unpleasant!) A very good crowd of South Oxfordshire people, and we enjoyed it enormously. Zandra was not there. She had gone off to the Southover Old Girls' Day – apparently, as Rupert described her, like a Zulu painted for war!

Mother, Father and Dickie arrived back from Wales on Friday night. A great failure. No water, no fish and Mother got something wrong with her tummy. She hasn't really recovered yet – poor thing.

I got a letter from Johnnie[137] on my return here. He wants me to go up on the 11th. Couldn't you stay down - if you do come south - till then, and we could go up in the train together? I go to Dumfries - or Thornhill, he says either will do. Is that on the same line?! My plans are that I shall stay with him till the 17th and then go to John Joicey who also wants me to shoot till the 19th – then on to Kit till the 24th.

DRUMLANRIG CASTLE,
THORNHILL,
DUMFRIES-SHIRE.

Aug. 12th.

Shooting at Drumlanrig: 12th – 15th August 1947

It was such a lovely weekend. Thank you so much for making me so happy. It is only when I am with you that I am entirely happy, and now that I am away from you something is always missing to make me feel complete.

But this is the most lovely place – and luckily Johnnie has organised a very good party – not at all frightening and grand! Tony Gibbs and his wife Mary, Geordie Leslie Melville, a man who has been to Manderston and seems to know all of you quite well called Professor Dunlop (who is charming), Elizabeth Fitzmaurice, Caroline[138] and Elizabeth Northumberland (so pretty and nice). It really couldn't be much better.

I had a very good journey – finished a book and started your mother's – and it all seemed to go very quickly. I was met by Caroline (who is nicer this time!) and we arrived here for tea.

It is not a really beautiful house in itself. But enormously impressive, and full of character. It is situated quite perfectly – surrounded by wooded hills and mauve moors – and in the evening I have never seen such heavenly colouring. Of course the castle is crammed with wonderful picture and furniture. I have not seen them properly yet – but only stolen a quick look round.

Aug 13th: To continue – we walked for miles yesterday over the most glorious country. The grouse were very disappointing though – but it really didn't matter – I really have never been in such country. From the top of the hills I looked down towards the castle and could see only one or perhaps two homes set in the valleys. I felt so isolated from the world. My shooting was satisfactory – as far as it went – but I think I only shot 3 brace or so. Johnnie is a first class shot – and organises the whole show very well.[139]

We went out riding this morning before breakfast – all along the river which flows past the castle away through the forests – it was so lovely. He is a most remarkable person. I wonder so much where he will end up – at the moment he really doesn't know that he wants to do. He has no close contact with either his mother or father and feels, I believe, rather lost.

In the meantime I have formed a more definite opinion about the rest of the family. Professor Dunlop is in a slightly mysterious role – but, as Johnnie himself says, the Duchess is obviously more than interested in him – and the Duke has gone to Bowhill and doesn't return to Drumlanrig till Saturday! She is a most attractive person – I don't think there is much doubt about that. However, we have been getting on very well and have our little jokes together! But never may I get the wrong side of her! Goodness knows what could happen.

Elizabeth N'humberland is terribly nice – we have long gossips. She is very beautiful and intelligent and easy to talk to. Caroline I simply can't make out – but she really has been awfully nice and amusing. So there we are.

We shot all day today. About the same number of birds – and a wonderful day. I have never been so hot. We had a late tea and then all went off to bathe at Morton before dinner. This is a most beautiful lake about three miles up in the mountains above Drumlanrig. The Scott family used to live at Morton till about 1680 (when Drumlanrig was built). The water really was hot and lovely.

Aug 14th: This letter must go today. But there has been so much to tell you about. I have just come back from a ride with Johnnie before breakfast. He is a most extraordinary person. I know him, I suppose, better than most people – but really I feel that I met him for the first time a week ago!

We aren't shooting today at all – tennis and bathing seems to be the order of the day. But it's boiling hot again and everybody is being very lazy. Oh, I do so want you here – and Mary and Tony Gibbs make me feel so envious. They are very happy people (and very nice).

I never told you that Derek and Claudia came to tea here the first day that I was here (11th). Wasn't it fun seeing them? Both in very good form and loving Lanarkshire. I would like to go up there to see them – but it's simply not possible.

Must post this.

More about Drumlanrig; staying at Blenkinsopp, then with Ros: 2st August 1947

Thank you for your lovely letter dated 15th which arrived safely at Blenkinsopp (so glad that they are in *Who's Who*).

The last two days at Drumlanrig were possibly more fun – as we all got much more chummy and less formal, etc, and laughed a tremendous amount. The house continued to get fuller and fuller and on the last night we sat down 24! Poor servants. The Duchess kept on saying "I really don't know what I'll do unless I get some servants" – but there was a butler (late Lt Col in the R.Es!) and 3 footmen there. Don't forget to tell your mother (who seems most interested) that Rees (the late butler) went to the Elphinstones at Carberry Towers (lucky chap!).

One of the newcomers to the castle was a most amazing American girl called Lorraine Dreselhanser. She arrived off the night train one morning, dressed – as she explained – for the moors in shoes whose heels were at least 6 inches high and clothes that would have looked overdressed in Bond Street. She quite solemnly shook hands with every single person sitting round the dining room table – and until my turn came I couldn't understand why everyone winced when she shook hands. However, I was soon quite clear – as she was wearing the most enormous sapphire ring which acted like a knuckle duster on the ordinary mortal. In the end she never came out shooting but retired to bed! Only to get up in time to dress for dinner that evening. We all laughed most unkindly at her behind her back.

The last evening Lord Linlithgow arrived. What an amazing man he is. He got definitely tight and sang doubtful songs, etc, etc, after dinner. But during dinner he was most interesting about India and he believes that there will be the most ghastly civil war there.[140]

It was a very pompous dinner party – and during it we had Jerusalem artichokes. I was sitting next to the Duchess who suddenly said "You don't know how to eat an artichoke, Ignoramus." I said that of course I did and the subject was dropped – then suddenly she pulled my plate away from me – adjusted her glasses and began cutting my artichoke about till she produced the bit at the bottom which she plonked on her fork and made me eat off it! I really like her very much – and we had a lot to laugh about. Professor Dunlop and she spent a whole day away together by the sea – only to return in the evening with the Duke whom they had picked up at Bowhill!

It was very sad having to go. I drove down to Carlisle with Mary and Antony Gibbs[141].

We found John waiting for us in the hotel. So lovely seeing him again. We talked and talked about everything all the way back to Blenkinsopp. It's a beastly house – really nasty and in bad taste! Father Joicey is the perfect hen-pecked husband, and Violet[142] is the typical music hall girl in antique! But awfully nice! Poor old John is pretty fed-up with both of them!

We shot one day that I was there but there was precious little to shoot at. However, it was a lovely day and such a beautiful place. We wrote a long combined letter to David one evening – quite a funny one! He told me all about the pram incident with Sue which he did think was funny! But you don't understand him!

I drove over to Holly Lodge with them yesterday. The house is, as you say, quite nice. But how much nicer it could be. Of course Ros is not feeling like doing much I suppose – and is anyway considered by Kit to be only treated very gently like the most valuable of brood-mares! I don't, however, think that either of them mind what sort of a house they live in though, like Mother, she wd. hotly deny that!

However it has all been the greatest fun. We spent all day today at the show.[143] The ground is terribly hard so we decided not to jump till tomorrow and Saturday. However we showed both horses – did so well. Kit was 4th and I was 5th in a class of 5!

Oh – it's so late. I must go to sleep. (Am writing in bed!) But I wonder so much how you are getting on: and Ann. I do so hope that you enjoy yourself somehow. Perhaps it will be lovely scenery – and I'm sure you'll laugh!

About 8th – it's not at all easy. My Tutor has set me a fantastic amount of questions to do – and I've not really started them. Therefore I shall have to get down to them between now and when I come north. However I must see him before I come north, but I can't on the 6th as we are shooting at home. So I planned to see him on the 8th. But if you really want me to come and won't go without me, etc, everything is possible! It is rather important though, isn't it?

I think that I must elaborate a bit on the horse-coping Ros had said that she would kill me if I allowed Kit even to contemplate buying yet another horse. In the event, having driven to Bert Cleminson's yard, a super looking horse (Red Hackle) was trotted out. I rode him round the field and we walked the horse home having left the new car with Cleminson!

Stayed at Nunnington, then Holly Lodge; tried to see Sgt Edmunds: 25 August 1947

I stayed last night with Peter and Susan Clive at Nunnington which was rather fun. We drove up to the great house to have a look at it. What an impressive place it is – quite enormous and very beautiful it must have been in its original state when it was built – but a large wing was later built on to it in the last century, which is more hideous than is possible to describe. Peter is their agent – an awfully nice fellow. He has a tremendous amount of work to do – but obviously does it very well.

I enjoyed staying at Holly Lodge very much and avoided any arguments with Ros! Kit and I lived a fairly narrow life of horse coping – which was lovely! He took me over to see a horse coper friend of his and, needless to say, bought another horse. A really nice one (which would have done your father down to the ground). The Fordson van + £300 (from the dealer) purchased the horse – which was a good bargain considering that he wanted £350 for the horse.

I left there yesterday and drove down to Doncaster where I had lunch with Peter and Katherine(sic). They live in a flat which is impossible to describe, it is so horrible – but the great thing is that they don't seem to mind, in fact they think that it is quite nice. They were both in good form. They are very worried about Harry who, they say, has got thoroughly tied up with Diana Lindsey! And don't think much of her.

I was able to drive down as Father arrived up by car last Saturday. The old boy was in very good form (as he so often is when he is away from the worries of Adwell) and seemed to enjoy himself. We all went to church at Hexham Abbey on Sunday. Oh! It is a beautiful church. Some of it very early (about 600) and most of it Early English or Transitional. I seldom have been so impressed by a building – or by the service which was taken most beautifully.

I am writing to you from a little country pub just outside Loughborough – before going on to Adwell. I hope to arrive there for dinner. I hope you are having a lovely time – anyway the weather has been perfect. In fact we are all terribly worried about the lack of water, and Father says there is no grass at Adwell. I am sending this to Manderston as I don't know whether you will still be with the Palmers when it arrives.

Adwell, August 20th: I had a lovely drive down. How frightened you would have been! I did drive so fast. I called in on Sgt Edmunds outside Mansfield – but wasn't allowed to see him as I arrived outside a visiting hour. I was furious - but I do see that they can't make exceptions. I saw his doctor who gave me a pretty bad report on the poor chap. He says that there is about at 50:50 chance of him getting better. I do wish I could do something for him – he saved my life so often – but I don't really see that I can do much. It really is a perfectly awful catastrophe for him – and he is being so courageous and patient over it.

I then went on to see the Herberts outside Loughborough - but unfortunately he was away. But Mrs Herbert was very nice and showed me a very nice new horse that Ivor (the boy) has just bought. She was most interesting about 'the crisis' (which is now just taken as a fact by the public without them enquiring why there is one!). The coal situation is, as Mr Herbert says, an admittance of failure. Less output and more cost is all that nationalisation had done for our greatest export article. I have become terribly bitter against this government – and if this is socialism, I hate it.

But what terrifies me is when are the public going to put their foot down? Where is this dreadful controlling (or taking away of freedom) going to lead us? This last Emergency Bill was opposed by one sincere Labour Member (Blackburn) and the Conservative Party – but otherwise the public just sat back never lifted a finger. Some of us might hate being controlled – but I don't believe that the majority of the people do. They hate thinking for themselves. Enough!

Mother got back from her 'holiday' with 15 children and Doris by the sea last night. Looking quite exhausted. Poor thing – I wonder when she will break up. Can you imagine anything so appalling?

Very sad news – in fact I can't get over it. Lady Duncan[144] has a tummy riddled with cancer – and has been given a year to live. Isn't it appalling? What makes it worse for her is that she is a Christian Scientist. And, of course, by her belief she should never have got it.

The other bit of news is that Cynthia has got a house and will be leaving Adwell on 15th September. Of course it is lovely for her but I shall miss her dreadfully. I don't know what I shall do without her there to go to.

I hope that the book (that your mother lent me) arrives safely.

John Joicey to stay; difficult relationship with Father: 29th September 1947

An age since I have written I'm afraid – how hopeless I am, and how little I show my love for you; but please don't judge me by my capacity as a correspondent! There hasn't been time to write – because, as you know, I have to have at least a spare hour in front of me in order to get down to it. I always think as I write – and when I think about you, I can't write as well!

Thank you for your two lovely letters. What a pity that the Oban Ball was such hell – poor Darling. How absolutely dead beat you must have been when you got back – and then those meetings. However you must have felt (rightly) extremely virtuous – so perhaps it was almost worthwhile.

There is so much to tell you from this end. To start right at the beginning, I rang up Father from the Maurices and immediately realised that he was in a filthy temper! A wonderful conversation then took place – "What's all this about some friends of yours coming down here for the weekend?" "Oh, only John Joicey and the two Thompson Glovers." "I've never heard anything like it – Mother away, no kitchen maid, no food, Jones ill – they can't come. You must put them off, now." "We'll talk about it at the Thame Show. I'll be down at 2 pm. GOODBYE."

I then went down by train, wondering what the hell to do about it – knowing how tricky Father could be. However, having found him there I managed to calm him down a bit and he said that he supposed they could come – but only till Sunday night! Meanwhile, John had rung up and said that he couldn't get here till Saturday.

The next difficulty was the lack of any female in the house – and Father's insistence on one being there for dinner. So, after long discussion Aunt Iola[145] was rung up and persuaded to come.

Meanwhile, no word from Peter as to when he was coming, etc. I waited all Friday afternoon – and at last Aunt Iola arrived and was furious to find nobody there except Father and me! During dinner the telephone went – this was Mother to say that she supposed we knew that the T-Gs were not coming as they had written to her a week ago saying that they couldn't. I was very nearly 'rude to my Mother'! Slightly exasperating.

Father and I went shooting at West Wycombe on Saturday morning – a tremendous lot of partridges – and picked up John at the station at 12.30. After a quick lunch the house was emptied save for John – and we went off to the wedding. Perfect manners for the newly arrived guest. The wedding was great fun – all the S.Oxon buddies in great form. I was a most efficient usher.

Back again for tea and out shooting and changed for dinner – Lavinia Holland-Hibbert and Marigold Whittaker came to help cope with John – and afterwards we were joined by Colin Balfour, Elizabeth Aubrey Fletcher, Rachel Clerke Brown and Mavis Honey and we all went to the Thame Fair which was great fun – John Joicey screamingly funny as usual!

I rang up John Berry and told him to bring Sue over to play tennis on Sunday but he gibbed badly and only came himself. It was such fun – John Goldsmid also turned up – followed by Colin Balfour and two friends of his and Mavis Honey. Tremendous tennis then took place – and a great 9th Lancer gossip afterwards.

John went on Monday morning. It really was fun having him – and Father really quite enjoyed it and liked John very much. He went off to Wales with the Maurices on Monday – and I was left alone here. It is rather a good opportunity to get things done – and besides doing a lot of Law, I have been pottering about clearing things up and trying to make things a little less like a disused slum area! I have been dining out every day – with John Glyn, Dick Fanshawe, Miss Jane, etc, and rather enjoyed it.

Mother rang up on Wednesday to say that Ros had had a son successfully – on the night that the nurse arrived! She came down on Thursday with Christopher and has now gone to 141. This leaves me absolutely alone – nobody at all in the house. I cook my own breakfast and go out for meals! This is far preferable to 141! I decided against going to Cynthia as there was too much to be done here.

I have been shooting all day to day at Culham with Mr Morrell. Tremendous fun. We got 100 brace and I have seldom enjoyed a day more. I decided to go and look at the Aunt afterwards – and arrived to find a cocktail party in full swing! She was dashing about – quite mad – and couldn't get a word in edgeways! She told me that she had seen Puss and your mother in London – and that all seemed to be going well. That's good.

I wonder how the Perth Ball went – hope it was better than Oban.

Johnnie was President of the Oxford University Conservative Association. I was not a member (don't forget that I was the first ever Chairman of the Eton College Labour Club!). Nevertheless he wrote a note to me which said (I think): "Dear Bill, you may not be a member of the Conservative Association (which you should be) but I want 5/- (five shillings) off you as a subscription to buy a bicycle. It is for a girl here called Margaret Roberts who might well be a future Conservative Prime Minister. She is a most splendid girl and has no bicycle which is necessary for her to have as she has to deliver my notes to members by hand." I paid up and when I saw Lady Thatcher a year or so ago she remembered!

Discussions about sin:
22nd October 1947

I simply can't remember when I last wrote to you – and perhaps I haven't turned over a new leaf at all. Anyway, I have had to resort to a 'little book' and am, from now on, going to put down in it when I write to you.

Your letter arrived on Monday – bless you for it. I am glad that Christopher[146] behaved himself, and that you are now a confident baby watcher! I have never seen Mrs Marriot but Mother always says how very odd she is! I wonder what your mother made of you looking after him!

I hope that you are having a lovely time with Sue – but you seem to be fearfully busy with all your meetings. I have had a pretty hectic time – and not very satisfactory. In fact, sometimes lately I have felt dreadfully depressed. I am reading a frightfully difficult subject this term – and simply can't cope, and occasionally I feel like giving up (and do!) and then feel unutterably gutless.

And then I wonder where it is all going to lead – and when I can marry you, and it is all so hopelessly vague. But I suppose that it is only a passing phase – and mostly because you are not here to hold my hand and give me confidence. It is an awful condition to allow oneself to get into – when I simply feel that I can't do it – and that I hate Oxford and all the pettiness and childishness that goes with it.

I am so hopelessly weak at times. I miss Johnnie and John terribly – as I hardly ever see them these days. Johnnie lives miles away over Folly Bridge – and John lives on the Banbury Roundabout. Actually I am having dinner with Johnnie tonight which will be lovely. He came in for a moment this morning. He tells me that he is almost certainly going down at the end of the term, and is getting a job under Lord Woolton in the Conservative Head Office where he will learn to speak and find out how the Conservative Party works (which will take quite a bit of doing).

By the way, have you got the shortened form of the Industrial Charter? If so, could you lend it to me? I suppose that I ought to read it sometime instead of shouting about something I don't know.

John Bickersteth came into my room on Saturday night and talked to me about sin – for hours. It really was just like the old days when John Synge and I used to talk. The whole discussion centred on the proposition: A man, A, who has slowly degenerated to be of low moral standards and a man, B, who is of high moral standards are confronted with the same temptation and both yield to it. Who has committed the greater sin – or have they both sinned equally?

I argued that A has sinned less than B because his conscience would not be equally aware of his sin as would B's conscience. We talked about this for ages – and I decided to go and see Mascall[147] about it. So, after dinner on Monday I put the question to him.

He was awfully helpful. His answer was that they have both committed the same sin. It is because A has become morally degraded on account of his past sins that his conscience is not pricked and although he would, no doubt, 'get a good mark' if he had resisted the temptation (because it would be more difficult for him to do so than it would be for B) it is a poor argument to say that because of his low standard of morality he commits less of a sin than B. If this, he added, was the case then one could let oneself go to the dogs in order that one could be satisfied if, at the end of it, one resisted a temptation.

I then talked to him about prayer – and how awfully difficult I found it was nowadays. He told me that this was a perfectly natural reaction – but a very difficult time to go through. (And so it is.) But he has persuaded me that I must struggle on – even if the whole thing seems pointless – in order that I can show God that I believe it to be worth the struggle.

John Smith, Ann Sutton, Clayre Campbell, Harry Graham-Vivian and I all went out to Adwell for tea on Sunday. It was a 'hectic' atmosphere all afternoon – and I came away feeling quite exhausted. The Maurices[148] were staying there. Alec annoys me intensely! But I felt very sorry for him - he was 'waiting to go fishing' – "But when are you going?" I asked. "I don't know, the day of our departure fluctuates as to whether your mother remembers that she has got (a) a County Council meeting, (b) a Rural District Council meeting, (c) the bench, (d) a wedding – or funeral, (e) the Pekinese is going to have puppies, (f) Jones, the cook and Edna are going on holiday."

I thought it best to ask – and got the satisfactory and definite answer from Mother that it was to be Tuesday – and from Father that, because Mother had an S.S.A.F.A. meeting, Wednesday was the day. I feel very sorry for Father often!

I had no idea that Puss was going to be at the concert. Four days ago Antony Gibbs asked Johnnie and me to go down and shoot with him at Briggens – and so I accepted to go. I am disappointed. It was all rather difficult anyway as I had previously asked Clayre to come with me – and it was tricky putting her off. She was definitely rather 'dark' about it.

The Hunt Ball will be HELL. Mother has accepted for us to dine and go with the Scotsgrove party. I was not consulted and am livid. Poor John Bick doesn't like the idea of being forced into their party much either! However, Humphrey and Cynthia will be there.

We are beagling at Adwell on that (14th) afternoon! Can you come on Friday and stay till Sunday night? I must be back for dinner in Oxford on Sunday I'm afraid. It's a very short time.

I must stop and work.

Johnnie going down at the end of term;
I go to a Labour meeting with Lavinia H-H:
2nd November 1947

Your last letter arrived yesterday morning. Such a lovely long one. I am so terribly happy for you that things are going so well at Manderston – and that you are beginning to feel really interested in everything. There is obviously so much that you can do to really assist your father – and you have only to prove yourself for him to have faith in your capabilities. And this you are obviously doing. There are such endless interests for you there – and you can learn so much that will help you in your political work.

Thank you so much for sending the Industrial Charter. Actually Johnnie gave me a complete copy of it the other day as he was so horrified that I hadn't read it. But yours is much better, as I shall never get down to the full copy. He is almost certainly going to the Conservative Central Office when he goes down (probably at the end of this term, alas) and will work there under Lord Woolton. Anyway he has gone quite dotty and never stops going to political meetings practically every night.

However I left him on Thursday night and went to a meeting of the Labour Club with Lavinia Holland-Hibbert! Very odd – but the fellow speaking was fairly reasonable, and seem to lack the beastly party viciousness with which all the Labour M.Ps and Winston Churchill are making themselves so unpleasant. How sad it is to see such a great man use such small, low weapons. He is doing unutterable damage to the Conservative Party, don't you agree?

Lavinia is now working in a school for German P.O.Ws at Beaconsfield – teaching them to be good citizens. Pretty presumptuous of us – but it may be justified so long as they are not taught to be socialists (which I rather suspect).

I can't remember this fellow Robertson – obviously a bounder! Anyway, I'm glad you don't like him.

It must have been fun having Sue. I should think that you are just about right about her. But don't become a suffragette! Bless you – I don't think you will. Or a haggling, domineering old SPINSTER – a wife (if I have anything to do with it!)

I am sorry to hear that Puss is causing complications. I quite agree with your mother that if she is working so hard it would be better for her to live in London. Nothing is so exhausting as rushing up and down in a train – and it is such a waste of time. Why is it such tripe? I am FURIOUS that you opened my letter to her. How do you know that it wasn't very private, may I ask?

Most efficient – I'm glad you agree. Took hours and days to discover the fellow, but was determined to do so!

I'll see you in less than a fortnight. What a heavenly thought. Please come down early on Friday. I think there is a 9.45 (Pad.) to Oxford, arriving 11.25. I could meet you and in the afternoon and we could go beagling!

The party will be: Father, Mother, Humphrey and Cynthia, John Bick? John Ashton? Rosemary Clarke Hall? Me, You. Rather fun – of course we will be going from Adwell now and not Scotsgrove.

Father and Mother came back from Wales on Wednesday night. Not a successful fishing escapade – but they had a lovely time chasing grouse and walking for miles like a honeymoon couple! And have returned looking much better and less tired. Father lunched with me on Thursday and we had a gossip. He was in V.G. form really.

I shot at Woodleys yesterday (with John Bick!). Great fun just going round the hedgerows and shooting anything we saw (which wasn't an awful lot).

Uncle Charles is resigning his seat (Sevenoaks, Kent) at the next election as he says that there is a 'young chap' who wants to stand. But actually, John (who is in his constituency) tells me that they all felt that, however much they liked him, they were not represented enough in the House!

Juliet gets back on Monday – it will be lovely seeing her again. She isn't here for long as they all go to South Africa in the winter. I wonder what she will make of John Smith now. I have seen a good deal of him – and although I still think him pretty amazing, he is a nicer sort of person than I thought. He is dining with me on Thursday with Richard Ollard (such a dear).

**Oxford life; beagling and shooting;
40 people for tea; Doris and 141**

In this letter I mention shooting with Bobbie Manners at Avon. I first shot there on my birthday (7th December) in 1941, when I was eighteen and still at Eton. Except for the War years, I shot there every year until 2004. Once, when I was shooting there in 1991, a beater came up to me at the end of a drive and said "Excuse me, Sir, but do you remember what you were doing on this day (December 7th) fifty years ago?" "No" I said, "what was I doing?" "You were speaking to me on this very spot and you're now 68!"

The Manners family and Avon were a very special part of my life. I loved both Bobbie's parents. Lady Manners was a Cecil and she was always very proud of that. Lord Manners was known as "the nicest man in the Grenadier Guards" – and so he was. Bobbie had a great friend at Eton (whose name I forget) who had persuaded him to join him in the Air Force, rather than join the family regiment. This, I believe, was a major mistake. Whereas all of us in the Army made more friends, he went to India for most of the War and made no friends. He complained bitterly about this after the War when we were at Oxford together. I certainly found him very changed from the Eton days where he had many friends and great enthusiasm for life. Now he was much quieter, almost reclusive, and somewhat lacking in confidence.

3rd December 1947

A bad lapse I'm afraid! Please forgive me – just this once. I have been having a most hectic week – and have done precious little work as a result, which is depressing. However it has all been great fun.

Bless you for your letter which I got when I arrived back from staying with Bobbie.[149] I am glad you had such a lovely time with Nick – I must go and learn how he holds your hand and whispers 'my heart is full' into your ear; it obviously is lacking in me! No Darling, but I must try and see him soon – but now, I suppose, not till next term. I am thinking seriously of living out – as it really doesn't seem to be much of a success trying to work in college. However I shall see how it works out.

Doris obviously means that when I am with her the spark of fun is not evident. Sue is just about 100% right! But then why should she, of all people, make me sparkle? I admit that I am not my best at 141 – in fact I always feel sick there!

I am afraid Gravesend[150] was very disappointing – not much one can say about it except that a Jaeger coat does not go down well amongst the dockers! Richard Acland is a very strong, and very clever opponent – and no doubt won them over by ingenious argument. I think that you are right about the municipal elections.

I am so glad that you are enjoying staying with the Ps – amazing to hear that J now stands in a fish queue etc. What married life does do for one . . . . .

We had a very good day at Tetsworth on Friday. Masses of people out, all of whom came back to tea at Adwell afterwards! Doris, needless to say, came out of Oxford with Mother and arrived at the meet looking too extraordinary. At tea I thought she was going to have a stroke, she became so excited over all the boys!

Mother was marvellous and gave us a all a tremendous tea – and considering there were over 40 of us, it was no mean effort – particularly as I told her that there would probably be only 20 people there, so many having gone to Fortune H Smith's dance.

I got back at 7 and after a bath drove on to Hampshire with Bob. I enjoyed my weekend very much. They live in a house that could be made charming – but they care very little about it. Everything is ultra mod in the house (by that I mean labour saving to the last degree) as they moved there (from the big house, Avon Tyrrel) in 1939. Amongst other pieces of equipment they have a washing up machine. Frightfully good and efficient. But never have I been so hungry! They eat nothing – talk about Dresden china!

We had a very good day's shooting – 60 brace. But they were all very disappointed that they didn't shoot more as they were expecting to get at least 100 brace. I couldn't have enjoyed myself more!! (although one drive I shot abominably which was a pity!).

Julian Jenkinson arrived to stay on Monday. I like him very much. I asked George Rich (Bays) to come and have dinner in Hall with us that night – and we then had a Chatham Club Meeting in my rooms after dinner when Lord Duncannon came and spoke about France. Considering what an interesting subject he had, we all thought him pretty boring – and Johnnie D went fast to sleep.

Yesterday I hunted hounds again as Bobby suddenly had to go to London. We met at Chislehampton (the village where we turn left to Abingdon after Stadhampton). The bus was full to standing capacity – and luckily we found a hare quickly and ran such as I have never run before. Unfortunately there were far too many hares and we kept changing – so that it took rather a long time to get a hare away. But once we did so, we had a wonderful hunt – a four mile point and really fast, ending up in a chicken run where I decided not to take hounds.

The round of cocktail parties has begun! We went back late and arrived at Ch. Ch. at 6.30 – only to find ourselves immediately involved in a party – not having even had a bath! Julian, Vivian, Harry and I then went off to a little club dinner – the Gridiron this time! Great fun. John Smith made a most amusing speech. How I wish that I could do that.

I am going out to Adwell with Harry and Vivian on Saturday morning early and we shoot all day. I then start for Oakham on

Monday – leaving London after tea. What fun. I shall stay there till Wednesday then go to Kit and Ros till Friday morning and on to Johnnie that day. May I let you know later when I am arriving at Manderston? (Probably getting a lift with the Duke of B!) How lovely that will be.

The last week has been great fun – but so very superficial. I always want you to be there to share things with me.

Hunting with Jenkinsons and with Kit: 12th December 1947

Your lovely birthday present arrived at Holly Lodge yesterday. Bless you for such beautiful socks and silk handkerchiefs – absolutely fit for a duke!

I have been having a perfect time – hunting practically non-stop! We had a very good day on Tuesday – not such a big field as before, and therefore more room to move without the risk of being cursed into heaps![151]

I arrived at Holly Lodge on Wednesday evening – and yesterday Kit and I hunted all day. Such a good hunt on the best cob I have ever ridden. He was bought for Ros – who quite obviously hasn't a hope of ever riding him! Far too good a hunter. Goodness knows what Kit paid for him – but an awful lot. However, he is worth anything! Never have I seen a little horse take on such big places. I enjoyed myself no end.

I can't get over the organisation of the whole of the domestic side. Really rather shocking. That is, we would hate it – but the great thing is that they are blissfully happy, and that is all that matters. Ros has far too much to do at the moment – and somehow copes. Dick Taylor (who knows all of you) came to dinner last night – and she laid on an excellent meal, etc, having put the babies to bed first.

I had lunch in the Northern Counties Club today with Kit – and there saw Keith Bewicke – he was very nice and friendly but looked too debauched and unhealthy for words. He told me that Ann was coming up for Christmas.

I shan't look my normal beauty at Manderston as at the moment my lip is swollen to twice the normal size. I have a black eye, a cut nose and a lame leg – owing to various hunting accidents! I hope they won't affect my shooting tomorrow. All rather frightening – hope you think of me.

I haven't any more paper – so must stop. Write to me at Drumlanrig, knowing not when and where in St Boswells.

New Year at Adwell;
Lawn meet of beagles & David Laurie stays:
29th December 1947

A lovely letter from you this morning – <u>and</u> a diary. Bless you. We have been having a pretty hectic week – and almost too many people staying: Betsy, Barbara and Mary; Watty Winter (Andy's old uncle); Deborah Duncan; David[152] and Peter[153] – and because the house was 'practically empty' a completely strange 'light blue job' New Zealander arrived, Mother having written to the Colonial Office enquiring whether there were any lonely colonials who had nowhere to go for Christmas. Typical!

We had great fun – but I did miss the two girls and the children terribly. David and Peter were in tremendous form and went up to London this morning with Betsy, Barbara, Mary and the New Zealander – as you can imagine we simply never stopped talking, and everyone became very fed up with our conversation which must have been quite maddening – particularly as most of the language was incomprehensible to anyone save 9th Lancers.

Catherine couldn't come as there was a flap about the baby – however all is well now. David merely strutted up and down saying "my dear – they tell me the bambino nearly hit a tiny bell." I was very sorry not to see her – and of course David was more than disappointed.

We had a Lawn Meet of the beagles here on Saturday – and so David and Peter were dragged out to run, which we did to no time, the day culminating in the hounds going off on a fresh hare in pitch darkness and me arriving home with two couple of hounds. I was out at 11.30 trying to collect them, in which I was successful save for one hound who I later found dead on the main road – very sad, he was such a good young puppy too.

The whole party of us played Vingt et un after dinner. Needless to say, David had no idea how to play (he is more stupid at cards than me!) and we all laughed a lot at him. We three then gossiped till 1.30 AM – you can just picture the conversation with David going off to sleep every other moment and waking up with a jump.

We took the hounds back to the kennels on Sunday morning – a lovely drive by Cuddesdon – and back by Ruth Fanshawe, who has been delayed going to Ireland because Brian is in quarantine for I.P.

This (1948) was to be my last year at Oxford and I should, I suppose, have been working hard for my degree, having done extremely little work the previous year. But the War had been over only three years and the country was still in turmoil. Politically, we had a Socialist government under Attlee. It suited the mood of the majority of people, both soldiers and civilians, who had suffered five years of war and who blamed 'the ruling class' for their suffering. Nationalisation was the fashion and the lack of individual responsibility (which went with it) was welcomed by 'the masses'. And perhaps, we, returning from the War, were infected by this general attitude of irresponsibility. Most of us seemed unable to face the reality of life in the future.

But we did have fun! As I read these letters of the first four months of 1948, I cannot get over the time we spent hunting, dancing (often into the early hours at the 400– or some other nightclub), racing and, above all, talking in each other's rooms far into the night. Few of us ever went to a lecture (I certainly only went to hear Lord David Cecil – never a law lecture). There are constant statements in my letters that "I must go and work" – but very little work was done!

When I told Walter Clinkard, the Kennel Huntsman of the Christ Church Beagles, that I wouldn't be hunting the hounds the next season he replied "Oh you should hunt hounds. Don't you worry, Sir, they always give a degree to the Master of the Beagles."

The result was disastrous for almost all of us. Johnnie Dalkeith left Oxford early without a degree, John Bickersteth failed to get one at all and the rest of us got Thirds! (Harry Graham-Vivian was awarded an honorary Fourth in

Agriculture.) Even the brilliant John Smith followed the fashion!

We were, however, jolted into activity after this rather shaming experience. I did work very hard at my Bar exams and managed to be called to the Bar in record time – thanks, mostly, to the tuition of Mr Hart. He had lost an arm when wounded in the Navy. He used his metal arm to hit me when I couldn't remember some important legal decision!

Lady Buxton, the wife of Lord Buxton, the Governor General of South Africa before Lord Athlone, was a hugely intelligent and loveable person who influenced the lives of many people, including mine.

She lived in her widowhood with Dame Meriel Talbot at Newtimber, a most charming Queen Anne moated manor house. Mary Ponsonby (my first cousin) and I escaped there to do some essential work before the dreaded finals in June.

Mildred Buxton's daughter married Charles FitzRoy (later Duke of Grafton) and was Hugh Grafton's grandmother.

FROM
COUNTESS BUXTON.

TELEGRAMS & TELEPHONE
HURSTPIERPOINT 3104

NEWTIMBER PLACE,
HASSOCKS,
SUSSEX.

Newtimber Place, Hasocks:
4th January 1948:

I was catching the coach up to London from Tetsworth on Friday afternoon when the postman came up and gave me your letter. My poor Darling – how beastly for you with your tummy. Oh I do hope that there is nothing radically wrong with you, and that you feel better soon. Nothing makes you feel so miserable. However, I am delighted to hear the more cheering news about the Junior Unionist Council – a very well deserved reward for a great deal of very hard work. Well done, Darling (though I don't trust your chairman an inch!).

I am sorry that riding The Poet astride wasn't much of a success – but perhaps your decision is right. But do remember that Daisy and

The Poet are not at all the same to ride, and that you are bound to feel a bit odd at first on such a big horse. It is lovely that you are enjoying your hunting again – I believe you might prefer it to skiing one day!

I forget if I told you that I decided to come here to work. It was rather difficult leaving Adwell, as they couldn't quite understand why I found it just about impossible to get down to it there – however, here I am in perfect surroundings with Lady B and Dame Meriel Talbot and Barbara and Mary[154].

We have a lovely day: working morning and afternoon, and the rest of the day talking to these two wonderful old ladies – both over 80, and both of frightening intelligence. It is such fun. They have the most wonderfully developed minds – and never stop talking about the most interesting things with the greatest authority.

Mary and Barbara are very good companions – and both rather different here compared to Adwell. They seem somehow happier and more alive. This has given me 'food for thought'. I wonder whether Adwell has become rather a difficult place to live in? Of course, when Father is ill an ugly gloom spreads through the house, but Darling, as you know - however much I love every corner of it – I do find it very difficult to live there.

Cynthia was down on Thursday night – very depressed about their future as the Regiment are moving to Salisbury and of course they can't get a house anywhere. So Cynthia asked me what I thought of them coming to live in the flat. It is difficult: I should, of course, simply love to have them. I believe that it might work. But they, quite naturally, insist on living absolutely apart from the rest of the family. It will be interesting to see what happens. Otherwise she was in very good form and looked so well. I haven't seen the boys since August – too long.

I had a very good day with the Bicester on Thursday, riding Hugh Trevor Roper's[155] horse. Lots of nice people out – Lavinia H-H and Mrs, General John Coombe, the two Gosling girls, Peter Hodgson and Robert Lonsdale (the latter 'dogging' Lavinia all day, to whom she just occasionally threw a bone and then rode on!). Oh! How I wish that someone would marry her[156]. She would make such a good wife – and it is all so wrong that she isn't married. People forget that she is a year younger that Cynthia.

I stay here till Friday – when I go up to London to see my tutor and I hope lunch with David Whately and David Wentworth Stanley. I then go back down to Pavenham where I see Roddie and John J and Desmond McInnes Skinner. Apparently things are not quite what they ought to be between David and Roddie as her family think David is after her money, and nothing else! However Roddie seems to like David very much – and so perhaps all will come out in the wash!

Most interesting about Elspeth. I wonder what the fellow is like. I hope he is worthly of such a lovely head!

I am sending this to Newton Don in the hopes that you will be well enough to go there. I do hope you can, and that you enjoy yourself. Give my best love to Gina!

Sorry I forgot to thank you for your lovely Christmas card from you and Daisy. Father thinks it the best one we had!

I was rather proud to be made President of the Chatham Club. This was quite a serious Oxford Institution and the President's job was to organise meetings addressed by well known personalities – not necessarily, but often, politicians. The highlight of the proceedingws was the Summer Dinner at the Randolph Hotel. I managed to get three good speakers, Lord David Cecil, John Betjeman and Evelyn Waugh. David Cecil was, of course, charming and 'civilised' in every sense of the word and spoke without a note. John Betjeman got hold of a menu card halfway through dinner upon which he scribbled some jottings and then spoke in rhyming verse for ten minutes. Evelyn Waugh stood up with a sheaf of notes from which he read for a quarter of an extremely boring hour! He stayed at Adwell for two nights and gave me an inscribed and signed copy of Put Out More Flags *on leaving.*

Christ Church, Oxford
5th February 1948:

I haven't heard from you for an absolute age – I shall hold it against you for always!

I wonder what you have been doing with yourself – I thought of you so much last week-end with the 9th Lancer contingent! I wonder how they went down – particularly my friend Gnochi! I haven't heard from either of them yet – but no doubt I shall soon have a full report.

David, Gnochi, John Joicey and Desmond McInnes Skinner are all planning to come down to race at Cheltenham on March 2nd – it will be lovely seeing them. But I can only go one day – and it is therefore fairly difficult making plans for them from here – all hotels booked up, etc. However I think I have found one for them now.

I went up to see Cynthia on Tuesday – poor little thing – she looked rather pathetic lying all about in bed waiting to be operated on. She was dealt with today, but as yet I don't know how it all went. I missed Humphrey this morning – who visited me when I was out. I hope that I shall see him tomorrow.

They have now bought a house at Chorleywood – near Amersham – really in the suburbs, but it looks quite a nice little 'villa' – and very convenient for them as, apparently, Humphrey is now a marked man and after his course at Greenwich he goes to the Combined Staff College (near Amersham) and then back to the War Office (for ever as far as I can see!).

I am rather pleased (!) I have been made the President of the Chatham Club. It isn't one of the 'stupid little clubs' – and it is going to be very interesting. The rough object of the Club is to get hold of really big men to talk to members of the University on political or cultural subjects. It will take up a certain amount of time – but I think that it is well worth it – and therefore, after some misgivings, I have taken it on. I don't honestly think that I shall cope very well- but there it is!

One of the House Clubs[157] met last Monday night! Tremendous fun. We had all seen each other at lunch the same day – and still wanted to see each other, which you always seem to think is so very odd. After a most excellent dinner we played a game which is apparently called *The Game* – and I was considered most curious for not having ever played it – or anyway known of it before.

But, nothing daunted, I was 'picked' by John Synge. He was the first of our side to act – and on coming back to us after being told what to act, he demanded that I got on my hands and knees – which I did. He then proceeded to milk me! This was his interpretation of "the milk of human kindness!"

I was rather flummoxed when asked (by Ludo Kennedy) to act the *Rape of Lucretia* – difficult to cope with, in fact I couldn't.

I had tea with Landia on Tuesday!! Francis Dashwood asked me to come along and, as he hadn't warned me, I couldn't get out of it. What a girl. Clare Beckett is staying with Susan Gibbs tonight – and we are going to a play (*The Millionairess* by G.B. Shaw) this evening. Do you know her? Christopher is her brother – and is exactly like her. She seems rather nice – and most unlike him in everything save looks. In fact, I must go now or I shall be late.

Father flies away on the morning of the 8th – oh, I do hope that he keeps well. It is an awful strain for Mother – and she will be worried until he gets back. Poor thing – but I am certain that it is right him going.

Do write to me soon – I feel rather lost not knowing what you are doing.

Christ Church, Oxford
18th February 1948

I really shouldn't be writing to you as I have a crisis over my work – however there it is! Sometimes I find it so unutterably boring that I have to use all the willpower in the world to work away at it.

Thank you so much for your letter which arrived this morning. It never ceases to amaze me how keen you have become on foxhunting – and it does make me so happy. What fun you seem to have had. Quite right anyway attempting to ride Jorrocks – and you will be able to manage him soon. You still have to get stronger – and then you will be all right.

The most extraordinary thing is that I had tea with Richard Ollard on Monday (yesterday) and I happened to mention it – and he said that he thought he knew Elspeth's name and wasn't she a friend of yours, etc? I said that she was and he then told me that Susan Hamilton was going to be married. I was amazed and didn't know quite what to say – but he quickly came to my assistance and said that the whole thing left him pretty cold.

Apparently she is marrying John Wylde who was married to Helen Leslie Melville before she died, I suppose two years ago. He has two boys (3 and 5 I should think). I wonder whether you know all this – Richard told me in the greatest confidence, etc, and said that it wasn't to be known until it appeared in *The Times,* etc! I wonder how she will be as a mother to two children – will she be able to cope at all?

Cynthia is now miles better – and that crisis is over! I go and see her every day – and today arrived to find John Bickersteth sitting on her bed talking to her! C adores him – so you'll have to fight over him. Humphrey has gone back to Bordon – feeling, of course, completely serene and happy again. What a really good person he is. It has been lovely seeing so much of him lately. He is dining with me on Friday night before the Chatham Club meeting when Quentin Hogg is coming down to speak, which should be quite interesting.

I forgot to tell you that the Boys' Club came down on Saturday. It really was rather fun – they were so nice, and the football matches went off very well. But oh! Why should they take so much for granted. That is the general trend now – to sit back and let everything be done for you – including your thinking. They love the control of the Labour government for this reason. It is a very great danger today.

I spent a lovely Sunday with John Bickersteth – we lunched at *The Rose and Thistle* in Abingdon and then walked out to Sutton Courtenay to have a look at the old camp site by the river, and then on to the village – such a very beautiful one – and then back again to Abingdon and home in time for evensong in New College Chapel. The choir there are simply miles better than the Cathedral one – and it is such a lovely service.

This is a very scrappy quick letter – and I must try and do some work now.

This is the fist time, apparently, that I mention the subject of the importance of a man's profession, having priority over marriage; whereas "a girl's object is to be married".

Christer Church, Oxford
28th February 1948:

    I've not written to you for over a week – pretty bad, as usual. I'm sorry – but, oh dear, I've not been able to cope over the past week. Time really flies – and I seem to have achieved so little. I am really trying to do so much work – and I suppose that, at the same time, I try to fit in all the other 'ploys' – and it really does, at times, become quite desperate! I love Oxford – and everything that goes with it far too much – and as a result I never seem to stop much!

    Your last letter arrived on Monday – bless you for it. And I did so love your beautiful postcard.

    Poor Sue and John[158]– they've got such a long way to go – but, though it's pretty ghastly, it must be worth it in the end. But at times I must admit it all seems pretty awful. Poor Darling – I wonder how often it is that you must think it unbearable. More often than I do, I'm afraid. A girl's object is to be married and have a lovely family – so is a man's, but it must be a secondary object; his first being his profession.

    And so at Oxford there is so much to think about and so much to do. I still do not spend enough time at my academic work – but I hope that I shall never be accused of wasting my time here. For I believe that ultimately the most important thing in life is to know oneself – and then to know something about others – and then surely one has a basis on which to work. So often I see people in Oxford who are pointed out as being "brilliant brains – got a first in Greats you know" – but what of him! So often he turns out to be such an uncompromising bore!

    Later: As usual – at 11.45 pm – two maddening people came in to see me! I most hypocritically entertained them with port and biscuits while they talked about early Venetian opera!

    Do you know what is wrong with David? He has eczema all

over his face – and, of course, is more worried about it than a normal man would be if he had his nose cut off! If fact he says that he doubts whether he will be able to come to Cheltenham, even though he is under the care of the very best specialist in London whom he visits every day!! In his last letter he adds a post-script "As this eczema on one's face sounds so awful, please keep it to yourself"!!

I have been planning Cheltenham for them flat out – and have now just about organised them with vouchers, hotels, taxis, etc, etc. We are having an enormous party for them on the night of the 4th which should be great fun. The party is so big that I have booked a 'bus to take us all out to the Brimpton Grange to dance!

Such an awful thing happened the other night: I had the most appalling row with John Smith. And, oh! over such a particularly petty thing. Such a prime example of a super intelligentsia having no sense of values. As I told you we have started the Bullingdon Club again – and he has not been made a member. Therefore he was very hurt – and tried to make me very uncomfortable that he was not a member. Of course the whole thing is out of my hands as the election was by ballot – but really, have you ever heard anything so utterly pointless? There it is though – we were both very rude and I am v. sorry (though I think I was, for once, in the right!). What a stupid affair it all is. He was now written to apologise – so I suppose I shall have to do something about it instead of forgetting about it, as it should be.

Vincent's Club, Oxford
19th March 1948

Bless you for your letter which arrived on Tuesday. I've been in a bad way, and this letter will be rather a bleat!

I don't think that I told you that I have been having beastly headaches for nearly 3 weeks – not much fun anyway, and hell if one is trying to work. I simply don't know what to do. However today I went to see Ching, the dentist, as not only does my head ache but also my teeth – but nothing seems to be wrong with them. So tomorrow I am off to see Dr Hobson, and on Wednesday I have an appointment with the oculist. I am quite determined to leave no stone unturned. It's pretty maddening, isn't it? And, of course, it has come at the worst possible time. But there we are .....

I want to see you so terribly – when is the earliest that you can come down here? Do come soon Darling. Three months is a ghastly long time. I've quite forgotten what you look like.

I had a pleasant week end with David at Pavenham.[159] It is rather odd staying there, as one really does nothing! But of course I always enjoy it. John Joicey and David Whately were both there which made it nicer than ever. You must meet David W who is a great buddy of mine. At the moment he is in the Stock Exchange which he loathes – and is wondering what on earth he can do for a profession.

We all behaved like girls! Giggling and gossiping! As soon as it was time for bed we all congregated in one of our rooms and talked till the owner of the room was in his pyjamas – and the party then moved on to the next room and the procedure was repeated until all of us were undressed – and then they all came and lay on my bed, until by tactful agreement the other two left so that David could talk to me about Roddie! It was all too obvious that he wanted to discuss something as he walked up and down the room and round and round till he more or less drove them out!

The situation is really pretty unsatisfactory isn't it? I don't believe she can be too terribly keen to get married. Betty – who I like more and more – is against the whole plan as she says that, although she likes Roddie, she feels that she really is only out for a good time, and has no idea of marrying David. But that does not quite seem to be David's idea of the situation – and he only blames the Warren Pearl family as being too possessive!

I then went up to London and saw James Attenborough[160] who is all against me coming to him for 6 months and says that I would learn very little. So I am going straight up to London in July and working there till May '49 when I am taking my Bar Finals. It is going to be a ghastly year – but the end seems now in sight.

I am going to live with Cynthia and Humphrey from July till September (when I do my Part I Bar Exam) and then go to London

House (I hope) to live for the winter, as it is obviously not practical to go up and down in the winter. Do you think it a good plan? I do! In fact I can think of nothing better that living with C and H.

How amazing Gerald Legge marrying Raine McC[161]! He isn't at all debish or stupid!

Dickie will be home (my mind switches, or rather naturally turns to him!) in three weeks or so. How lovely it will be to see him again. It does seem quite an age.

I wonder what you have backed for tomorrow's race – how I wish I was going. It is the greatest thrill in the world. Have a lovely day.

I will write again – but I haven't got your letter here!! Photograph will be returned.

Adwell
5th April 1948

I haven't written for a week – and then only a beastly short note to you. Bless you for yours which arrived here on Wednesday.

Darling, about coming south – when shall I see you? Of course you know that there is always a bed for you here so come as soon as you like. I go back to Oxford on 23rd, but any w/e is perfect. We must make plans! Couldn't you come def. on w/e 23 -25?

I shall be working flat out now till the ghastly June 10th. Really pretty grim, particularly as things aren't going too easily.

I have now got to go into the Acland Home to have these teeth done, which really is about the bottom, particularly as they can't let me know when it is to be. I am rather frightened by the whole idea! Perhaps you will be down in time to come and hold my hand.

My future plans are these: June – leave Oxford, holiday for a fortnight, and then to Cynthia where I am living till September. I will be working under Law Tutors in London called Gibson and Weldon and take my Part I Bar Exam in September. The final is in May, and I shall, I think, live in London from September until April as I will have to be running about the Inner Temple more then. All being well, I will be a barrister in Sept. '49.

I was so sad to hear about Ann – though I rather feared the worst.

Sad primarily for her sake – but also for you as you were such a friend of hers. Can she still be helped? I know that it is hard to want to help her – but if there is any chance I feel that you must try. You owe her a great deal for the past (as she does you). But friendship cannot be placed on a footing of a commercial transaction – now that she is in trouble, surely she must be helped if it is humanly possible?

I don't think that I told you that there is a great building scheme going on here. All the rooms over the garages past my room are being turned into a self-contained flat – kitchen, bathroom, h & c in all bedrooms, etc. Nobody quite seems to know who is going to live there[162] – and the plan seems slightly pointless. But it is going to be very nice. It has taken up quite a bit of time organising the building while Father is away. Likewise other business. I enjoy doing it all very much, but I have rather a guilty feeling the whole time that I should be working.

The new gardener is proving a great success. He is such a nice fellow – and really is getting things done: amongst other extra jobs the swimming pool is being re-done, ie, all the pipes are being re-laid and the numerous cracks filled in. And the tennis courts are a constant 'ploy' for anyone who is doing nothing in particular. We spend hours sweeping it clear of all loose gravel so that some more surface covering can be put on. So much to do .....

I spent the morning selling tickets at the South Oxfordshire Pt to Pt on Saturday – only yesterday but it seems so long ago! I thought so much of you! There seemed to be comparatively little decrease in the number of cars – there were all the policemen standing around laughing at them – and refusing to make any enquiries as to why they were on the road. It really is the most absurd situation – and the law is being openly violated. No law can ever be effective if it is not respected by the community: and the Labour government has done too much to undermine the authority of the law for it to be passed lightly over.

One quite interesting situation occurred: Sir G. Fox M.P. drove up in a large car drawing a trailer. Naturally horse-trailers were allowed in free, so I waved him on. But one of my assistants was quicker than me. He stopped the noble knight and said "Have you got a horse in that trailer Sir?" Before he could answer, the tail board of the trailer was dropped and there, before our eyes, sat 8 PEOPLE (including your friend Gina). Not only was our member acting strictly illegally by using a car on the road, but he was also trying to swindle the South Oxon Hounds! Quite a commotion – and a v. embarrassing one for me ensued. It was not till after quite an argument that I extracted £2 from him for a car park ticket. Can you beat it? Needless to say, the story is now well round S.O. So good for the name of the Conservatives.

The Pt to Pt itself was the greatest fun possible. Masses of people (who didn't arrive in their own car) came by 'bus – and all the old faces were around. I saw Sue and John arriving in Cousin Button's Bentley – purring through armies of enquiring policemen! – but not again. This was maddening as I have fixed the money question for them in Paris which is helpful.

I then drove to High Wycombe with a girl called Heather Collier – do you remember her – and her brother and we caught the train for London and then went to a play called *The Relapse*, a real Elizabethan bawdy comedy – very well done. Cyril Richards was superb – but really rather vile! However, we laughed a lot. The party was given for Susan Gibbs who was 21. We then all went off to change – as were still in our Pt to Pt clothes – and met again at the 400! Goodness knows when I was last there! I rather enjoyed it – surprisingly – and saw lots of buddies again, etc. But stayed up much too late, and felt awfully tired this morning.

We all went to church at St Martin in the Fields – a very good service. I hoped to see Pat (!) (married to Mavis, twin, son died) but he appeared to be off duty.

Adwell
8th April 1948

Your letter arrived this evening. Bless you. And I'm writing back by return which you must admit is pretty good of me!

First of all – plans. Mother would, I think, prefer you to come here on the w/e 23rd – but she said that I was to be sure to say that it doesn't really much matter. But come then – and I shall see you sooner. It's a bit of an effort to wait, knowing that you are in the south (and spring is here again!).

I take your word about Christopher – though I am very sorry to hear your judgement. What a pity. He was so charming and, I thought, outstanding. Isn't it quite extraordinary how David influences all these people? He has been described as a weak character before now – but it is strong enough to completely change other people's!

What fun the Conservative w/e must have been. Florence Horsborough is a great ally of Mother's and came down here during the War to see the children, etc. In fact her influence at the Min. of Health saved the future of the children, who would have been sent back to an institution.

I have been writing round to all the big Conservatives; Anthony Eden won't answer my letter to ask him to speak to the Chatham in June - but I have collected Field Marshal Maitland Wilson to speak about the Middle East and General Paget to explain the workings of Ashridge, both of which would be very interesting.

I have been in Oxford all day – WORKING (you're rather unkind about that. I can't work for 12 hours per day. And anyway I wouldn't take a word in.)

I had tea with Mother at 141[163] – Doris in rattling form. I have pretty well changed my mind about the children and now feel that a really pretty wonderful job has been done. I have had long talks with Mother and Doris – and we are now all in fairly amicable agreement about it all! How odd it is – if you appear to agree with a plan from the outset and skilfully make suggestions to improve it, then so often the suggestion is at least received cordially. But if you show disapproval of a plan from the outset, then woe betide you if you make a suggestion. It is treated as a totally futile criticism and flung out on its ear (and yours too if you're not very careful!).

Must go to SLEEP. Bless you as always.

Will Pott was my mother's cousin and he, though much older than me, became a great friend and adviser. It was he who, having been in the 9th Lancers, persuaded me to join the Regiment and, some years later, introduced me to Sir Guy Ropner, who gave me my first job when he was President of the Chamber of Shipping. The story surrounding my being offered the job of Legal Officer to the Chamber is worth telling. I had decided after a few years at the Bar that, what with marriage and a baby on the way, I should try and earn more money than the somewhat paltry sums made in Chambers (at 4 Paper Buildings with Teddy Ryder-Ricardson). So, when Sir Guy suggested this job, I thought that I should apply for it.

Two others were shortlisted for the interview – both with much better credentials than mine. But my interview went rather well and I was called back after a few minutes and told that I had been chosen. "Have you any questions?" asked Sir Guy. I said that I hoped it was in order to enquire what was written in the note from Mr Gorick (the General Manager of the Chamber of Shipping) which had been passed to Sir Guy. I was given the note. It read "I think you should know that Birch Reynardson is an MA and the other two only BAs." Not a bad investment of £5 for an MA at Oxford!

Somberby Grove, Grantham
11th April 1948

Your note arrived at Adwell just when I was starting off to stay up here with Jerry Pott. I'm afraid that I simply can't come to Sue's party – and I know that you will understand. Oxford will be up and I really must make an effort to be there for a last minute gallop – whip well out. It is beside the point, and obvious that I am frightfully disappointed – and that I feel most self-righteous about it all.

The week-end was great fun. Jerry Pott is an old flame of Mother's – who was in the Regiment about a century ago. The kindest person that you can imagine. Here he is – living all alone in the middle of the Belvoir Country - and he has managed to remain a really good man, amonst so many bad men. Oh dear, what an appalling lot so many of them are. All off with other people's wives – hunting, drinking hard as 2 inch (at least) nails! And yet Jerry always makes his personality felt – and everybody admires him enormously, even the very worst. The answer to his great influence amongst them seems to be his entire lack of priggishness – and his Christian heart.

We went to the Belvoir Point to Point yesterday which was the greatest fun. I saw a lot of friends – David Burghersh, Rupert Watson, Jean Lockett, Eddie Digby (who now has his own aeroplane in which he flew up to the course from London!), the Jenkinson girls (alas no Mrs Baird!), etc. And then last night we had a large dinner party and went off to dance at a place called Craven Lodge: the haven (and/or heaven) of the worst of the hunting community! Amongst others dining there was a girl called Ann Horton who, apparently, is a great friend of Judy's – with whom she was at school.

We are going over to the Belvoir kennels this afternoon, and then I go back to Oxford this evening. I am now reading all the Latin part of Roman Law – and as I have forgotten most of it, I am having to read it with a funny old man in Oxford four times a week. Rather a bore – and most expensive. It means that I have to be in Oxford most of Monday, Tuesday, Thursday and Friday.

I must stop now and go out before luncheon for a toddle with Jerry.

I can't think about the budget. How sad it is – but read the history of the social revolution in (a) 1680 and (b) 1820. It was much worse then!!

Adwell
19th April 1948

Dickie is back – and, oh! it is so lovely having him with us. Mary and Susan had their twenty first birthday party on Thursday and he arrived back just in time for it – having got to Windsor that very day.

He is quite changed in so many ways. When I last saw him he was a baby – or at least a boy, who was trying desperately hard to be a Grenadier – and now he is a man. As Humphrey says, he could be nothing other than a Grenadier, but he is a very nice one. He has grown a large red moustache, and become quite fat (that will soon go, poor chap).

We had had only one long talk about since he arrived, as Mother and he went off to the Bicester Pt to Pt yesterday, so I hardly saw him all day. I went and dined with the Fox family. A most amazing party!

Thirty of us sat down to dinner – and afterwards we danced in the drawing room. Really rather fun. Lady Fox is a pretty ridiculous individual – but very kind and, I believe, fairly sincere. Gifford is more boring (and perhaps stupid) than is possible to imagine. He seems to be very upset about the death penalty (I agree) – and even opened his mouth in the House on Friday about it. Thank goodness this is a rare occurrence.

Mary's party was the greatest fun – we all went to *Bless the Bride* – and then went on to The Berkeley where Galbiati[164] gave us a frightfully good dinner. The party consisted of: Susan and her sister (Mary Macdonald) and her brother Peter, Audrey Wills, Mary, Betsy and Barbara, John Pott, John Bickersteth, Anthony Birley, Keith Egglestone, Betsy Pryor, John Synge, Heather Collier and Dickie.

One quite funny situation occurred when we were collecting taxis for the girls and Dickie, in blues and a blue hat, arrived on the running board – only to be approached by a theatre-goer with a large tip in his hand to tip whom he thought was the commissionaire! We laughed a lot – and so did he (which a year ago would not have been the case!).

I have been going into Oxford nearly every day – which is an awful bore, but it's got to be done.

Extract from my letter to Lorna dated 26th April 1948
Oxford

...I do want you to realise how unutterably unhappy the thought has been for me to think of you waiting and waiting for this indefinite time, without any fixed limit. For me to expect you to do so would be unforgivably selfish and beastly.

From my own point of view – so much less important – is the ever growing feeling that I must get my qualifications over – even at the price of skimping some of them - so that I can stop this waiting for you. And there, of course, is the crux of the matter.

If – perhaps some, even you, would say – if I loved you enough that should be my wish, and that all my desire should be to get my work done, and marry you. You know – and you always have – that I am not ready yet. Will I ever be?

How can I expect you to just hang on at my convenience? I love you too much for that – and too much to ask you to marry me before I can honestly believe that I will make you a husband fit for you. Before I am qualified as a barrister – and have a profession – I know that I should be incapable of doing so.

And so I feel that this present situation has become impossible. For you – and for me – the strain is awfully bad, both mentally and physically, perhaps spiritually too.

Extract from Lorna's letter to me dated 30th April 1948

You put everything perfectly and I am quite convinced that we are doing the right and only thing possible, hard though it is going to be ...

We just never faced up to it – that's the trouble. We knew it had to come but just always hung on with our heads in the sand, hoping that 'something' would happen ...

Darling, I know it's right and I feel terribly strongly and almost confidently that it will come out in the wash. If either of us changes we shall be thankful that it ended here and now. If not, and in however many years to come it is, we'll be certain and sublimely happy ...

Footnotes to Part V

104. Worth about £18,500 today.

105. The name of the fountain in Tom Quad.

106. Sir Richard Goodenough, eldest son of Sir William.

107. Tommy Hutchinson, Treasurer of Christ Church and Secretary of the Heythrop Hunt. A very brilliant man. His daughter Judy became a great friend; the first female High Sheriff of Oxfordshire.

108. Her landlady, wife of Canon Williams.

109. Tony Meyrick

110. Zandra Brett

111. Christopher Beckett's father, Ralph.

112. June Ponsonby, afterwards Lady Grimston, daughter of Lord de Mauley, my mother's uncle.

113. Winifred Ponsonby, later Mrs Christopher (Kim) Holman, sister of June.

114. Sir William Goodenough, my father's great friend. Later Chairman of Barlays Bank, he made my father a local director of the bank in Oxford.

115. There used to be a particularly beautiful avenue of elm trees running from the ha-ha into the park. All died of elm disease forty years ago.

116. He had been in South Africa on a fundraising tour for London House (where I lived – see later).

117. Major Morland; a great friend of my father in South Africa. Toni was his very pretty daughter who Colin Balfour and I used as a 'bait' to stop cars for us on the A40 road at Adwell Lodge; we then hitch-hiked up to London!

118. Memorial Service for Douglas Bailie.

119. He had T.B.

120. Later became Master of the Horse.

121. This was the first time that I heard Kathleen Ferrier sing. She dined with us and, as Bruno Walter was late arriving from London, she sang to us "to fill in the time". I'll never ever forget it.

122. Bosahan, on the Helford River. A huge Victorian house which Harry Graham-Vivian had inherited. I had recently been made a Trustee (with Michael Joicey) of the Aberavan Trust which included the house and land in Cornwall. Later the house was demolished and a more manageable house built. Sad but necessary.

123. Eresby House, Rutland Gate. This was a haven for all us. If no bed was available there was always the floor, or a bolster down a double bed with Juliet the other side!

124. Harry Graham-Vivian, perhaps my greatest friend. He was my best man at our wedding. I became his Trustee of the Bosahan Estate in Cornwall and also his mother's Marriage Settlement Trustee, so I was closely involved with the family!

125. John Synge, later a well known picture dealer. Died young.

126. Clare Beckett. John was very fond of her, but this was not reciprocated.

127. Lavinia Ponsonby, who married Sir Michael Hamilton MP, son of the Dean of Windsor and Sue Hamilton's brother.

128. Lorna helped Ros move from Holly Lodge, Northumberland, to Nunnington, Yorkshire.

129. Typing the list of names attending the ball.

130. Richard Faber, later Publisher
131. Christian Carnegy, who later married Sir John Smith MP.

132. At Sutton Courtenay.

133. Irene Kearsley, always known as Miss Jane – goodness knows why! A huge friend of my parents', who spent the last part of her life at Lawn Lodge, Adwell.

134. General Rowan-Hamilton.

135. Rosemary, formerly Elton.

136. Caroline Lascelles, later Viscountess Chandos.

137. Dalkeith.

138. Scott.

139. I remember that it was very hot and grouse were scarce, but as we arrived at the top of a hill, a large covey of grouse got up – but not one was shot because, below us was Star Loch and in it were bathing the female members of the house party, all naked, led by Elizabeth Northumberland.

140. Somehow (can't remember quite how) he is related to us, and always called me 'Cousin William.'

141. Mary (née Tyser of Gordonbush where, later, we used to stalk) and Antony (later Lord Aldenham) who, when staying at Drumlanrig, was surprised at being given half a grouse at dinner. "What an extraordinary thing to carve a grouse" he was heard to exclaim rather too loudly!

142. Violet Loraine – a famous Edwardian actress. John's father was sacked from the 9th Lancers for marrying her!

143. Newcastle Show. Kit and I did enter the Open Jumping on two of his hunters. They had never seen a show jumping course before. My horse didn't do too badly. Nevertheless, when I rode out of the ring the commentator said "Well, the last rider certainly had a smashing time."

144. Married to Sir Patrick Duncan, late (and last) Governor-General of South Africa.

145. Aunt Iola Ashton, my father's sister. Married to Colonel Sam Ashton, a really lovely old-fashioned man; a great port drinker with my father!

146. Christopher Marriott.

147. Canon Mascall of Christ Church Cathedral, a good friend and adviser.

148. Alec and Pam Maurice, great friends of my father.

149. Bob Manners, later Lord Manners.

150. I went down to Gravesend to do some Conservative canvassing.

151. Hunting with the Cottesmore from Ranksborough, the Jenkinsons' house. Mrs Baird always looked magnificent riding side saddle. She never hesitated to tick you off if she considered your riding below par!

152. Colonel David Laurie.

153. Peter Gibbs.

154. Lord Buxton's son, Denis, killed in the First World War and his grandson, John Ponsonby killed on Christmas Day 1943, the son of Phylis (married to Maurice Ponsonby) the eldest surviving daughter of Lord Buxton who died in 1942. On Lady Buxton's death in 1955, Newtimber was inherited by Betsy Ponsonby, the elder sister of Barbara and Mary.

155. Hugh Trevor Roper, Regius Professor of Modern History at Oxford. He wrote numerous books including the Life of Archbishop Laud and *The Last Days of Hitler.* He was later created Lord Dacre. He married Field Marshal Haig's eldest daughter, Alexandra (Zandra) Howard-Johnston.

156. She married Peter Orde and went to live in Northumberland.

157. This must have been a Loders dinner. We had a lot of totally irresponsible fun – and always overdid the drink! We dined at the Feathers in Woodstock and decided to go and visit the Duke of Marlborough at Blenheim! He was not very pleased but gave us a drink!

158. Sue Mattingley and John Berry.

159. Pavenham Bury, the Laurie house in Bedfordshire.

160. A close colleague of my father's in the War Office; he later resumed his practice as a solicitor.

161. Raine McCorquodale. Married, first, Gerald Legge (Earl of Dartmouth) and later married Johnny Althorp and, therefore, became the step-mother of Princess Diana.

162. Later to be Lorrie Wollerton's house, but we lived there first before we moved into the house in 1959. Before it was renovated it was occupied by Leslie Jones (as a changing room) and Walter Merritt (the footman).

163. 141 Banbury Road, Oxford, where 'the children' lived.

164. Galbiati, the Head Waiter in The Berkeley Restaurant (when the hotel was in Berkeley Square). He was a great friend of many of us and always asked whether we could pay now or later!

Epilogue

And so the parting occurred. I suppose it was almost inevitable. We had met when we were very young and I returned, having participated in the Italian Campaign, a much older and experienced man but with no job. And there was another factor. Lorna was the heir to Manderston and I was the heir to Adwell. How were we going to cope with two estates? Where were we going to live?

We were both, of course, very miserable at the time, but life had to go on. I had to qualify as a barrister and start earning some money. I worked very hard and managed to pass my Bar exams in quick time. Lorna returned to Manderston and began to take over the reins (or anyway the snaffle rein) from her father (who never released the curb rein!). She married Gordon Palmer[1] on May 6th 1950.

And then, in the summer of 1950, an incident occurred which was to change my life. My cousin Ashley Ponsonby rang me up an asked me whether I was free to come to a performance of *The Marriage of Figaro* at Covent Garden. He explained that the party would consist of Margaret Elphinstone, "a girl recently returned from Southern Rhodesia" and us two. Of course I should have smelt a rat as Ashley was not what you would call a regular visitor to Covent Garden. Anyway, I accepted with alacrity.

On the chosen evening I arrived at the Opera House punctually at 7.15. Nobody was about. I went to the ticket desk. "Oh yes, we have a ticket for you but the performance commenced at 7.00 pm." I should have remembered that Mozart operas begin half an hour early. I was allowed in at the first 'break' and shown to my seat in the dark. It was an aisle seat. "Why are you late?" whispered my neighbour. "Kept in chambers, important case," I replied. "Are you sure or did you forget it was a Mozart opera?" We dined at the White Tower in Percy Street. When I got back to Adwell I told my mother that I had met the girl I was going to marry. I did this six months later on November 29th 1950.[2]

---

[1] Gordon Palmer, of the Huntley and Palmer Biscuit company, was a particularly charming man. Although a Territorial soldier, General John Mogg always claimed that Gordon taught him how to be a soldier. He became Humphrey Prideaux's Vice-Chairman at Morland's Brewery in Abingdon (where Lorna was born). A hugely popular Lord Lieutenant of Berkshire.

[2] See photograph on page 303.

ELEANOR, MRS BAILIE AND LORNA
AT MANDERSTON

[Eleanor was very much the reluctant debutante,
hence her expression.]

Eleanor Bailie's Ball at Manderston, 1949

Back Row: Michael Joicey, Tony Bicket, Major G. Bailie, Ronnie Callendar, Dick Palmer
Second Row: Gill Savoy (Younger), Eleanor Bailie (Retallack), Lorna Bailie (Palmer), Rosemary Portman (Pease)
Third Row: Elizabeth Grenfell, Ba Sclater-Booth, Mrs Bailie
Front Row: Derek Bibby, Gavin Rowan-Hamilton, Robin Stormouth Darling

1947.

Ben Cunningham — December 18th – 19(?)
Julia Cunningham — " "
Susan Hattersley
Henri
Pom[?] Carr — October 15th – 29th –

1st November 1947.

1948.

Jimmy Stewart-Stevens — 2-4 Dec.
Greville Stewart-Stevens — 2" 4" December
Bill Bird Livingston — 18th to 21st December
Mrs E. Crew — Jan 19" 23rd
Par Blake — Jan 30 – Feb 1
19.4.8.

David Zaretie — car – 30 – 25 /

EXTRACTS FROM MANDERSTON VISITORS BOOK.
THE DATE 1948 (IN BOLD) IS NOT CORRECT. I STAYED AT MANDERSTON IN DECEMBER 1947.

Left to Right: W.B.R., Cynthia Prideaux, Colin Balfour, Prue Balfour, Jean Maclagen, Humphrey Prideaux, Michael Maclagen, Nik Humphreys (later Birch Reynardson)
Red Hat Ball, Grosvenor House
1950

Our Wedding
St. Bartholomew The Great, Smithfield
November 29th 1950

W.B.R.
INNER TEMPLE
1952

CHARLES PONSONBY, GLADYS PONSONBY
AND LESLIE JONES (BUTLER)
1958

Lt Col David Laurie M.C.
1960

P.M.B.R.
1975

P.M.B.R., W.B.R., Clare and Juliet
Adwell 1960s

THOMAS AND NIK WITH THEIR TERRIER GLENNY
ADWELL 1960s

Back row: RONALD STEWART-BROWN, W.B.R.
Middle: IMOGEN B.R., T.B.R. (WITH EDWARD) JULIET S-B, ADRIAN HOPKINSON, P.M.B.R, CLARE H.
Front: WILLIAM B.R, HENRY S-B, IOLA H, WALTER S-B, DIANA S-B, FREDERICK H, GEORGE B.R, DAISY B.R, CUTHBERT H, GORDON H.
1995

Appendix 1

Song

The golden hours of June have fled
Beyond the western seas,
The lilac long ago has shed
Her petals to the breeze;
And now no more the nightingale
Sings to the dreaming trees.

The golden hours of Youth have fled
Beyond the bourne of years,
The rose of Love that bloomed so red
A paler livery wears –
No more, no more the waking heart
A song at morning hears.

by H.B.R.

Appendix 2

Verse written by H.V. Sones for W.B.R.

As I've hobbled round the table
Serving soup and fish and meat,
Oft my hands have been unable
To endure the oven's heat,
But I've stuck it like a Trojan
Firmly setting teeth and jaw,
Face devoid of all emotion
Butlers are not men of straw.
How I've polished that old table
Smoothing scratches, moving grease,
'Til I got it smooth an' sable,
Yet my efforts did not cease.
As I worked I wove in fancy
Stories round that aged wood;
Luckily for me, I can see
Romance – any poet could.
For around that grand old table
Hosts of generations past
May have gathered when the blackness
Of the night no shadows cast.
Shades of Jones, and Webb and Newell,
Birch and Reynardson, maybe,
"Lord Abingdon in the corner"
May have joined their company.

Years will pass and at that table
You may sit as Squire and Host,
To the company assembled
It will be no idle boast,
If you speak of brave Sir Samuel
And his trade on Turkey's coast,
London's Mayor, and loyal subject
Of King Charles – when needed most.

These are solid facts not fable,
But I must not linger long
For your food is on the table
And I soon must sound the gong,
So, reverting to our duties
We will leave the Phantom throng
To the cobwebs, and the rafters,
And the past where they belong.

Notes on the foregoing (written by Mr H. V. Sones):

Adwell (Oxfordshire), mentioned in the Domesday Book, had a sucession of owners, many of whom lived to a ripe old age (see v3). "Lord Abingdon sat in the corner" was a wooden panel, with a Dutch painting on it.

Sir Samuel Reynardson was Lord Mayor of London in the reign of Charles I. Having sworn allegiance, he refused to sign the King's death-warrant' was thrown into the Tower of London, and fined a large sum of money by the King's enemies. Later he founded and endowed the Merchant-Taylor School. Master William was a direct descendant. I was his grandfather's butler from 1925 to 1935.

Appendix 3

Extract from article, written by an Italian civilian on 20th September 1975, describing the battle at Montecieco on 20th September 1944

'Goodbody knew that his artillery (H.A.C.) could not perform miracles nor even his infantry (the KRRC); Hull's order meant slaughter. And at 10.50 am the Queen's Bays coldly launched themselves towards their own massacre.

From the crest, along which runs the road, to Hill 153, there are 1800 metres of open ground without any hedges. The Bays were reduced to 27 Shermans from the 52 they had three weeks before. How many would remain of those up there on the road?

The Germans saw them appear on the summit of the hill. The German artillery was incredulous at the sight. The Shermans presented themselves, within range, like targets in a shooting gallery. It was a massacre. From all directions perforating tungsten grenades rained down on the English tanks. At least six 88mm cannons were placed at the houses Balducci and Conti and now fired on the backs of the advancing Shermans. "For the most part," cited the English report of the battle, "our tanks were under fire almost immediately." Some were put out of action with broken turrets, or body and tracks immobilised. The survivors threw themselves out of their vehicles, some darting into the open to get back to the infantry up on the crest, but they were almost all cut down by German machine gun fire. The wiser ones flattened themselves on the ground and awaited nightfall. All the tanks that had taken part in the attack, with the exception of three, were destroyed.

24 out of 27 Shermans were thus eliminated. 64 men fell, killed or wounded. Among those killed was the observation officer of the H.A.C. whose Sherman got a direct hit.

It was now up to the 9th Lancers, who should have renewed the suicidal attack, passing between the burnt out shells of their comrades' Shermans in flames on that infernal slope. But Col Price now forwarded a new report to Goodbody telling him to suspend the attack and "consolidate his positions." Besides, another attack would have been even crazier and more useless, for by that time the Canadians had already broken through the German lines at San Fortunato.'

This article was sent by Stug Perry to Jack Price. It was written by an Italian civilian who sent it to the 9th/12th Lancers H.Q. in 1975. The article mentioned that we were fighting the German 90th A Division, commanded by the legendary Major General Baade (the 'Hero of Casino').

Appendix 4

W.B.R's Address at Michael Joicey's Memorial Service

During the last few days I've been thinking quietly about Michael and I've been talking to his friends. He seemed very near. As Canon Scott Holland wrote in the passage read at the service last week, he seemed 'only to have slipped away into the next room'. And memories of him turned into quite clear visions.

My first vision is of him at Eton. I suppose it must have been the winter of 1940. There he was, out beagling, standing aside from the rest of the field. He had seen a hare and he was pointing in that funny way he had - left shoulder dropped and that special look of joyful enthusiasm tinged with excitement. You know what I mean? And another thing I remember was that, unlike the rest of us who in those days wore breeches and change coats and those rather smart spotted stocks, he was wearing a white cricket jersey - rather big and floppy. Michael was not a follower of fashion.

I left Eton before he became Captain of the Oppidans. Not everyone knows of his scholastic prowess. He was, of course, the last to flaunt it.

But his intelligence was the basis for his extraordinary wide spectrum of knowledge.

We went our different ways in the War. He joined the Coldstream Guards and, I'm told, was a brilliant staff officer. We came back to Oxford together after it was all over. Oh! What fun we had. Work was not a major consideration.

And here's my second vision for you. We were sitting on the terrace at my home in Oxfordshire with my Mother. We were - or so I thought - busy catching up on some revising before our Oxford Finals. After a morning of complete silence I observed Michael sidling up to my Mother. "Mrs B.R." he said, "I thought you'd like to know that I've seen forty seven different species of bird fly into that Virginia creeper this morning". And he produced a meticulous list of them for her. He could have done the same with butterflies, of which he had an encyclopaedic knowledge.

After Oxford we went to London. It wasn't quite the happiest period of Michael's life and it didn't last too long. But, nevertheless, there was plenty of laughter at his flat in Rosscourt Mansions. It was a wonderful quadrille - I use that word advisedly instead of a quartet, it seems more descriptive consisting of Michael, Philip de Zulueta, Henry Douglas Pennant and Andrew Harding. Andrew used to describe how, when the rest of them were bustling off to the City, Michael would quietly dial TRU (Trunks) and check up on the progress his mother was making with the Times Crossword puzzle. Those of you who knew Michael's mother will know that the morning calls were brief.

But the main thing about London was that it was there that he met and married Elizabeth in 1952 and here their loving partnership began.

They returned to his beloved Northumberland in 1953. In 1954 he took over the mastership of the North Northumberland hounds, a position he held for nearly twenty years - with Jack Howells his devoted huntsman.

We were constant visitors to New Etal to hunt or shoot there. And here's another vision. Elizabeth had a donkey called Tuppence. I can see Michael fussing round our daughter Clare as she sat astride the donkey making sure that the saddle and bridle were all in order just as if he was saddling a Grand. National runner. His love of children was proverbial and his capacity to take trouble for them - as indeed for all with whom he came into contact - was infinite.

But life was not only hunting and shooting. He served on numerous county and local committees and was on the County Council for many years, attaining the office of Alderman.

Michael and Elizabeth and the children moved to the Manor after his father's death in 1966. Immediately Michael set to work. He was not only efficient but immensely practical. The stables and garden were modernized and improved and maintenance work on the estate commenced. Michael made it a rule that he didn't ask people to do things which he couldn't do himself. He could not only gralloch a stag but he could butcher it - he could clean a fish quicker than the most experienced gillie - he could shear a sheep - he was an expert gardener.

And he was determined - verging on stubbornness! What about that day shooting on the Till at New Etal when a woodcock fell into the river? No dog could be persuaded to venture into the very cold and fast flowing water. But Michael announced that his dog - I think it was Donna - was going to retrieve the bird. Nothing doing, Donna didn't like the water either. Eventually desperation overcame him and grabbing her in his left arm he proceeded to wade into the water and launched her onto the floating woodcock.

Dogs became more and more part of his life - not only his German Pointers but also his sheep dogs Shoofty and Smiler. That's another vision as he quietly worked a dog with the fleet footed and jumpy Hebredian sheep - speaking and whistling. You can see him - can't you - with his arm outstretched directing the dog to right or to left or to lie down.

I have spoken to many of his friends in the dog world. He was on a number of committees of the Kennel Club and however much he disliked London he regularly attended their meetings.

"What did you feel about him?" I asked one of the Kennel Club Chairmen. "Well, he respected us for what we were - experts in our own particular sphere. Sometimes he might disagree with us but, if we were in the majority, he'd always support our view. He was a real man - a man of honour."

And what about the way he ran the estate? He has been described as an 'immaculate landlord'. But his attitude was that of a custodian rather than an owner. He aimed at being the best possible steward of his inheritance. He worked zealously to maintain and improve the many cottages and buildings on the estate. His forestry management was of the highest quality. The way in which he diversified into areas other than agriculture was impressive - do you know that since the opening of Heatherslaw Mill and the Lady Waterford Hall over half a million people have visited them.

But his main concern was the well being of his thirty five tenant farmers and the fifty people who worked with him - not for him. I've spoken to some of them.

"He'd always have time for us - and if we didn't see him he'd come and see us." People mattered to Michael because of what they are not who they are. But at the very centre of his concern for others was his love of his family. We grieve so much for Elizabeth and for James and Andrew and Katie - and for the six grandchildren, Hanna, William, Richard, Lucy, Helen and Robert. But we thank God that he died from a heart attack and didn't linger on unable to live the full life he loved.

And this leads me to his religion. Michael was, of course, a very private person. He was disinclined to discuss things about which he felt deeply. He was much more of a listener. And his religion was the last subject for discussion. His religion was the core of his life - his corner stone. You heard James read 'They that put their trust in Him shall understand the truth.' Michael was trusting and faithful; he understood the truth.

And he practised what he believed. Here at Etal he was churchwarden and lay Chairman of the PCC. Further afield he was a member of the Deanery Synod, he was on the Newcastle Cathedral Appeal Committee and he was on the Diocesan Standing Conference on rural evangelism. His gifts to charity were generous in the extreme.

You will all be familiar with that part of Saint Paul's letter to The Corinthians when he describes charity. Nevertheless, I'd like to read a short extract to you:

"Charity suffereth long, and is kind; charity envieth not; charity vaunteth not itself, is not puffed up, does not behave itself unseemly, seeketh not her own, is not easily provoked, thinketh no evil; rejoiceth not in iniquity, but rejoiceth in the truth, beareth all things, believeth all things, hopeth all things, endureth all things. Charity never faileth."

It seems to me that these verses perfectly describe Michael's character.

But what about us? May we all learn from his example as we gratefully honour his memory.

Appendix 5

From *The Times* Obituaries 2nd September 1991

NIK BIRCH REYNARDSON

Nik Birch Reynardson, former Oxford county councillor and president of the Henley Conservative Association since 1993, died on August 6 aged 74. She was born on June 15, 1923.

A tireless figure dedicated to the service of the county in which she lived for nearly 38 years, Nik Birch Reynardson could at first sight have been mistaken for a conventional product of the British class system. But that would have been to do her a great deal less than justice. The brisk, courageous determination she brought to every aspect of living was originally reflected in the way as a child she tackled the challenge of tuberculosis.

The elder daughter of Lieutenant-General Sir Thomas Humphreys, Nik Humphreys (as she was until her marriage) spent her early years in India, where her father was serving at the time. At the age of six, as a result of a riding accident, she contracted tuberculosis and having returned to England, spent the next seven years lying on her back encased in plaster from head to toe.

She was first sent to a T.B. sanatorium, where a governess gave her a good general educational grounding. But academic salvation came with her arrival at the home of two maiden aunts living in Kent (her parents were still in India). One of them had beds made up for both herself and her niece in the dining-room and there she taught Nik an almost complete syllabus of subjects ranging from botany to history, languages to geography, music to mathematics.

So well did she do her job that at the age of 13 though still on crutches the young daughter of the Empire passed easily into St Mary's, Wantage, where she spent the next four years, even playing hockey on crutches in goal. Finally, however, she came to manage simply with the made-up shoe that she wore for the rest of her life in order to cope with a faulty hip-bone.

Fortune then once again took a turn for her future. One school holidays the local M.P. came to call at her aunts' home and - struck by her determination and ability - insisted that she should be sent to a crammers to learn Ancient Greek. This she duly did, going up to Oxford in 1942 with an exhibition from St Hugh's College, where she took a good second in Philosophy, Politics and Economics.

With the Second World War over, she then cast about for a job. It was typical of her lifelong concern for others that the one she chose should have been looking after Displaced Persons in Germany. After that came 12 months in Salisbury, Southern Rhodesia, serving on the staff of the Governor where the atmosphere in those palmy, post war days was presumably rather different from refugee camps in Germany. Her spell in Southern Rhodesia proved, however, to be her last paid job as in 1950 she married a friend she had made at university, Bill Birch Reynardson, a maritime lawyer, who lived near Thame in Oxfordshire.

But the energy that might have gone into a career was now merely diverted into raising her family and into a powerful amount of voluntary work. In 1967 she founded the South Oxfordshire Conservative Women's Advisory Committee, later being elected first for Chinnor and Tetsworth and then for Thame onto the Oxfordshire County Council. A strong supporter of her local M.P., the former Deputy Prime Minister, Michael Heseltine, she eventually became president of the Henley Conservative Association, having served for many years as chairman of its Tetsworth branch. She was, in turn, a member of the Oxfordshire District Health Authority and of the Oxford Regional Health Authority, subsequently becoming a trustee of the Nuffield Medical Trust.

She was a passionate Tory. But she also possessed a gift of listening, and her interest in other people always lay in what they wanted to say rather than in what she felt they ought to be told.

She and her husband lived in a lovely country house which they made into a welcoming family home surrounded by a beautiful garden on which for almost 40 years she lavished great affection.

She is survived by her husband Bill and a son and two daughters.

Appendix 6

HUMPHREY PRIDEAUX

He was born in 1915. After Eton and Trinity College Oxford, he joined 3rd Carabiniers in 1936. He had a distinguished career as a soldier during the war, serving first with his Regiment (surviving the retreat to Dunkirk) then at the Staff College as a student and instructor. He joined the Guards Armoured Division, finally going to Washington as P.A. to Air Marshal Sir William Elliot. He left the Army in 1953 having been invited to join the Board of N.A.A.F.I. (Navy, Army and Air Force Institute). Later he became Chairman of Oxo, Brooke Bond, London Life Insurance and Morlands Brewery, Deputy Chairman of W.H. Smith and a Director of Grindlays Bank. He was also Chairman of Lord Wandsworth College.

Appendix 7
The Evacuees at Adwell 1939 to 1945

REAL HOME SOLVES HOMELESS CHILDREN'S PROBLEM

Foster-parents can be trained for the full-time, paid career of bringing up this family of 150,000; can give to the unwanted children of this country the home-life and mother-love that so many institutions lack

Every young life is of value to Britain today, if our forty-seven millions are to pull their weight in the days ahead alongside the more numerous millions of Russia and the United States.

Healthy, happy childhood is the State's, as well as the parents', affair, far more so now than ever before —especially where it concerns the child whose parents, for a variety of reasons, cannot be entrusted with its upbringing, and the child who has no known parents at all.

The great human problem of the legion of children denied the elementary birthright of proper home life has been enormously aggravated during the last few years. First are the problem-progeny bred of the fleeting friendships formed in the artificial excitement, anxiety and separation of war.

There are the orphans of the blitz; others whose parents have disappeared without trace and may be dead or alive; and those deserted by the contemptible few who vanished to avoid paying billeting charges.

At least a hundred and fifty thousand unwanted or unclaimed children are known officially to have no normal home life—the unofficial figure is estimated to be scores of thousands more.

The Gough case flashed a lurid light on just one sordid aspect of the problem. And now the Home Office committee, headed by Miss Myra Curtis, principal of Newnham College, is touring the country, inquiring into the provisions made for children deprived of normal home life, studying the good and bad of the existing system in order to recommend a new charter of what foster-parenthood should and should not be.

What it can be is illustrated by the picture-story on these pages of a unique six-year experiment in the bringing up, as brothers and sisters of one big family, by one foster-mother, of twenty-one children, most of whom have never known what it is like to have parents of their own.

The joyous life brought about by their change of fortune, and evidenced by their smiling faces, will touch many hearts. More, this constructive story can be an example to authorities and well-wishers of what can be done to help every fostered child to grow up into a valued and useful citizen, instead of into a backward and delinquent one.

The cottage home, with one and the same foster-mother caring for a good-size family of "brothers and sisters," avoids the impersonal and motherless atmosphere of institution life. It offers safer and easier inspection than when odd children are scattered

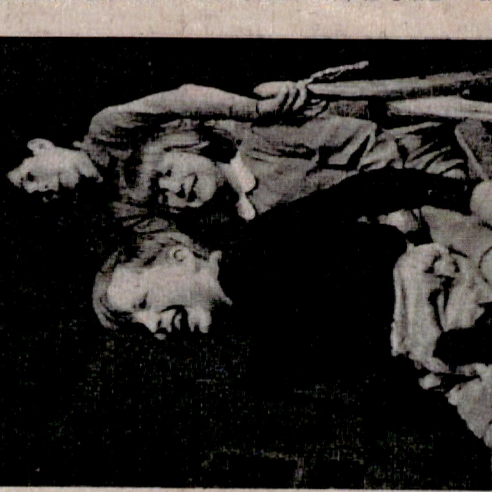

The Slide. Gay and grave studies of two "brothers" and a "sister" as one cries excitedly: "Here we go!"

OVER

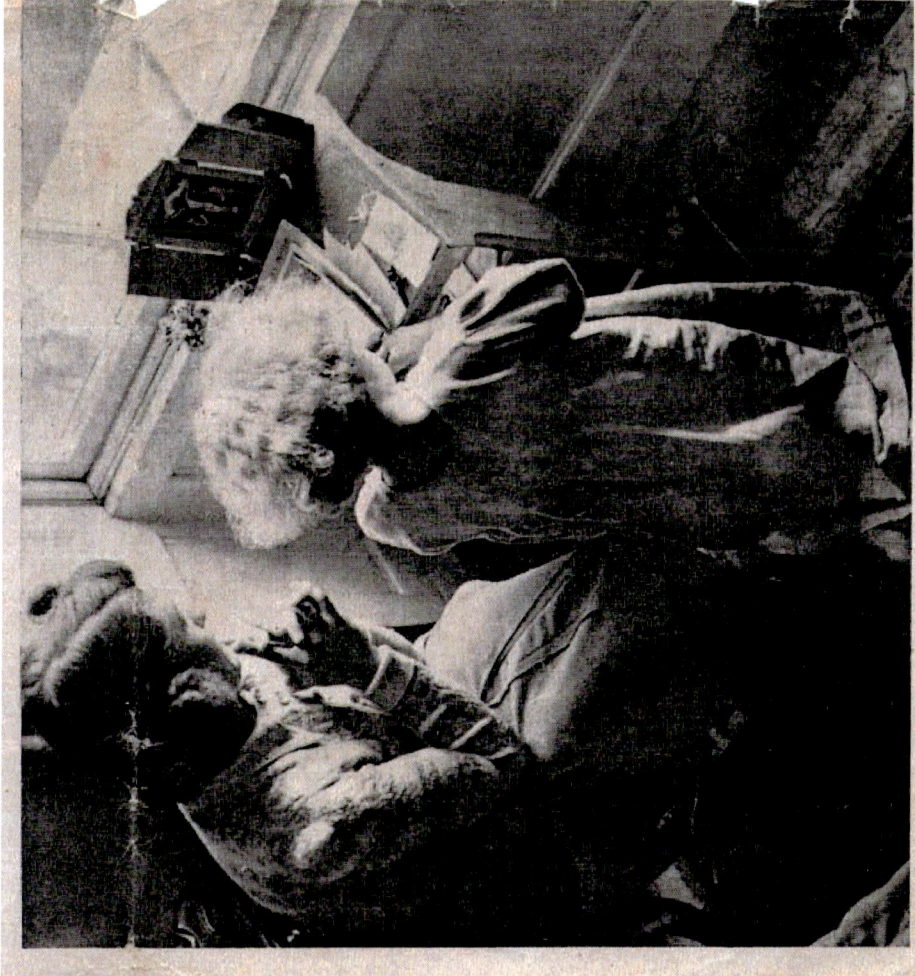

among private families, and the motive of profit is sometimes stronger than that of love.

The cottage home as the ideal foster-family unit is, I understand, being urged on the Curtis Committee by some of the most experienced bodies and individuals concerned with unwanted and ill-treated children.

More than two hundred officers of the National Society for the Prevention of Cruelty to Children favour it. They suggest a family of eight or nine, with a mother who is preferably a widow and whose affection for her charges is her foremost qualification.

Affection is rated even higher than efficiency, for the first inborn desire of unwanted children is to feel they are *wanted*.

If the problem is handled the right way there is no reason why they should not enjoy both. But this will come about only if motherhood ceases to be regarded as an amateurish business, and one hears less about choosing "the right sort of foster-mother," instead of a trained and qualified one.

Nobody talks about the "right sort of teacher" where a child's education is concerned. It is taken for granted that a teacher is trained and qualified. Why shouldn't a foster-mother be also?

A child's home life, by which its character and moral outlook are largely formed, is every bit as important as its schooling. And a foster-mother who brings up a family, or series of families, should be following a vocation recognized and paid for as a skilled and noble job.

Such courses of training already exist at the best types of nursery schools, where a potential foster-mother soon discovers whether she loves child-care sufficiently to go on with it as a lifetime career.

Foster-Mother Doris Sayer, whom you see with her charges in these pictures, was not only trained at a nursery school, but is a certificated teacher able to give them their schooling as well. This is exceptional and is not essential. What does matter, if foster-children go out to school, is that they have a mother to come home to—the same one all the time.

This is the reverse of institution life, where they have no one person as mother, and pass through the hands of several if moved from home to home or school to school.

The children you see pictured here at Adwell House, Tetsworth, Oxfordshire, the home of Colonel and Mrs. Birch-Reynardson, have been brought up to know Foster-Mother Doris Sayer as their one mother.

The colonel's wife, who is the presiding genius behind the adventure of this super cottage home with

Prayer Time in Foster-Mother Doris's room. For children who have never known a real father it is a delight to say "Our Father." They also say another little prayer which has been devised for them. It is: "I want God and God wants me

its fostered family of twenty-one, and who throughout the six years has taken her turn with everything from bathing the children to putting them to bed, is regarded as an extra special mother. Five young relatives and friends of the family, who have given their services free throughout the war, take turns as additional helpers.

Now, the German war over, the family is at the parting of the ways. Seven children with homes will go back to them. One has been adopted by the Adwell cook. Thirteen with no homes will, if funds can be found, go with Foster-Mother Doris Sayer into a smaller house and be brought up and schooled by her till they are sixteen.

Friends will provide a house rent-free, and the institutional authority concerned will contribute generously; but the utmost economy still leaves a need for more money, if the thirteen are to enjoy a future as rich in promise as the lives they have led for the last six years.

But thousands of children have never enjoyed such happiness. They have remained in institutions, known only the impersonal life of this system. It is not the fault of the institutions; in well managed ones, everything possible is done for the child. It is the system that is wrong; the cottage home may prove the solution.

With the institutional system should go all the outworn psychological approach to the problem of unwanted children. In some quarters they are still made to feel different from their fellows by being labelled as "waifs and strays." In others the smug words "moral care" creep in. Elsewhere there is an atmosphere of "pity."

The Ministry of Health has shown daring and enlightenment by decreeing that every unwanted child and its mother shall have all the special medical attention and food allowances that others enjoy. Indeed, as the Ministry official in charge of child-care told me, children without normal home life need if anything more care than those born under a luckier star.

The happy foster-family pictured in these pages have all, since they were toddlers of two or three, been brought up, if not born, under such a star. They are not to be pitied, but envied. They enjoyed what poor little Dennis O'Neill deserved, but did not get, at Gough's farm.

He will not have died in vain if the heart-searchings his death started, and the nation-wide Curtis inquiry now going on, bring about a more humane deal for the Unwanted Child !

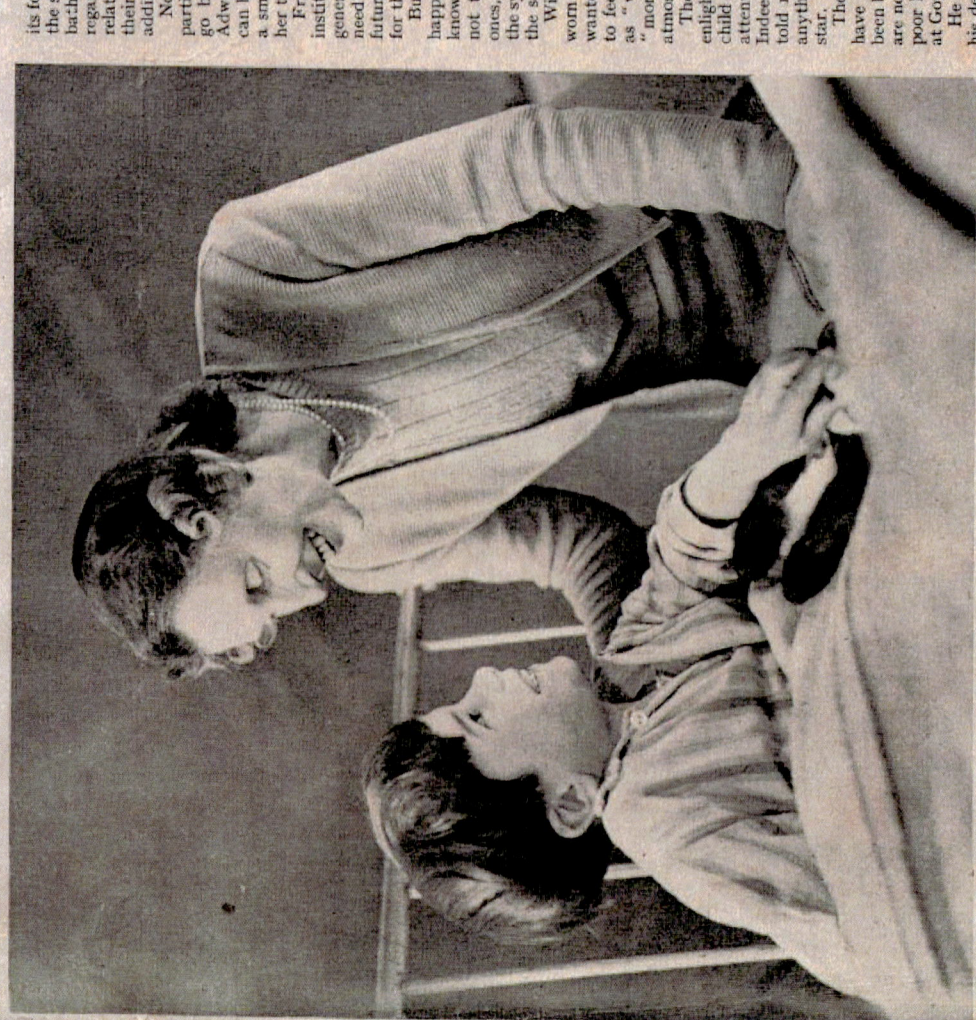

JOHN CASHEL.

And so to bed. The Colonel's wife, whom the children call " Mummy Di," bids Brian " good-night." Mrs. Reynardson, herself a mother of four, has a way with children and a deep and tender insight into the psychology of unwanted ones

325

These Children, some of the twenty-one at Adwell House, Tetsworth, have been brought up as brothers and sisters with one foster-mother; have played together for six years

High Expectations—on stilts, a picture symbolizing a real-life fairy story, the rise in the world of a model foster-family—thirteen of them once 'Unwanted Babies'

HOMELESS CHILDREN'S PROBLEM—continued

Home Farm at Col. and Mrs. Birch-Reynardson's Adwell House has helped with the rationing and feeding of their big family. The calves are always a popular turn with the children

Shaggy Donkey called Margaret gives rides to the children. Here Sylvia, as girls will, leads Louis, mounted, up the garden path. Children play in surrounding meadows and woods

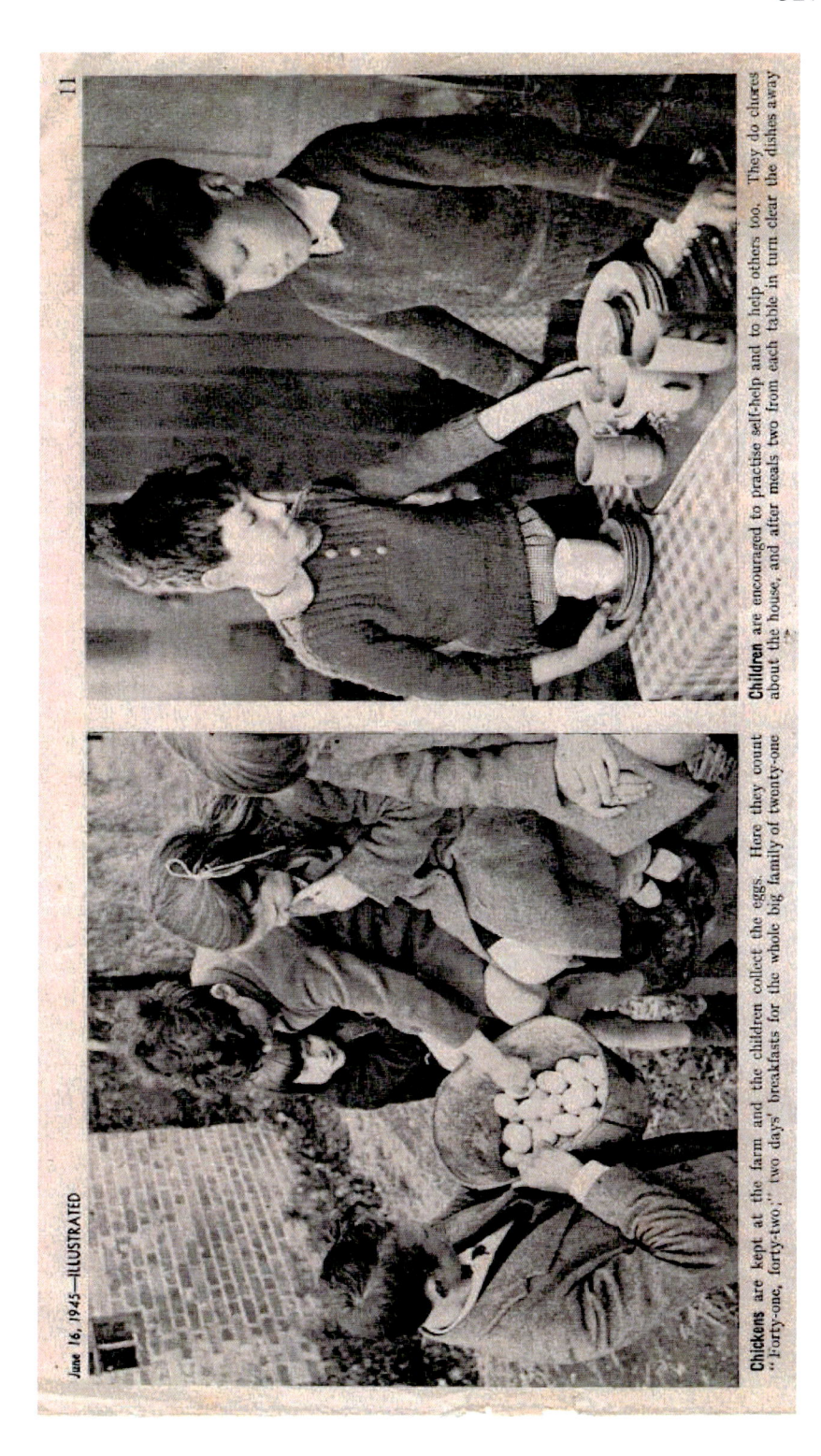

Chickens are kept at the farm and the children collect the eggs. Here they count "forty-one, forty-two..." two days' breakfasts for the whole big family of twenty-one

Children are encouraged to practise self-help and to help others too. They do chores about the house, and after meals two from each table in turn clear the dishes away

Appendix 8

KIT EGERTON'S AWARD OF THE M.C.
DESCRIBED IN THE OFFICIAL DIARY OF 15/19 HUSSARS 1939-1945:

24th September 1944 3rd Troop (Lt. Egerton) was again in the lead and it fought an action of great skill and distinction. The leading tank was hit by an 88mm [gun] and three members of its crew wounded. 3rd Troop found itself in an awkward predicament - Lt. Egerton observed from an exposed position in view of the enemy gun. After firing one or two shots the Challenger was hit in the turret by another gun and two troopers were killed. The troop leader then moved his own tank into position to engage the original gun and knocked it out with his second shot. The enemy withdrew during the night and in the morning three 88mm guns were found which had fallen victim to third troop. For this action, the culmination of several outstanding performances, Lt. Egerton was awarded the M.C.

Appendix 9

Scotsgrove and the Ashtons

I want to write something about Scotsgrove (near Thame) and my cousins, the Ashtons. My Uncle Sam Ashton married my father's sister, Iola. He was the grandson of the owner of the largest cotton mill in the western world who had made a very large fortune 'in trade' at Manchester. For this reason my grandfather, who disapproved of 'new money', was exceedingly doubtful about his daughter marrying Sam who had arrived at Oxford in 1909 not only with a car, but also with a chauffeur! However Sam, one of the most delightful men I've ever met, won over my grandfather with his charm and he married my aunt in 1911. (It should be remembered that my father always insisted that we were Birch not Reynardson, the latter having been 'in trade' when Lord Mayor of London in 1642!).

They had four sons (one son had died at birth) John, Jim, Pat and Charles (the latter twins). Charles, the only survivor today, is an extremely sprightly 91 – the other three are now, sadly, no more.

In 1919 Sam purchased Scotsgrove with a farm of some 260 acres and settled down to that not uncommon way of life in those days of hunting (he was Master of the South Oxfordshire Hunt), shooting and fishing. His main agricultural interest (which was limited) was breeding a herd of beautiful but uneconomic Shorthorn cows. But so what, money was not the object! He and my father were great friends. They drank a great deal of port together and shared the tenancy of a small fishing lodge and a lengthy beat of the River Cothi at Edwinsford.

Being a non fisherman, I only went there once (when I was nearby on a military scheme from Sandhurst). I slightly resented this! However, to revert to the sons all a good deal older than me but all extremely nice to me. Here are some 'visions' of them.

First, John (who was born in August 1912) came back after the War to become, amongst other things, Secretary of the South Oxfordshire Hunt. We hunted regularly together. One day he came to me to tell me that the Treasurer of Christ Church (who also acted as land agent) had complained that the Hunt had drawn the Christ Church woods (near

Forest Hill) without notice to him. Wasn't it monstrous? "Good God, if we had to ask permission of everyone to draw their coverts we'd have to write so many letters that we wouldn't have time to hunt". When the hounds went to the woods a second time without permission, locks and chains were put on all the gates. The chains were then cut through by John – and the hounds were immediately prohibited from drawing the coverts. Not unreasonably! But things were different 60 years ago. Anyone who 'warned off' hounds from their land was a social outcast. There was a huge row and only after much negotiation were the hounds allowed to hunt the following season on Christ Church land. (I was heavily involved as Hunt Chairman!)

Next Jim. He was keen on the girls and a great dancer. He arrived at Adwell dances and Hunt Balls with a spare collar because his sweat produced from enthusiastic dancing reduced the first one to wet rags. My mother, observing him dancing with one girl twice in succession, remonstrated with him and prohibited him from dancing with her a third time! Safety in numbers.

Then the twins. First Pat, who was one of the first people to enter Belsen Camp. He was ordained after the War having, at Oxford, been a most successful huntsman of the Christ Church Beagles. He went to Sandringham as Rector where he remained for fifteen years. He was an extremely good shot and, for that reason, was often invited to shoot by the Queen. On one occasion he was shooting next to Prince Philip. The first drive started with Pat shooting two right and lefts and continued at that standard. Prince Philip turned to his loader and said "That's what I call the Church Militant."

And finally Charles. He left the Army after the War having won an immediate D.S.O. at Anzio when aged 27. He had married Cis Butler and they started farming at her home in Wiltshire where they still live. There was a lot of hunting, shooting and fishing – all of which sports Charles excelled. I've already mentioned the Cothi, in Wales. Once, when fishing on a somewhat unpropitious day he hooked a fish which 'took off' down stream. He was fishing with an 11 foot trout rod (normally adequate for the comparatively small salmon in that river). The fish took him quickly into a pool at the end of which he saw, to his horror, a fallen tree with all its branches spread out in the water. His wife Cis was within hailing distance (Charles has a loud voice). He directed her to fill her skirt with stones, climb along the fallen tree trunk and throw stones at the salmon when it approached too close to the branches. This worked and the fish, weighing 23 pounds was safely landed after 15 minutes.

I have written at some length about this family but the Ashtons were all a great influence in my life. We had such happy days at Scotsgrove and they all came to Church at Adwell most Sundays. Jim was Humphrey Prideaux's best friend at Oxford and it was on one of the visits to Adwell Church that Humphrey first spied 'the little girl cousin' Cynthia singing in the choir.

Appendix 10

The 400

From time to time I have reminisced about the 400 nightclub and I feel that I should write in rather more detail about it because it was such an important rendez-vous for so many of us. The entrance was on the East side of Leicester Square (there is a cinema there now) and one went down stairs to get to the very dark club room. It was lined in red velvet and there was a tiny dance floor and a small band presided over by 'Snakehips' Johnson at the piano. But the most important person there was Rossi who was the head waiter and a friend to all of us. He certainly looked after us. He took telephone calls for us but always said to the caller (even though he might know that we were there) "I will see if he (or she) is in the Club." He would then come and tell us that we were wanted on the telephone by so and so, and did we want to speak.

Once, when Lorna arrived wearing a particularly beautiful brooch on her overcoat she was appalled, when she put it on again, that the brooch was not there. She rushed to Rossi. "Oh Miss Lorna, don't fuss. I always remove good jewelery before giving things to the Cloakroom attendant."

The place was always full of friends but there was a convention that one normally didn't talk to them! The Club closed at 4.00am! Any unconsumed bottles of wine or spirits were carefully marked with the members name and stored away for the next visit.

Found later!

LAVINIA LASCELLS AND DELIA HOLLAND-HIBBERT

Visited me in hospital at Ancona, South of Rimini, in November 1944. They assured the Matron that they were 'my sisters' and she reluctantly agreed to let them see me.

THE GARDEN HOUSE
ADWELL
THAME, OXFORDSHIRE OX9 7DQ
TEL. 01844 281 204   FAX. 01844 281 300

As I have already made clear this book which covers, perhaps, the most important period of my life, would never have been contemplated had not Adrian Palmer made this collection of letters (long forgotten) available to me. So he deserves, and receives, my most sincere thanks, shared with his brother Mark and their aunt Eleanor Retallack. They have all encouraged and helped me in this endeavour.

Then there has been the laborious and often tedious job of typing out the hundred or so selected letters which I had written in circumstances which made my writing particularly illegible. This was done by the ever cheerful Helen Batten who made the additions and corrections without demur. I am most grateful to her.

Diana Holderness was a superb instructor in the mysteries of editing a book of this kind. Tactful in her criticisms, generous in her compliments, firm in her advice and tolerant of many of my suggestions, she was the mainstay of this project. To her and to her assistant Celia Summers I owe a special debt of gratitude.

I wish to thank Mr Mike Galer of the Regimental Museum for kindly providing photographs and documents from the Derby muniments. They were invaluable.

And last, but by no means least, I have to thank Lorrie Wollerton. She has put up with our family for over fifty years and, had she not looked after me I would certainly have been quite unable to spend the time producing this book.

Autumn 2008

W.B.R.

Abbott, Thomas (Footman at Adwell) 9
Abel-Smith, Mrs 160
Abraham, Major General Martin 69
Acland, Sir Richard Bt MP 271
Addlestrop 161
Adwell 1 et. seq.
Agar, Herbert 84
Airlie, General 112, 114
Aldenham, (Walter) Lord 224
Alexander of Tunis, Field Marshal Earl,
    KG, GCB, DSO, MC 128, 153, 200
Algiers 63, 68, 71, 73
Alice, Princess GCVO GBE 4
Allan, Cpl (my Wireless Operator) 101, 135
Allhusen, Hon. Claudia 178-9, 181, 185, 190,
    193, 198, 258
Allhusen, Derek 78, 81, 92, 96, 99-101,
    104-5, 107-8, 123, 125, 150-1, 166-7,
    171, 178-9, 181, 190-2, 196, 204, 206,
    209-11, 219, 258
Althorp, Northamptonshire 45
Althorp, (Johnny) Viscount (*later* Earl
    Spencer) 42, 44-6, 56, 87, 242
Ambler, John, m. Princess Margarita of
    Sweden 33, 58
Amy (our Cook in South Africa) 4
Anderson, W.A.C. Brigade Major 195
Arbuthnot, Sir Hugh Bt 16, 252
Armstrong, Sir Thomas 62
Ashton, Charles DSO 149, 158, 329, 331
Ashton, Iola (Aunt) m. Sam Ashton 101,
    264
Ashton, John 94, 114, 239, 269, 330
Ashton, the Revd Pat 287, 329-30
Ashton, Sam 239
Astor Club 49, 50
Athlone, Earl of KG, GCB, GCMG, GCVO,
    DSO, m. Princess Alice 3, 4, 56, 276
Attenborough, James 284
Attenborough, Mrs 83
Attington 157-8
Attlee, Clement (*later* Earl Attlee KG),
    Prime Minister 31
Aubrey Fletcher, Elizabeth 264
Baade, Major General 313
Bacon, ('Mindy') Sir Edmund Bt 27

Bagshot Common 53
Bailie, Major Hugh (Lorna's father) 27, 300
Bailie, Douglas (Lorna's brother) 35, 61-2,
    74, 157
Bailie, Eleanor ('Puss') m. Tim Retallack
    33, 84, 176, 239, 243-4, 265, 268-9,
    299-300, 333
Bailie, Lorna, m. Hon. Gordon Palmer
    1 et. seq.
Baird, Mrs 240, 252, 289
Balfour, Anne, m. General Sir David Fraser
    GCB 41
Balfour, Colin 11, 35, 264, 302
Balfour, (Prue) Mrs Colin 302
Barbirolli, Sir John 213
Barclay, Ursula 68, 111
Bari 80, 107, 109-11
Barnard Castle 60, 63, 78
Barnard, Evie 159
Barton Abbey 230
Beaman, David 236
Beckett, Hon. Christopher (*later* Lord
    Grimthorpe) 195, 206-7, 236
Beckett, Hon. Clare m. Peregrine
    Crewdson 246, 280
Beckley 52, 232
Berkeley Hotel 184, 291
Berry, John 123, 158, 172, 233, 264
Betjeman, Sir John CBE (Poet Laureate)
    106, 278
Beveridge Report 31, 34
Bewicke, Ann 24, 31-2, 34, 39-40, 43-5
    47-50, 57, 59, 70, 74, 78, 88, 102,
    115, 142, 154, 158-9, 163, 203,
    232, 247, 260, 273, 285
Bewicke, Verly 47, 50, 232, 273
Bewicke, Major (Ann's father) 50
Bibby, Derek 300
Bicester, Lord (owner of Roquilla) 63
Bickersteth, John (*later* Bishop of Bath and
    Wells) 225, 247, 251, 266, 268-9,
    275, 281, 291
Bicket, Tony 300
Bingham, David 240
Birch Reynardson, Clare (Daughter)
    m. Adrian Hopkinson 9, 306, 308, 315

Birch Reynardson, Diana (Mother)
    31 et. seq.
Birch Reynardson, Dickie (Brother) 3,
    13-4, 21, 32, 51, 53, 57, 83, 92, 105,
    223, 235, 242, 244, 247-8, 256, 284,
    290-1
Birch Reynardson, Edward 308
Birch Reynardson, Henry Lt Col CMG
    (Father) 3 et. seq.
Birch Reynardson, Thomas 307
Birch Reynardson, William (Bill) 21, 107,
    308, 311
Birley, Anthony 291
Bishops School, Rondebosche, South
    Africa 4-5
Blackdown 27, 30-1, 33-4, 36-8, 41-2
Bland, Sir Simon (*later* Equerry to the Duke
    of Gloucester) 200
Bolton, Duncan 26
Bonham Carter, Mark (*later* Lord Bonham
Carter) 240
Bostock, Christopher 64, 247
Bostock, (Jo) Mrs Christopher 64
Boughton 250, 255
Bowhill 257, 259
Bradstock, Mike 116
Brett, Brigadier 236
Brett, Zandra 236, 256
Bridgeman, Jeannine, m. Alan Scott &
    Admiral Josef Bartosik 41, 159
Bridgemans, the family 228, 236
Bridlington 58-9
Brooke, John (*later* Lord Brookeborough)
    116, 149
Browne, Pam 238, 241
Browne, Percy 238, 240-1
Bruce, Rosalind 244
Buccleuch, (Molly) Duchess of 257, 259
Bulkley, Tony 206
Bullingdon Club 3, 283
Burghersh, (David) Lord (*later* Earl of
    Westmoreland) 240, 289
Burnaby Atkins, Andrew and Mollie 240
Burt-Smith, Annette 14
Butt, Dame Clara 56-7
Buxton, Countess 160, 276-7

Buxton, Earl 276
Caladon 199-200
Caldecott, Andrew (Imogen Birch
    Reynardson's father) 81
Callas, Maria 79
Callendar, Ronnie 300
Camberley 31, 33-4, 39, 44, 48, 56
Campbell, Hon. Clayre, m. Hon. N. Ridley &
    Lord Richard Percy 246, 267
Capel Cure 45
Capel, Ann m. Hon. Edward Ward 58
Capel, June m. Franz Osborn & Jeremy
    Hutchinson 58
Carberry Towers 259
Caro, Peter 81, 98
Carr Wilson, David 144
Casablanca 74-5
Caserta Palace 113-4, 149
Castle, Jack 15
Cavalry Depôt, Spahi 72
Cecil, Lord David 106, 233, 275, 278
Chatham Club 38, 106, 250, 272, 278-9
    281, 288
Chaworth-Musters, Bobby 144, 200
Chaworth-Musters, John 3
Chenevix Trench, Anthony 254
Chichester, Desmond 209
Christ Church 27, 67, 239, 241, 246, 251,
    254-5 278, 280, 282
Christ Church Beagles 3, 226, 254, 275,
    330
Christ Church Boys Club 225, 248
Churchill, Randolph 106
Churchill, Sir Winston KG, Prime Minister
    269
Clarelli, Marchesa 116
Clarendon, Earl of 3-4
Clarendon, Countess of 4
Clark, General Mark 128
Cleminson, Bert (Horse dealer) 261
Clerke-Brown, Arthur 49
Clerke-Brown, Rachel 15, 156, 264
Clifton, Peter 68
Clinkard, Roy and Walter 225, 252, 254, 275
Clive, Peter and Susan 261
Cobbold, Bill 113

Codrington, Simon 80
Collier, Heather 287, 291
Colt, Matty 50
Cooke, Lt Col Tony 175, 180, 190, 192, 196, 204-5
Coombe, Major General John, CB, DSO 187, 189, 205-6, 277
Coriano Ridge, Battle of 80, 100
Crampton, Ribton MC 144, 253
Cropper, Gay 38
Cropper, Nancy 176
'Cuffie' Mademoiselle Hubler 34
Culham 227, 253, 255, 265
Cumming Bell, Ann 50
Cummins, Brian 42, 47, 56
Cunningham, Bill MC 154, 157, 159, 161
Dalkeith, (Johnnie) Earl of (*later* Duke of Buccleuch) 26, 55, 226, 232, 241-2, 244, 249-50, 256-8, 272, 275
Dashwood, (Helen) Lady 237-8, 241
Dashwood, Muriel 228
Dashwood, Sarah m. Lord Aberdare 237
Dashwood, Sir Francis Bt 238-9, 241, 259, 280
de Burgh, Michael 126
de Chair, Mike 16
de Zulueta, Philip 315
Dickinson Sgt 101
Digby, Eddie (*later* Lord Digby) 289
Diggle, Christopher 167, 171-2, 204
Ditchley 11
Douglas Pennant, Henry 315
Dowdeswell 236
Dragon School, Oxford 45, 53
Dreselhanser, Lorraine 259
Drumlanrig 256, 258, 274
Dudding, Pat 156, 166, 187
Dudgeon, Ian 103
Dudgeon, Joe 114
Duino 200
Duncan, Deborah (dau. of Sir Patrick) 274
Duncannon, (Eric) Lord 272
Dunlop, Professor 257, 259
Dunn, Archie 41
Eden, Anthony MP (*later* Earl of Avon KG MC) Prime Minister 288

Edmunds, Sgt Jack MM 71, 81, 97, 144, 151, 239, 261-2
Edwards, Lionel 43, 161
Egerton, (Kit) Col Christopher MC 16, 36, 38, 43-4, 57, 104-5, 140, 151, 178, 229, 231, 233-6, 256, 260-1, 272-3, 328
Egerton, Mrs Jack 104
Egerton, Rosamund (Sister) m. James Marriott GM & Kit Egerton 7, 16, 21, 35-7, 42-3, 51, 58, 62, 64, 68, 81-3, 140-2, 172, 180, 204, 218, 230-1, 233, 235-6, 250, 260, 262-3, 266, 274-5
Egerton, Vice-Admiral Jack CB 16
Egglestone, Keith 291
Elgar, Sir Edward 47, 213
Elizabeth, Princess (*Later* Queen Elizabeth II) 55
Elphinstone, Hon. Margaret LVO (Lady in Waiting to Queen Elizabeth the Queen Mother) m. Denys Rhodes 55, 298
Elton, Lord 41
Emerson, Cpl (my Driver) 74, 101, 105, 135
Eridge 46
Errol, (Diana) Countess of 245
Erskine, Malcolm 94
Eton 7, 9, 14-6, 27, 32, 38-9, 61, 176, 193, 225, 248, 265, 270, 314, 321
Eton Beagles 225
Euston, (Hugh) Earl of (*later* Duke of Grafton) KG 43, 95, 209, 276
Evacuees and 141 Banbury Road, Oxford 12-3, 159-60, 184, 265, 270-1, 288, 322
Faber, Dick (Publisher) 247
Fairbairn, Penelope, m. Michael Hughes Hallet 235
Fairfax, Hon. Peregrine 116, 149
Fairfax, (Tom) Lord Fairfax of Cameron 40, 49, 53
Falk, 'Foxy' 34
Fanshawe, Brian 275
Fanshawe, David 163
Fanshawe, Dick 14, 32, 37, 42, 47, 51, 265
Fanshawe, Ruth (afterwards m. Lord Dulverton) 14, 156-8, 230, 275
Fanshawe, Sir Robert 14-5, 51

Faris, Sandy 33, 46
Fez 74-5
Filkins 228
Fitzmaurice, Lady Elizabeth m. Charles Lampton 50, 56, 84, 257
Fitzpatrick, Ivor MC 119
FitzRoy, Lady Anne m. Colin Mackenzie of Farr 14
FitzRoy, Lord Charles 276
FitzRoy, Lord Oliver 95
Flemings, the family 230
Fooks, Elizabeth 72
Forbes Watson, Ian 245
Foreign Legion at Sidi Bel Abbes 74
Forli 109
Forsyth Forest, Peter 114
Fowler, John (Colefax & Fowler) 12
Fox, Lady 290
Fox, Sir Gifford MP 291
Galbiati 227, 291
Galbraith, Jimmy 35, 38, 41, 51, 141
Galer, Mike 333
Gardner, Lorry 236
Garsington 225-6
Gatiens, Cpl 171-2
Geddes, Willie 42, 56, 59, 87, 121
Gibbons, Carol 145
Gibbs, Ann, m. Ian Mitchell 243
Gibbs, Antony & Co 224
Gibbs, Antony (*later* Lord Aldenham) 224, 257-9, 268
Gibbs, Edna 14
Gibbs, Sir Geoffrey 224
Gibbs, Mary (*later* Lady Aldenham) 233-5, 237, 247, 253, 257, 259, 274, 277
Gibbs, Mary, m. Sir Somerled Macdonald of Sleat 290-1
Gibbs, Peter 274
Gibbs, Susan, m. Richard Carr-Gomm 280, 287, 290-1
Gilbey, Mark 80
Gilby, Giles 121, 141
Gilmour, Trp. 153
Gladstone, Charles 15
Gladstone, William ('Willie') (*later* Sir, KG) 225

Glyn, John (*later* Lord Wolverton) 157, 265
Glyn, Audrey (*later* Lady Wolverton) 157
Glyn, the family 157-8, 228
Goldsmid, John 80, 99, 126, 135, 171, 175, 196, 264
Goodbody, Lt General Sir Richard KBE, DSO 80
Goodenough, the family 228, 236
Goodenough, Sir Richard 225-6
Gordon Lennox, Reggie 41, 49, 69
Grafton, (Rita) Duchess of 160
Graham, Euan 38
Graham-Vivian, Catherine 244, 249, 274
Graham-Vivian, Harry 242-3, 247, 249, 251, 261, 267, 272, 275
Grant Baillie, Steven (my Tutor at Oxford) 223, 225
Grenfell, Elizabeth 300
Gridiron Club 35, 272
Hannen, Guy MC 82-3, 117, 119, 123, 232
Harding, Andrew 315
Harding, Field Marshal Sir John (*later* Lord Harding of Petherton) GCB DSO MC 150, 154, 183, 200, 206
Hardwidge, RSM 147, 153, 192, 194
Hare, Rosemary 227-8
Hastings, Hermione 249
Head, Judge Adrian 123, 138, 173
Head, Viola 14, 37
Hedges, Jim 17
Heathcote, Bill 231
Heber-Percy, Colonel 240
Helena Victoria, Princess 4
Henderson, Canon 13-14
Herberts, the 262
Heseltine, Michael MP (*later* Lord Hesletine) 320
Hesketh, Bill and Diana 230
Heythrop Hunt 6
Hezlett, Micky 116
High Winchendon 159, 233
Hitchcock, Joyce 179
Hitchcock, Major Rex MC 120-1, 131, 135, 143, 179
Hodgson, Peter 277

Holden, Diana 68, 110-1, 112, 114, 149
Holland, George 8, 10, 16-7, 63
Holland-Hibbert, Audrey 7
Holland-Hibbert, Delia m. Bill
    Cunningham 14, 58, 110-3, 149, 154,
    158-61, 163, 190
Holland-Hibbert, Lavinia, m. Peter Orde
    42, 47, 63, 80, 149, 152, 232, 264,
    268-9, 277
Holland-Hibbert, Michael (*later* Viscount
    Knutsford) 52-3
Holland-Hibbert, the family 7, 230, 232
Honey, Mavis 230, 264
Hopkinson, Adrian 308
Horton, Ann 290
Houldsworth, Diana 231
Howard Johnston, Lady Alexandra (*later*
    Lady Dacre of Glanton) 255
Howells, Jack (Huntsman North
    Northumberland) 315
Hugh Smith, Owen 240
Hughes Sgt 81, 94, 98
Hull, Field Marshal Sir Richard KG GCB
    DSO (last Chief of Imperial General
    Staff) 80
Humphreys, Lt General Sir Thomas KCB
    CMG DSO (Father-in-Law) 319
Humphreys, Matnika ('Nik') m. W.B.R.
    220, 222, 302, 307, 319
Hussey, Marmaduke ('Dukie') (*later* Lord
    Hussey of North Bradley) Chairman
    of the BBC 54, 74
Hutchinson, Judy, (dau. of Tommy
    Hutchinson, Treasurer of Christ
    Church) 157
Hutchinson, Tommy 227
Huxford, SSM, DCM 126, 144
Ingleton-Weber, Inky 8, 14, 84-6, 110
James, Arthur 42
Jenkinson, Clare 240
Jenkinson, Julian 272
Jenkinson, Lavinia 240, 244
Jenkinsons, the family 238, 240, 273, 290
Johnson, ('Snakehips') 332
Joicey, Andrew 317
Joicey, Elizabeth 315, 316-7

Joicey, Major E. 260
Joicey, James 317
Joicey, Major John MC 72, 74-5, 98, 100-1,
    104-5, 108, 126, 131, 135, 141, 143-5,
    150, 153, 165, 182-3, 199-200, 206,
    208-9, 256, 263-4, 278, 284
Joicey, Katie 317
Joicey, Michael 225, 242, 251, 300, 314-8
Joicey, Robert 317
Jones, L/Cpl 151
Jones, Leslie (Butler) 7-9, 16-7, 263, 267, 304
Kearsley, Irene (always known as 'Miss
    Jane') 120, 253, 265
Kearsley, Nigel 120
Kelly, Sir Gerald 55
Kemp, Doctor 101
Kennedy, Sir Ludovic 225
Kimberley, (Johnny) Earl of 95
Lacey Thomson, Bobby 237
Lambart, Lady Elizabeth m. Mark
    Longman 44, 236
Lambert, Constant 113
Lambert, Rachel 52, 54
Lansdowne Club 45, 49-50, 235, 237
Lascelles, Lavinia, m. Edward Renton,
    Gavin Maxwell & David Hankinson
    113, 157, 208
Laurie, Betty 231
Laurie, Charles 50
Laurie, Lt Colonel David MC 54, 82-4, 97,
    99, 101-2, 105-9, 113, 115, 118, 121,
    123, 125-6, 130-1, 135, 138-45, 147,
    149-52, 154, 156-7, 161, 165-8, 171-3,
    175-6, 178, 181, 190, 192, 195-6,
    199-201, 203-5, 207, 211-3, 231-2,
    236, 260, 274-5, 278, 282, 284, 305
Laws, Tim 35, 38, 41
Leak, Humphrey 81
Leatham, Paddy 116
Lee, Hugh 87
Leese, Lt General Sir Oliver Bt CB DSO 80
Legge, Hon. Gerald (*later* Viscount Lewisham
    and Earl of Dartmouth) 284
Lennor, Pat 83
Leslie Melville, Geordie 257
Leslie Melville, Helen 280

Leslie Melville, Mike 42
Lindsey, Colin 80
Lindsey, Diana 249, 261
Linlithgow, Marquess of KG. Viceroy of India 259
Lockett, Jean m. Angus Rowan-Hamilton 289
Loders Club, Oxford 3, 26, 38
Lonsdale, Robert 277
Lothian, (Peter) Marquess of 26, 82
Lowe, Dr 225
Luddington, Bill 60
Lumley, Colonel 63
Lyle, John 59
Lyle, Robin 38
Lynam, Jock 5, 75
Lynam, Humphrey 5
Macdonald, Peter 291
Mackworth Praed, Stephanie 228
Maclagen, Michael and Jean 302
MacNeal, Mary 34
Mahoney, Honor 14
Manderston 1 et. seq.
Mann, Disney 14
Mannellia 50
Manners, Bobbie (*later* Lord Manners) 225, 248, 252, 270-1
Manners, Lord and Lady 270
Marriott, Christopher 16, 82, 265-6
Marriott, Captain Jimmy GM 16, 81-3, 140
Marsdens, the family 193
Martin, Andy 49
Mattingley, Sue, m. John Berry & Robert Murdoch 172, 197, 235, 243, 248, 250, 260, 264, 266, 269, 271, 282, 287, 289
Maud, Dorothy 6, 194
Mayes, Andrew 247
McCorquodale, Raine, m. Earl of Dartmouth, Earl Spencer & Count de Chambrun 284
McCreery, General Sir Richard GCB DSO MC 185
McCullen, Major Mike 68, 70
McInnes Skinner, Desmond 153, 190, 192, 196, 198-9, 208, 211, 278
Meredith Hardy, Tony 68

Merrick (Gunner) 101
Meyrick, Ann 179, 195
Meyrick, Major George 170, 179, 181, 191, 195, 199, 203
Meyrick, Tony ('Tone') 109, 230, 236
Michael of Kent, Prince 230
Middleton, John 121, 141
Middleton, Molly 41, 44, 139
Mildmay, Harry 240
Miller Stirling, Hubert 230
Miller, Alastair 156
Milne, Johnnie 157
Mirabelle 103
Mogg, General Sir John GCB DSO 49, 298
Monck, Mr (Agent at Adwell) 17
Monck, Colonel 32
Moncreiffe, Sir Iain, of that Ilk, Bt 245
Mond, Julian (*later* Lord Melchett) 95
Montgomery of Alamein, Field Marshal Viscount KG GCB DSO 132
Morgan, David 249
Morland, Major 238
Morland, Toni 238, 241, 256
Morrell, Jim 227
Mortimer, Sir John QC (Author & Playright) 5
Moule, Michael 116, 181
Mowlem, Mr (Surgeon) 158, 160, 171
Myrrdin Evans, George 54, 247
Nanny, Miss Turner 4, 48, 56
Naylor Leyland, Sir Vyvian Bt 111, 272
Newtimber 276
Nichols, Cpl 101, 125, 127, 135, 151, 239-40
Northcot, John 251
Northumberland, (Elizabeth) Duchess of 257-8
Nott, Sylvia 37
Nunnington 16, 261
Ollard, Richard 270, 280-1
Ozanne, General 27
Paget, General Sir Bernard GCB DSO 154, 170, 288
Palmer, (Adrian) Lord 1, 333
Palmer, Dick 300
Palmer, Hon. Mark 333

Palmer, Lady Mary (Lady in Waiting to
   Princess Elizabeth) m. Lord O'Hagan
   & St. John Gore 86
Parifitt, Sgt 129
Parker, Bill 171, 178, 203
Parnell, Charles 179, 237
Parnell, Laura 179
Pearce, Dickie 36, 103-4
Peek, (Joan) Lady (Aunt) 49, 236
Peek, Sir William Bt 72, 84, 141, 167, 173,
   178, 205
Perkins, Will 16
Perry, ('Stug') Lt Col R.S.G., DSO 101, 313
Philpotts, Sgt 148
Ponsonby, Sir Ashley Bt MC 144, 149,
   234, 236, 240, 298
Ponsonby, Barbara, 274, 277, 291
Ponsonby, Betsy, m. Judge John Clay 52,
   190, 227, 231, 233, 274, 291
Ponsonby, Sir Charles Bt MP 62, 224, 246,
   270, 304
Ponsonby, Diana, m. Revd Mark Meynell 3
Ponsonby, Edwin (Grandfather) 10
Ponsonby, Gerald (*later* Lord de Mauley)
   236
Ponsonby, Juliet, m. Rt Hon. James
   Ramsden MP 41, 51, 53, 62, 87, 190,
   236, 240, 245, 270, 294, 306
Ponsonby, June, m. Lord Grimston 236
Ponsonby, Lavinia, m. Sir Michael
   Hamilton MP 62, 236, 245, 248
Ponsonby, Mary, m. William Barnes
   14, 41, 86, 231, 235, 247, 276
Ponsonby, Priscilla, m. Sir Edmund Bacon
   Bt 27
Ponsonby, (Winifred) Lady (Aunt) 224,
   236, 249
Ponsonby, the family 27, 43, 223, 245, 247
Portman, Hon. Rosemary, m. Sandy Pease
   300
Pott, John 291
Pott, Will 288-90
Price, Col Jack DSO 90, 105, 117-8, 123,
   125-7, 130, 139, 147, 151, 155, 158, 163,
   165, 168, 170, 184-91, 193-6, 198-9,
   203, 211, 214, 223, 242, 245, 313

Price, David (*later* MP) 230
Prideaux, Cynthia (Sister) 3, 6-7, 13, 21,
   32-4, 39, 43, 46-7, 49, 58, 71, 158,
   163-4, 181, 230-1, 233-4, 238, 249,
   255-6, 263, 265, 268-9, 277, 279, 281,
   284-5, 302, 331
Prideaux, Humphrey (*later* Sir) 7, 11-3, 34,
   39, 43, 46, 49, 57, 158, 160, 230-1,
   233-4, 249, 256, 268-9, 279, 281, 284,
   290, 298, 302, 321, 331
Prideaux, Julian 48, 58
Prideaux, Nicholas 34, 43-4, 58
Prideaux, Walter 144
Pryor, Betsy 291
Pytchley Hunt 45
Queen Charlotte's Ball 60
Queen Elizabeth (*later* Queen Elizabeth the
   Queen Mother) 55
Rachmaninoff, Sergei 33, 58, 114, 158
Randolph Hotel, Oxford 258
Ranfurly, (Dan) Earl of 224
Ranfurly, (Hermione) Countess of 112
Ransom, Bridget 231
Raveningham 27
Reid, John 189-91, 194, 198-9
Reid-Scott, Sandy 206
Renton, Lord 1
Rich, George 208, 272
Rich, Martin 81
Richards, Cyril 287
Rickets, Fred 253
Rigden, Mrs (Proprietor of The Cockpit at
   Eton) 53
Roberts, L/Cpl 151
Roberts, Margaret, m. Denis Thatcher (*later*
   Lady Thatcher LG) Prime Minister
   265
Robson, John 121, 141
Rodzianco, Col 116
Roi, Boso 145-7
Roi, Memina, 144-5, 171, 174, 182-3, 185
Roi, the family 144-6, 173, 169, 173-4,
   176-7, 201
Romford, Kennelly 56
Ropner, Guy 289
Ross Club 51

Rossi (Steward at 400) 332
Rowan-Hamilton, Gavin 300
Rowley, Susan 111
Ruggles Brice, Jane, m. Anthony Birley 44
Russell, Dr 199
Ryder-Richardson, Teddy 289
Sale, Brigadier Richard 236
San Savino, Battle of 81, 96-7, 99, 178, 185
Sandhurst 27, 31, 33, 36, 38, 41-5, 52, 55, 58-9, 329
Sayer, Doris 14
Sclater-Booth, Ba 300
Scotsgrove 157, 160, 268-9, 329, 331
Scott, Lady Caroline, m. Sir Ian Gilmour Bt MP (*later* Lord Gilmour of Craigmillar) 226, 256-8
Sergison Brooke, Timothy 111
Shepley-Shepley, Nigel 255
Shuttle, Mrs (our Cook) 10, 14, 231
Simmonds, Mrs 57
Simpson, Alec 147-8, 267
Slessor, Judy (dau. of Marshal of the RAF, Sir John Slessor GCB, CB, DSO, MC) m. Lt Col. Jack Price DSO & John de Lazlo 76, 78, 81, 84, 90, 95, 105, 109, 119, 123, 138, 140, 150-2, 154, 156, 157, 161, 163, 165-8, 170-3, 175-9, 181, 184, 186-7, 189-92, 194-5, 197-9, 202-4, 209-11, 214, 242, 290
Smith, Fortune, GCVO (Mistress of the Robes) m. Duke of Grafton KG 256, 272
Smith, Sir John MP 240, 267, 270, 272, 275, 283
Smyly, Colonel Denys 205
Somerville, Sir Donald 230
Sones, Mr (our Butler) 10
St Aldwyn, (Michael) Earl 49
St Aubyn, Tommy 80, 165
Steel, Major David DSO, MC (*later* Sir David, Chairman of B.P.) 144
Stevens, Cpl 82
Stevens, Pat 190, 205, 208
Stewart-Brown, Ronald, Juliet, Henry, Walter and Diana 308
Stormouth Darling, Robin 300

Stourton, Hon. Charles *(later* Lord Mowbray, Seagrave and Stourton) 26, 245
Stratton, Desmond 245
Stuart, Peggy 161
Stuart, Robert 82, 98, 102, 116
Stubbs, Pamela 111, 157-8
Sutton, Ann 267
Sutton, John 33, 50
Symonds, Anne 37
Synge, John 26, 80, 246, 266, 279, 291
Talbot, Dame Meriel DBE 276-7
Taylor, Dick 273
The 400 Club 49, 50, 54, 56, 78, 275, 287, 332
Thomas, Mr (Hairdresser) 84, 115, 230
Thompson, John (*later* Sir John, Chairman of Barclays Bank) 157
Thompson, (Elizabeth) Lady 157
Thompson-Glover, Katherine 261
Thompson-Glover, Peter 167, 169, 195, 235, 244, 249, 264
Thwaites, Otto MC 79, 119, 126, 129, 135, 192
Toller, Captain Charles 114
Toller, Tom 165
Tree, Michael 20
Tree, Ronnie MP (Nancy Lancaster's first husband) 11
Trenchard, (Katherine) Viscountess 37
Trevor Roper, Professor Hugh (*later* Lord Dacre of Glanton) 227, 277
Tufnell, Carli 44
Villa Maser 175-8
Villa Roi 169, 171
Vincents Club 63
Volpe, the family, owners of Villa Maser 176-7
Wakefield, Mary, m. Alexander ('Sandy') Stirling 232
Wakeford, Captain VC 106
Wales, Prince of (*later* Edward VIII & Duke of Windsor) 3, 213, 251
Walker, Mrs (Mother's maid) 4
Walker, Peter 116
Wallace, Jean 49-50, 157, 161, 236

Wallace, Ronnie MFH 49-50, 157, 161, 225, 236, 252
Walter, Bruno 294
Walter, Gladys, m. Victor Ponsonby 304
Walters (my Scout at Oxford) 225
Warren Pearl, Roddie 231, 278, 284
Watson, Rupert (*later* Lord Manton) 68, 289
Waugh, Evelyn 106, 278
Wavell, Lady Felicity, m. Peter Longmore 88
Weatherby, James 41, 78, 138
Wentworth Stanley, David 82-3, 107, 113, 118, 125, 129, 135, 144, 181, 206, 232, 277
Whately, David MC 123, 126, 144, 154, 187, 205, 249, 277, 284
Wheatley, Mike 81
Whitaker, Marigold 41, 248, 256, 264
Whitaker, the family 248, 256
Williams, Mrs 232
Wills, Audrey 291
Wilson, Bill 32
Wilson, Field Marshal Sir Henry Maitland GCB GBE DSO ('Jumbo') (*later* Lord Wilson) 111-3, 136
Winter, Watty, Brigadier 274
Windsor (Other) Viscount (*later* Earl of Plymouth) 16
Woodhead, Mike 116
Woodleys 6, 157, 246, 269
Woodperry 229-30
Woollerton, Lorrie 334
Woolton, Earl of, CH 266, 268
Worsthorne, Simon 80
Wylde, John 280
Yates, Billy 255
Yates, Donald 247

Back Cover

I thought that it might amuse you if I tried to make a collage to illustrate the main interests of my life. I'm sure that I should put HUNTING first so here, top left, is a picture of me with my friend Alastair Mann riding down the drive at Adwell. I am on the best horse I ever had, Royal Event. Alastair was Master of the South Oxfordshire Hunt and I was Chairman. I had so many happy days with him. Then, top centre, I am SHOOTING near Spring Covert at Adwell. We have always kept the shoot as a family affair; such a relief not to have paying guns complaining about the lack of birds! Further over, on the right, I am PAINTING on the island of Siros, staying with the Musgraves. My best days were with your Granny Nik. We used to paint happily together all day completely unaware of the passage of time.

The middle picture is a composition of some of you playing at one of 'Grandpa's Christmas Concerts' at Norton Curlieu. Quite an achievement to find an orchestra or cello (Adrian Hopkinson), four violins (Clare, Gordon and Iola Hopkinson and Diana Stewart-Brown), trombone (Walter Stewart-Brown), two flutes (Henry Stewart-Brown and Cuthbert Hopkinson), clarinet (Frederick Hopkinson) and piano (Juliet Stewart-Brown). This is to illustrate my love of MUSIC, both orchestral and operatic. Thank you for giving me such pleasure hearing you all playing together.

Finally, at the bottom, I am GARDENING in the Crayfish garden at Adwell. I know I look a bit cross, but this is how I feel when I'm disturbed in my weeding by someone saying that I'm wanted on the telephone! Gardening has, perhaps, been an obsession since I won the gardening prize at the Dragon School nearly eighty years ago.